THE ESPERANZA FIRE

The
ESPERANZA
FIRE

Arson, Murder, and the Agony of Engine 57

◆ ◆ ◆

John N. Maclean

COUNTERPOINT | BERKELEY

The Esperanza Fire: Arson, Murder, and the Agony of Engine 57

Copyright © 2013 John N. Maclean

Library of Congress Cataloging-in-Publication Data
Maclean, John N.
  The Esperanza fire/John N. Maclean
    p.cm.
  ISBN: 978-1-61902-071-9 (hardcover)
1. Oyler, Raymond. 2. Arson—California. 3. Wildlife fighters—California. 4. Trials (Arson)—California. 5. Wildfires—California. I. Title
HV6638.5U6M33 2013
364.152'3092—dc23

Cover design by Faceout Studios
Interior design by Maria E. Torres, Neuwirth & Associates, Inc.

COUNTERPOINT
1919 Fifth Street
Berkeley, CA 94710
www.counterpointpress.com

Printed in the United States of America
Distributed by Publishers Group West

10   9   8   7   6   5   4   3   2

*To Ashlyn, Bronwyn, Evan Fitzroy, Larsen Muir,
and Paisley Kathleen, with love.*

ACKNOWLEDGMENTS

I was attending a fire conference in Reno, Nevada, when a Forest Service engine captain I knew, Richard Gearhart, strode up and asked in a bold manner, "Are you going to do a book on the Esperanza Fire?" Gearhart then brought over Norm Walker, the division chief who had been in charge of the Forest Service engines the day of the Esperanza Fire, and he went over the story and its aftermath. My efforts over the next five years to pull together this account would not have been possible without the cooperation of Gearhart, Walker, the three other Forest Service captains who were with Engine 57 at the fire: Anna Dinkel, Freddie Espinoza, and Chris Fogle; their crews, too, fully cooperated. The captains along with Dr. James Hepworth and Mike Rogers read drafts of the text; any errors, however, are my responsibility.

I gratefully acknowledge the cooperation of many Engine 57 family members, and particularly of Vivian Najera, Daniel Najera's aunt, who acted as informal family liaison for me. Rick Reeder, a fire behavior analyst and my first guide at the fatal site, generously shared his research and photo archive. Concerning the arson story, I especially thank Mike Hestrin and Mike Mayman, the prosecutors, and Detective Scott Michaels. Richard De Atley of the Riverside *Press-Enterprise* was a great help with court matters; his newspaper's general coverage of the fire could be counted on as thorough and reliable. Julie Hutchinson, Cal Fire's public information officer, gave important assistance. Many others, some of whose names appear in the text, made generous contributions of time and memories. A more detailed account of the book's making can be found in "A Time for Fire," a story I wrote for *Wildfire* Magazine that is available on JohnMacleanBooks.com.

THE ESPERANZA FIRE

1.

WHEN A JURY RETURNS TO a packed courtroom to announce its verdict in a capital murder case, every noise, even a scraped chair or an opening door, resonates like a high-tension cable snap. Spectators stop rustling in their seats; prosecution and defense lawyers and the accused stiffen into attitudes of wariness; the judge looks on owlishly; even the court bailiff, who experiences too much of humanity's dark side, often stands to attention for this moment. In that atmosphere of heightened expectation, the jury entered a Riverside County Superior Court room in southern California to render a decision in the trial of Raymond Oyler, charged with setting the Esperanza Fire of 2006, which killed a five-man Forest Service engine crew sent to fight the blaze.

The jurors cast quick glances around the courtroom, avoiding eye contact, and tried to wipe any hint of the verdict off their faces as they took their seats. For more than a week of deliberations, they had been "semisequestered," and sheriff's deputies had escorted them to and from the jury room. The special security measures had been put in place by Judge W. Charles Morgan, who had mysteriously stopped the trial during the final arguments, closed the courtroom, and called in the jurors one by one to question them. Speculation of a mistrial ran rampant when news leaked of an attempt at jury tampering. But the crisis passed, the closing arguments concluded, and the jury retired.

As the jurors found their chairs, an extra half dozen armed sheriff's deputies stood by the defense table where Oyler, in a sober gray suit, sat unshackled. Sheriff's Deputy David Holland, the court bailiff, warned the spectators against any outburst. "If your emotions get the best of you, please leave the courtroom," he said.

The spectators, some of whom had driven many miles and arrived breathless at the last minute, divided like families at a rivalrous church wedding. Firefighters, relatives of the victims, and their supporters filled pew-like benches on the side of the courtroom nearest the jury box. The fire people looked scrubbed, upright, and unspeakably sad. On the other side of the courtroom sat Oyler's family and friends from southern California's Banning Pass, where the 38-year-old auto mechanic had lived and where the fatal wildfire had burned. They were scattered along a couple of rear benches as far from the jury as possible. Several had napped, nodded, and cast hostile glances during the trial, but there had been no unruly behavior, at least not in the courtroom.

The Oyler clan appeared both hopeful and apprehensive. They had reason for a glimmer of optimism, for the trial had been lengthy and complex. The prosecution had presented no physical evidence to tie Oyler absolutely to the Esperanza Fire. Instead, prosecutors had sought to prove that a string of twenty-three arson fires in the Banning Pass beginning in the spring of 2006 had been the work of one person, and that that person was Raymond Oyler. The ignition devices and locations of the fires showed unmistakable similarities, the prosecutors argued, and followed a classic evolutionary pattern for serial arson, becoming more efficient and destructive over time, and finally deadly. DNA matches, witnesses, tire tracks, and surveillance camera images linked Oyler to several previous fires in the series, and the Esperanza Fire followed the general pattern: the ignition device, for example, was made, like many of the others, with stick matches bound to a Marlboro cigarette, his favorite brand, by a bluish-green rubber band. The prosecution's case depended on the jury understanding how the totality of evidence formed a pattern that had been engineered, as the chief prosecutor Michael Hestrin charged, by a lone "man bent on destruction." Adding to the suspense, the legal stakes in the trial were the highest they had ever been in a case like this one: to this date, no one had ever been convicted of murder for setting a wildland fire, even though arson wildfires had caused many deaths and hundreds of arsonists had been caught and punished with fines and prison time.

The jurors, eight women and four men, had fought a long, hard battle to reach a verdict. "I didn't want to give it away when we walked in, but it was hard to keep an expression off your face," said one juror. The foreman, Don Estep, handed the court bailiff a thick sheaf of verdict forms. As Judge Morgan read through them and minutes ticked by, the tension grew almost unbearable.

"It felt almost like we were in church or at a funeral while the judge read the verdict forms," said the aunt of one of the victims.

The case against Oyler proceeded with what for the legal system was nearly the speed of light. After the fire, Oyler was identified as a possible suspect in less than forty-eight hours, arrested in less than a week, and tried in less than three years. This happened even though Oyler had initially been dismissed as a suspect by nearly everyone—Riverside County homicide detectives, the FBI, and others. "We almost didn't investigate him," said Scott Michaels, a Riverside County homicide detective who pursued Oyler despite opposition. Senior investigators weren't impressed with the Oyler connection, not at first, because Oyler was linked only to a previous fire, days earlier, and he did not fit the standard FBI profiles for a serial arsonist. Overwhelmed by a flood of leads about the Esperanza Fire and concentrating on more likely suspects, Michaels' superiors ordered him to work on leads directly related to the Esperanza Fire. After a shouting match with his sergeant, Michaels kept after Oyler, at the risk of his career. His vindication came in dramatic fashion during a meeting of quarreling law enforcement officials, with news that stunned everyone and sent Michaels off to make an arrest.

The mass effort to find the Esperanza Fire arsonist may have followed a choppy course, but it did not come about by chance. Everyone behaves differently when fires break out in the zone where wildfire and civilization overlap: the citizenry becomes aroused, firefighters fight harder, and governmental officials and politicians take notice and intervene. When a serial arsonist is suspected of setting a fire in this critical zone, the wildland–urban interface, the entire community goes to severe threat alert. In short, Michaels was not alone in his passion for the hunt. Southern California is the nation's top hot spot for wildfire and one of the top three in the world, along with Australia and southern France. Sensitivity to any wildfire runs high, and arson is a regional scourge. Deaths by wildland fire occur with unhappy frequency, but never before had an entire Forest Service engine crew been wiped out by flames, not in southern California or anywhere else.

Though Detective Michaels made the first link to Oyler, his investigation was based on evidence painstakingly gathered by the state's Cal Fire arson squad. As part of a six-month-long investigation, from the time an arson series had broken out in May of that year, the squad had placed surveillance cameras around the Banning Pass in areas prone to fire. One of the cameras, mounted on a service pole along a roadway, captured the license plate number of a vehicle at the site of an arson fire four days before the Esperanza Fire. The car was Oyler's, though he had never bothered to register it with the state. Michaels, assigned to the Esperanza case on the fatal morning, backtracked the vehicle to a salvage shop and then traced it to Oyler in a series of quick, dogged, and lucky steps. "Investigations don't happen like this," Michaels said later. "They don't go this fast; you don't have arguments with police commanders and do cliché stuff like that. It was like being in a movie." Adding to the sense of unreality, Oyler at one point admitted that he had set the Esperanza Fire, though prosecutors decided the confession was too dodgy to use in court.

District Attorney Rod Pacheco decided to seek the death penalty after a review of the case by thirty regional law enforcement officials. A capital case changes things; if a jury found Oyler guilty of murder, the same jury would sit for a second proceeding and make a separate decision on whether to recommend the ultimate penalty. Prior to the Oyler trial, the closest the legal system had come to a murder conviction for a wildland fire involved John Orr, a longtime fire investigator and captain for southern California's Glendale Fire Department, located less than one hundred miles from the site of the Esperanza Fire in the heart of southern California's fire ground.

Orr had been convicted of four counts of murder, with victims including a grandmother and a 2-year-old child, for setting a fire in 1984 in a home improvement store in South Pasadena. After a complex investigation, he came to trial fourteen years later, in 1998. One investigator thought Orr had set more than two thousand fires, many of them wildland fires. The jury that found him guilty failed to agree on the death penalty, and Orr was sentenced to life in prison without possibility of parole. Orr, a would-be thriller writer, had helped seal his fate by writing a book, *Points of Origin*, based on the home improvement store fire, which he had helped investigate and for which he had won much acclaim because he insisted, despite opposition, that it was arson. Unlike Oyler, Orr almost perfectly fit a standard arsonist profile: the hero firefighter who sets fires to make himself famous. In his book, which figured at his trial, Orr addressed the question that haunted his and Oyler's trials: What sort of a person would do this? At one point Orr described the reaction of his fictional arsonist, Aaron, who bears many similarities to Orr, to the havoc he had created. "Aaron had already killed five people in one of his fires. He rationalized the deaths as he did everything. It wasn't his fault. The people just acted stupidly and their deaths had nothing to do with the fact that he set the fire. They just reacted too slowly. 'It was too bad about the baby, but, shit, it wasn't my fault.'"

◆ ◆ ◆

WILDFIRE ARSON, BOTH deliberate and unintentional, has grown in virtual lockstep with the expansion of the wildland–urban interface, though reliable figures about the impact of arson are hard to come by; for one thing, it's not always easy to identify arson. California is a special case on account of the density of population in fire-prone areas, the annual Santa Ana winds, and a large number of busy arsonists. (At the time of Oyler's arrest, California's state registry of convicted arsonists numbered 3,800; only two other states, Montana and Illinois, maintain such a registry.) Consequently, the Golden State keeps its own statistical records for arson-started fires. In California, 7 to 12 percent of wildfires in recent years have been identified as arson, so an average of 10 percent is a reasonable estimate. Nationally, the picture varies widely from state to state. In some southern states where lightning is rare and timber plantations plentiful, arson may account for 90 percent or more of wildfires; in some other states, arson is a negligible problem. Nationwide, the number of wildfires ranges from about 100,000 to 120,000 a year. Extrapolating California's 10 percent figure, arson may account for ten thousand to twelve thousand wildfires a year nationwide. About 10 percent of wildfire arson cases are prosecuted, according to veteran fire investigators and the few available statistics. But serial arson is common, and one prosecution may account for many fires, as happened in the Orr and Oyler cases. The problem is deadly serious: in California alone in the first decade of the new century, thirteen people died from confirmed or suspected arson wildfires.

Wildfire arson convictions don't come easy. Prosecutors say that arson is the second most difficult crime to prove, behind only adult sexual assault. Typically with wildfire arson, the crime scene is empty country, witnesses are few or nonexistent, and the arsonist may be long gone when flames spring to life. The simple ignition devices are often destroyed; a single match in light grass can start a blaze that can quickly spread into a major fire. Evidence can be inadvertently obliterated by firefighters hosing water, digging fire line, or driving fire engines. Deliberate arson is the crime of a coward: the perpetrator almost never comes face to face with a victim. The wildland arsonist's motives are harder to fathom than those of his urban counterparts, who often ignite buildings to collect insurance or to kill or injure a particular person.

For many decades, deliberately set wildland fires were treated more as a nuisance than as a major crime. Rural communities did not merely tolerate arson in their backyards; they often practiced it as a cultural prerogative, to clear brush and stimulate grazing land or wildlife forage, or to create jobs on fire crews. The problem became especially common in the wake of the Big Burn of 1910, which scorched more than 3 million acres in Idaho and Montana, killed an estimated eighty-seven people, and ushered in the age of mandatory federal fire suppression, the effects of which can be seen today in millions of acres of overgrown forest and brush country. Local communities revolted when deprived of their long-standing practice of deliberate burning. Things got so bad in California by the middle of the twentieth century that the Forest Service, calling the problem the Battle of the Brush, sent an undercover investigator to sample local attitudes. "Every person to whom I talked was quite elated over the fact that the fires of 1944 would improve the deer hunting and help the cattleman," reported the investigator, who traveled the Mendocino area in northern California. A local might favor brush burning for many reasons, the investigator reported, among them "a gripe against the Forest Service policy of no burning during fire season, or a conservation policy which prevents him from doing things 'the way Granddad did.'"

A few years later, in 1953, a ne'er-do-well young man, the son of a respected Forest Service engineer, ignited a blaze in the same area, on the Mendocino National Forest, to get work on a fire crew. A single match was all it took to spark the Rattlesnake Fire of 1953, which killed fifteen firefighters and became a stark example— one of the worst in history—of tolerance for wildfire arson. The arsonist, Stanford Pattan, did get a job as a fire camp cook, but he raised the suspicions of an arson detective as he served the lawman breakfast at the camp. His arrest and confession followed shortly thereafter.

That was a different age; a grand jury refused to indict Pattan for second-degree murder. He had not intended to kill anyone, people said, and make-work or "job fires," as they are still known, were part of country living, typically taking their toll in unoccupied forest where no one got hurt. Pattan confessed only after he was confronted with photos of the dead. "The pictures certainly helped break him," said the sheriff who arrested him. "When he saw those, I believe he realized for the first time what he had done." When I traced down and interviewed Pattan almost a half century later for the book *Fire and Ashes*, he acknowledged that the photos had left him shaken. He had never meant to harm anyone, he said, and had been distraught because he couldn't find a job and his wife had left him. Pattan ultimately was charged with two counts of "willful burning" and served just three years in San Quentin State Prison.

The Rattlesnake Fire set a lasting mark: those fifteen deaths remain the greatest loss of firefighter life on a wildfire since that year.

During the Oyler trial, photographs of the dead once again would trigger a turn of events, though this time the effect would be on the jurors.

As the growth of the wildland–urban interface has exposed a more urban-oriented population to wildfire, penalties for arson have ratcheted upward. Here, too, precise and instructive figures are hard to come by, though anecdotes abound. Federal surveys carried out in the first decade of the new century, spurred by concern about the mounting toll in lives and property from wildland fire, reported that about 9 percent of the land area in the United States, containing 39 percent of all houses, or 44.8 million units, can be classified as part of the wildland–urban interface. To no one's surprise, California has the highest number of interface housing units, about 5.1 million. But the eastern United States, which has a minor wildland fire problem compared with the West but a denser population, has the most interface land; in Connecticut, for example, 72 percent of the land is classified as interface. A few figures are both precise and instructive: nationwide in 2003, a bad fire year, 4,200 residences were destroyed, $2 billion worth of damage was done, and thirteen firefighter lives were lost in wildland fires. In addition, the calamitous "fire siege" that swept southern California that year took the lives of twenty-three civilians, most of them residents who waited too long to evacuate their homes, and one firefighter.

Before Oyler's case, perhaps the most notorious modern wildfire arsonist was Terry Lynn Barton, a seasonal Forest Service employee whose duties ironically included spotting smoke. Barton at first denied but later admitted to setting the 2002 Hayman Fire, at that time the largest in Colorado's history, which destroyed 133 houses, burned 38,114 acres, and forced the evacuation of more than five thousand people. Five members of the Grayback Forestry crew from Oregon were killed when their van, on the way to the Hayman Fire, swerved off a highway in western Colorado and spun out of control; Barton was never held responsible for those deaths.

One of the Hayman Fire evacuees happened to be Edward Colt, the state court judge who later handled Barton's trial. Colt acknowledged before passing sentence on Barton that he had seen the Hayman Fire's smoke in the distance and evacuated his home in the interface for a single night. He sentenced Barton to twelve years in prison, which was later reduced to six years after an appeals court said that Colt's link to the fire presented a conflict of interest. Barton offered several explanations for starting the fire, including that she'd done it accidentally while burning a letter from her estranged husband, but investigators concluded that her actions were deliberate and she meant to start a wildfire. She pled guilty to arson and served the six-year prison term, double the time Pattan had served for the Rattlesnake Fire, which had burned fifteen firefighters to death.

Women set far fewer arson fires than men, but it happens: a veteran California arson investigator studied the gender issue and turned up two cases in which women married to much older men took out sexual frustrations by starting fires. One woman would complain about a migraine headache when her husband wanted sex and then set out for the hospital, lighting fires along the way; the other would agree to sex, then afterward go for a drive and set fires. In a story that may have improved with the telling, the veteran investigator recounted a case involving a string of arson fires that seemed to defy solution. After months of chasing dead ends, he caught the arsonist by staking out a likely ignition spot. Embarrassingly, the arsonist was a very familiar figure: a grandmother who had served him tea when he had interviewed her as a potential witness. She had set the fires so a grandson could find work on the fire crews.

Since the Barton case in Colorado, many fire starters, intentional or otherwise, have discovered that the public and the judiciary are fed up. In 2004 Matt Rupp was driving his mower over a field of dry grass in northern California on an especially hot day when a passerby suggested he stop on account of the heat and drought conditions. Rupp reportedly responded, "Go to hell." Instead, he went to jail after his mower blade hit a rock and started a fire that gutted eighty-six homes. Rupp was sentenced to four years in prison and ordered to pay for $2.5 million in damages. Even his defense attorney, Jean Marinovich, who said Rupp had been "hammered" by the judgment, acknowledged that sentences in such cases "have to be harsh enough for people to pay attention."

The wildland fire community closely followed the case of Van Bateman, a Forest Service fire management officer and one-time incident commander of a national incident management team. Prosecutors charged that in 2004 Bateman set two fires on the Coconino National Forest south of Flagstaff, Arizona, to burn brush and give his crew from the Mogollon Rim District a bit of work. The fires burned barely 22 acres, but they cost Bateman his freedom and exposed a long-standing and more or less accepted brush-clearing practice.

"I'm not lily-white on this," said Bateman, who admitted to setting the fires when confronted with global positioning data from his cell phone. He claimed, however, that his actions were sanctioned by tradition, and more than fifty fellow firefighters sent letters to support him. "I'm saying I came out here and I was doing my job. Did I obtain the proper authorization? I did not. But I wasn't trying to start an arson fire. I was trying to clean this piece of country up. I would be shocked if there's anybody who has spent their career in forest management who hasn't done this." Eventually, the arson charges were dropped, but U.S. District Court judge Paul Rosenblatt sentenced Bateman, who had hoped for probation, to twenty-four months in jail for the technically illegal blaze. Another two-year sentence was imposed on a Forest Service firefighter a few years later. Perhaps concerned about the consequences of a public trial, Daniel Mariano Madrigal of Hesperia, California, entered a plea of no contest in 2011 to setting a 1-acre fire on forest land in July of the previous year, after first claiming the fire had resulted from a smoking accident.

The year of the Esperanza Fire, 2006, was a busy one for arsonists. A mentally ill homeless man who described himself as a nature lover accidentally started a wildland fire, the Day Fire, which burned for a month in the Los Padres National Forest in southern California, injured eighteen people, destroyed eleven structures, burned more than 162,000 acres, and cost over $100 million to suppress. Two years later, Steven Emory Butcher was sentenced to forty-five months in prison and ordered to pay $102 million restitution (rescinded because he was indigent) after a jury convicted him of starting the Day Fire by burning garbage at a campsite. The same jury also convicted him of accidentally starting another fire two years earlier, the Ellis Fire, which scorched 70 acres a few miles from where the Day Fire was started. The court ordered Butcher, described as suffering from paranoid schizophrenia, depression, and alcoholism, to submit to a mental examination and psychiatric care. The prosecutor, Assistant U.S. Attorney Joseph Johns, said the forty-five-month sentence was the longest he knew about for an accidental fire start in the wild.

A longer sentence, of ten years, was handed down for a willful arsonist, Jonah Micah Warr, after he pleaded guilty to deliberately setting nine wildland fires on national forest land in northwestern Montana from July to September 2006. Warr, who was 19 at the time, had a lengthy criminal record, including possession of explosives, and was described in court documents as a pyromaniac who abused drugs and alcohol. No one was injured in the fires, and most were extinguished quickly, but the largest one cost more than $6 million to contain.

The prosecution of Raymond Oyler was a far more challenging endeavor. Oyler faced a charge sheet with forty-five felonies: five counts of first-degree murder, with special circumstances justifying the death penalty; twenty-three counts of arson; and seventeen counts of illegal use of an ignition device. The real issue, though, was the Esperanza Fire and the murder charges. The link between Oyler and that fire hung by a thread: the notion that a series of arson fires started with stick matches, cigarettes, and rubber bands was the work of a single person. It helped that Oyler's DNA had been found on ignition devices for two of the nonlethal fires, that all the fires were fairly close together and near Oyler's home, and that the series evolved from small and ineffective blazes to larger and more destructive fires, one sign of a serial arsonist. The ignition devices also became simpler and more effective with time, a sign of successful experimenting by one person. There was, however, one vital exception.

The jury had been shown a photograph of the device that actually started the Esperanza Fire, a bundle of about a half dozen stick matches held around a Marlboro cigarette with a blue-green rubber band. It looked like a lot of the devices used to start the first arson fires, as defense lawyers had been quick to point out. If it was part of the arson series, it was a throwback. The device, discovered by an observant investigator amid the char at the fire's point of origin, had been carefully collected into a box and taken to a crime lab for analysis. When examined, it was found to bear no traces of DNA, no fingerprints, no absolute link to the accused man now seated at the defense table. At one point, late in the deliberations, the jury had reported to the judge that they couldn't reach a decision. Raymond Oyler and his supporters had good reason to hope for an acquittal or hung jury at least on the gravest charges, those connected to the Esperanza Fire.

2.

ON THE FIRST DAY OF what came to be called the Banning
Pass arson series, May 16, 2006, three tiny fires broke out
close together and minutes apart along roadways near the town of
Banning. No one was injured. The fires did no damage. Yet they
started a chain reaction that led, in less than three years, to the
Riverside courtroom and the capital murder trial of Raymond
Oyler. The locations and timing immediately raised suspicions
that the fires were the work of an arsonist, and a call went out to
the Cal Fire arson squad. Among those responding was Charlie
Dehart, a veteran of more than three hundred fire investigations.
Upon examination, he found large bundles of burned and partially
burned wooden matches at the sites of all three fires. There was
no mistaking the signs: the fires had been deliberately set. Dehart
put in a call to Mike Mayman, an assistant district attorney for
Riverside County who specialized in arson. Dehart and Mayman
were well acquainted.

"We got three fires in one day," Dehart told Mayman. "It's May
and it's not even hot out yet." Dehart took a breath. "Mike, it's
going to be a long fuckin' summer."

The fires that day burned less than 1 acre of ground altogether.
Started in grassland at times given as 2:05 PM, 2:14 PM, and 2:21
PM, the fire sites were within three miles of each other. The ignition

devices found by investigators followed a similar pattern: each was made of thirty-one to thirty-three wooden matches fastened together by a rubber band around a Marlboro cigarette. All three devices were found within ten feet of a roadway, less than a stone's throw, indicating that they probably had been tossed from a vehicle rather than walked out and placed. With slight modifications, a device made up of wooden matches, a Marlboro cigarette, and a rubber band would become the all-too-familiar signature of the Banning Pass arsonist.

California has about fifty state arson investigators, but there was only so much anyone could do at this early stage. With no one hurt and virtually no damage done, the fires didn't have enough priority even to justify running the ignition devices through the state crime lab for analysis. Authorities had a list of potential arson suspects, but there are legal constraints about going after individuals without specific or probable cause. So investigators assigned to the Banning Pass series carefully collected and stored evidence and awaited developments, which were not long in coming. Another three fires were started three days later, on May 19, within a fifty-minute period. These fires were slightly more spread out, within nine miles of each other, but once again ignition devices were found each time ten feet or less from roadways. And again, the fires caused little damage, blackening altogether less than 1 acre of ground.

Eleven more similar fires were ignited in the Banning Pass during the remainder of May, all alongside roadways and all with minimal damage. Arson investigators went to each ignition site and collected and stored whatever evidence they could discover. Sometimes they found no incendiary device; other times just a few matches. Concern heightened on the last day of May when a fire, the third to occur that day, was set on sloped ground and burned over an acre. Investigators worried that perhaps the arsonist had begun to appreciate a slope's magnifying effect on fire growth.

By happenstance, two of the arson investigators, Dehart and Matt Gilbert, attended a training session that spring at which Douglas Allen, the retired head of the Cal Fire arson team for southern California, was teaching a class. Allen kept his hand in the game as a consultant and instructor; later he would be a star witness for the state in the Oyler case, debating with a defense expert, David Smith, whether the Banning Pass series could have been the work of one man alone. At the spring training session, Dehart and Gilbert shared their worries about the Banning Pass series with Allen. The two investigators badly needed a break in the case, something to point them in the right direction. They asked Allen what conclusions a veteran like him would draw from the makeup of the ignition devices found at the fires, which was about the only clue they had at this point.

Allen offered them little comfort. "I told them that when the guy hits the same area, the same road, in one day with a large device—there were dozens of matches used in these early devices, a lot more than necessary—it indicates he's just starting up and experimenting," Allen said. "And it indicates he'll keep going. This wasn't a guy who got drunk and went out and lit one. It looked to me like the beginning of a series. These guys don't stop until they're caught."

The first unmistakable sign of a pattern of evolution in the arson series came on June 3, when a fire burned 3 acres of grassland in an open field at Sixth and Xenia streets in Banning. The address was right across the street from where Oyler lived and within four feet of a walking path through an open field routinely used by Oyler to walk to nearby stores and restaurants. Those connections became known only after the Esperanza Fire, when Oyler fell under suspicion. On June 3, however, investigators discovered something else at Sixth and Xenia that piqued their interest: a differently arranged ignition device.

The customary Marlboro cigarette was there, sure enough. But this time the remains of three wooden matches lay across the cigarette at a 90-degree angle. Just as with the previous devices, where the matches were arranged around the cigarette, the matches in this device would burst into flame as the cigarette burned down. Investigators estimated it would take four to seven minutes for the matches to ignite, plenty of time for an arsonist, especially one in a vehicle, to be long gone. The arsonist had learned that it takes only a flaming match or two and not a bundle of matches to ignite a wildland fire. The arsonist also had shown imagination and simplified his task, because the smaller device could be assembled at the scene from parts that would not cause suspicion if observed, unlike the previous, bulkier device, which most likely had to be assembled beforehand and looked unmistakably like an ignition device. Because the matches were placed on the cigarette, the arsonist would have to set the new device by hand and not throw it. Investigators dubbed their find the layover device and would testify later that the design was new to their experience.

From the beginning of June onward, the evidence pointing toward a single serial arsonist piled up. For a month, from June 3 to July 2, the arsonist consistently used the layover device to set no fewer than ten fires. By mid-June the arsonist had switched locations, graduating from mostly open, flat fields of dried grass and brush, where fires generally stay small and can be contained, to mostly sloped terrain leading to a mountain, with limitless possibilities for destruction. The tally of charred acres from each fire steadily climbed.

In one case that drew much attention, both at the time and later, an arson fire was ignited at 12:31 PM on June 14 at Broadway and Esperanza Avenue in Cabazon, barely a half mile from the eventual site of the lethal fire. Starting at the foot of Twin Pines Ridge, the blaze nearly got away into the mountains and was stopped only by a roadway that acted as a firebreak. Investigators recovered a layover ignition device made up of a Marlboro cigarette and about a half dozen matches resting on it at a 90-degree angle. The fire, the biggest in the Banning Pass series up to that point, burned 10 acres. Prosecutors later called it a practice fire, a trial run for the Esperanza Fire.

More fires burned in early July. Some were small; several were set on sloped terrain. One on July 5 scorched 62 acres. Then something strange happened. The series ended, or at least the arsonist took a break, beginning on July 9. Week after week, no arson fires were reported. Investigators thought the arsonist might have moved away, gone on vacation, or simply stopped setting fires, though veteran fire investigators doubted the latter explanation. Then, on September 16, after more than a two-month hiatus, two more arson fires were started in the Banning Pass. One of them, on a slope leading to a basin or wash, burned a hefty 1,580 acres. The next day, September 17, an arson fire in Banning swept over 1,658 acres of grassland. The Banning Pass arsonist, if it was one arsonist, was back at work and becoming more destructive.

Calculations showed that from the first fires on May 16 until June 14, the average land scorched per fire was 0.83 acres. From June 14 until October 26, the average rose to 223 acres per fire, excluding the massive Esperanza Fire. By the end of the series, more than half the fires were being set on sloped terrain and more than a quarter of them in a drainage basin in the mountains, which would greatly magnify their effect.

The Banning Pass arsonist was on a fatal learning curve.

◆ ◆ ◆

THE ESPERANZA FIRE began as a spot of orange-red flame no bigger than a match head flaring alongside a lonely roadway on the floor of the Pass. The fire came to life minutes after the taillights of a departing vehicle had disappeared around a curve on Esperanza Avenue, which divides the hardscrabble town of Cabazon from Cabazon Peak, a bulky 4,350-foot mass of loose boulders and chaparral that looms above the Banning Pass. A bundle made of stick matches fastened around a Marlboro cigarette by greenish-blue rubber bands was found within easy throwing distance of Esperanza Avenue—exactly twelve feet away—at the ignition point of the fire. Investigators concluded that an arsonist had tossed the device from a car window or had placed it there and then sped away before the smoldering cigarette ignited the matches.

The remoteness of the location, plus the curve in the roadway and the approximate 1:00 AM time of the fire start, delayed a sighting of the fire long enough for it to take hold and grow. Tiny orange flames spread in fits and starts from matchsticks to twigs and dry grasses, dying out here and carrying forward there into the next bunch of grass. The flames morphed into multiple pinpricks of light, as though someone had scattered seeds of flame across the dry landscape. The pinpricks of light burned into heavier brush in a nearby wash, dry at this time of year, and rose through the brush into the branches of a few scraggly trees. Flames crackled in the heavier fuels.

The location at the base of Cabazon Peak was a perfect spot for a fire to grow. The steep, uninhabited slopes of the peak, primed to burn after months of hot sunshine and scant moisture, rise dramatically from 1,700 feet at the desert floor to more than 4,000 feet. The slopes are boulder-strewn and dotted with chaparral. At the place where the fire was started, the slope forms a kind of bowl tipped on its side. The ignition point was on the lower edge of the bowl; a ridgeline formed the upper edge. Once the fire became established, it began to run upward, following the wash, which concentrated and accelerated it, fanning out into a broad flame front that continued to ascend the peak. As the fire progressed, the flames generated enough light to reflect off the night sky in a false dawn. Finally, a night security guard at a water bottling plant several miles away saw what was happening and called 911.

The official life of the Esperanza Fire began at precisely 1:11 and fifty-six seconds on the morning of Thursday, October 26, 2006. At that moment the Riverside County sheriff's dispatch office forwarded the security guard's fire report to the region's Emergency Command Center in Perris, a town to the west. For identification purposes, and with unintended irony, the blaze was named, as is customary, for the nearest prominent geographic landmark, Esperanza Avenue, itself named by the Spanish word for hope.

The fire report sparked an immediate reaction from the Perris command center. Considering that southern California is one of the most combustible places on earth, no fire authority in the region hesitates to commit a sizable response of manpower and equipment immediately upon receiving a wildfire report, and most certainly not in late October, at the height of fire season. That first report triggered an automatic call-out for a battalion chief, five fire engines, two twenty-person hand crews, and two bulldozers, or about seventy firefighters in all. A force that large instantly committed to a blaze of only an acre or two would drop jaws— and exceed capabilities—in many other parts of the country. Even before the fire report, however, firefighters knew that a spark at this time of year, at this hour and in this place, could cause major destruction.

The previous morning, Wednesday, October 25, the National Weather Service had issued a red flag warning, which means conditions are ideal for fire ignition and spread. For days, the NWS had issued red flag watches, cautioning that a Santa Ana wind might occur. On Wednesday meteorologists raised the level a notch, to a warning, and predicted the Santa Ana wind would arrive by the following dawn, now only hours away. Many of the worst fires in California, which holds records for destructive, costly, and deadly wildfires, have been whipped by the Santa Ana winds that devil the region from October through December. A Santa Ana can blow for days at forty miles an hour or more, with gusts above one hundred. The wind turns vegetation to tinder, strips fronds from palm trees, overturns garbage cans, litters streets with debris, and grates on the human psyche like a gas-powered leaf blower. It also stirs the dark passions of California's arsonists, many of whom are aware that a Santa Ana wind's greatest power is to transform a tiny spot of flame into an inferno.

Arson, too, was in the forecast for October 26, if only informally. When the red flag warning went out on Wednesday, several supervisors from Cal Fire telephoned a fire captain based near the Banning Pass, whom they regularly consulted as a weather sage. The captain, Tim Chavez, a fire behavior analyst and wildfire veteran, told the callers that he thought the weather service forecast had the timing right for the Santa Ana but had seriously underestimated the intensity. The wind would arrive in the morning, Chavez agreed. But the weather service had predicted a relatively moderate blow. "It looked to me like it was going to be a strong wind," Chavez said later. "It was late October. We'd had no rain. Forecasters are pretty good on timing, but intensity is harder." Then Chavez told the callers, in words they would well remember, "I sure hope whoever's setting fires in the Banning Pass doesn't set another one during the wind event."

Chavez and the fire supervisors had every reason for concern. The Banning Pass arson series had made the news only a few times, but the fire community was keenly aware that a serial arsonist was at work in their backyard. "It seemed like we were getting a fire a day," said one of the engine captains who fought the Esperanza Fire. Though none of the arson fires had yet caused major injuries or loss of homes, they were getting bigger, with several over 1,000 acres, and good luck would not last forever.

At the early hour when the Esperanza Fire began, the wind breathed gently through the Banning Pass. The more than three thousand wind turbines clustered in ranks on the slopes at the mouth of the Pass east of Cabazon Peak were models of indecision. The graceful white-bladed turbines, the tallest over 300 feet high with blades 150 feet long, would abruptly spin to life on a breath of wind and then, just as abruptly, halt as the wind died out. Accelerated by the narrows at the mouth of the Pass, the effect that explains the presence of the wind farms there, the Santa Ana wind when it arrived would overwhelm the weak prevailing westerly wind, set the white-bladed turbines spinning, and sweep the ten-mile length of the Banning Pass, which makes a perfect wind tunnel.

Normally at this time of night, with only a dim urban glow from the floor of the Pass to lighten the sky, Cabazon Peak would be shrouded in darkness, overshadowed by the looming San Jacinto Mountains. Topped by San Jacinto Peak at just over 10,800 feet, the mountains, including Cabazon Peak and a long west-running ridge called Twin Pines, make up the southern wall of the Banning Pass, the deepest pass in southern California. The opposite, north wall of the Pass is topped by San Gorgonio Peak, the highest in the region at just over 11,500 feet. The Banning Pass has been the main east–west land route into southern California since ancient times. First used by Indians, it became a major travel and trade route for Europeans in wagon trains and stagecoaches, one driven by the legendary Wyatt Earp. In modern times, a busy railroad line and heavily used interstate highway, I-10, follow in a general way the old stage trace. Dry, barren vistas invite the traveler to keep moving.

The Pass was formed tens of millions of years ago in part by the San Andreas Fault, the "transform boundary" between the Pacific and North American tectonic plates, which makes its famous big-bend turn to the east near Santa Barbara, north of the Pass. The bend in effect turns earth's plates against each other, so instead of sliding past they press on one another. The tremendous pressure this generates caused the fault to fracture into a spiderweb of smaller faults in the Banning Pass area. Geologists call the results "fairly complex" and offer only suggestions to explain the chaotic results. Ancient volcanic activity associated with the plate movement, followed by eons of earthquakes and erosion, gives the Pass its geologic character: the floor is sandy, the foothills are made up of crumbly granite and loose boulders, and the peaks are relatively solid granite.

The Banning Pass was known informally for decades as "the Appalachia of Southern California," too far from Los Angeles to be overwhelmed by sprawling exurbia, but not close enough to the desert playgrounds to attract the well-heeled. The Pass was what prosperous folk drove through on their way to and from Palm Springs, which lies just beyond the mouth of the Pass. In the great housing bubble of the early twenty-first century, a few tract housing developments and gated retirement communities—for folks "55 and better," as one come-on sign beckoned—made their way into the Pass, followed by cookie-cutter shopping malls with big box retail outlets. The bursting of the housing bubble ended headlong development, at least for a while. At the time of the Esperanza Fire, the string of small towns along the old stage trace, including Banning, Beaumont, and Cabazon, mostly retained their working-class atmosphere.

The Banning Pass had its loyal longtime residents, and one of them was Cal Fire's Andrew Bennett, the fire's first incident commander. Bennett had fought more than one thousand fires during his twenty-three years of service, most of it in the Banning Pass. Bennett looked every inch a firefighter—tall, fit, and ramrod straight, with a neatly trimmed mustache. The responsibility for the Esperanza Fire, from the first citizen report to the fire's climax, belonged to Cal Fire, though many other agencies would become involved and eventually share responsibility. Bennett was dispatched from Banning, about ten miles from the fire scene, within minutes of the first fire report.

As he drove along I-10, following the old stage route, he could see both the orange glow from the fire, reflected in the night sky, and the necklace of flame creeping up the slopes of Cabazon Peak. The peak was a well-known landmark. It was not only clearly visible from anywhere in the Pass but also had a specific name, which made it handy for fire communication; many of the deep ravines and prominent ridges in the foothills lacked names altogether. The most significant piece of geography in this story, for example, was christened only after the fire and then was called, blandly enough, the unnamed creek drainage. The Banning Pass excites fire behavior, but its hostile emptiness also deadens the human imagination, as the Esperanza Fire was about to demonstrate.

Bennett knew from the start that this was no routine blaze. He was a firefighter, but he also was an arson investigator and as such had been assigned to the Banning Pass arson series from the beginning. He had bought aluminum roasting pans and given them to fire captains so they could protect and preserve any ignition devices they found. If the arsonist wasn't stopped, one of the fires was bound to get loose and cause great damage. From what Bennett could see, the Esperanza Fire could be the one.

In the best of times, the Banning Pass is a landscape made for burning, and this was the worst of times—the driest, windiest time of year. Nighttime is the most favorable time to fight fire: the wind usually drops, temperatures moderate, and humidity rises. But on this night, darkness was an enemy not a friend. Sending hand crews into chaparral-choked ravines in full darkness is a prescription for disaster. Several hand crews in fact scouted the Esperanza Fire that night, but none found a safe place to begin an attack before daylight. One pair of hotshot supervisors who had scouted the face of Twin Pines Ridge without success found themselves driven back by advancing smoke and flames and wound up sheltering in their pickup as the fire passed by.

The slopes of Cabazon Peak have a history of regular wildfire, one every five years or so; in the area of the Esperanza Fire there had been eleven fires in the past fifty-five years. Most of the fires on Cabazon Peak, though, are easy to spot and are caught early and stopped. Or they burn themselves out before causing major problems. The peak is just that, a peak, so fires often just burn to the top and die out. Even though the peak is uninhabited, fires there get quick attention: if flames do break loose from its slopes, they can threaten the communities on Twin Pines Ridge and farther up in the mountains. The regularity and inconsequence of the fires are something of a local joke. One night a few years earlier, a veteran firefighter and his wife were awakened by yet another middle-of-the-night fire call. "Where's this one?" the wife asked grumpily. "Cabazon," her sleepy spouse replied as he pulled on his uniform. "Oh, come back to bed. That's just a pile of rocks," the wife said.

Sometimes, though, especially in October, a Banning Pass fire turns deadly. Dating from 1967, three such fires killed firefighters, all within a few miles of the ignition point of the Esperanza Fire. In October 1967, Frank Rios, a firefighter from Arizona's Tohono O'odham Nation, or People of the Desert, was killed on a steep slope during the Bailiff Fire. In September 1971, Robert M. Miller, a Forest Service firefighter, was killed on a similarly steep slope while trying to outrun the Mack II Fire. In October 1998, a pilot, Gary Nagel, died when the air tanker he was flying crashed into a mountainside during the Mount Edna Fire.

As Bennett approached the Esperanza Fire, however, he had many advantages, because nobody takes on wildfire the way they do it in southern California. The Golden State has more and bigger wildfires, more citizens and firefighters killed, and more structures burned by wildfire than any other state in the union. In terms of loss, according to the National Fire Protection Association, six of the eight costliest wildland fires in recorded history occurred in California. The 1991 Oakland Firestorm holds the loss record at $1.5 billion, adjusted to $2.4 billion in 2010 dollars. Consequently, acre for acre, nobody pours more money, manpower, and equipment, especially aircraft, into fighting fire than California, even when the state dips into a low point in its boom-and-bust economy. "We can put one hundred engines on a fire anywhere in the state within an hour," said one battalion chief who fought Esperanza. At the beginning of the twenty-first century, the U.S. Forest Service's budget for wildfire for the entire nation reached a record of more than $1 billion a year, not incidentally eating up half the agency's overall budget and draining funds from recreation, maintenance, forest management, and other nonfire programs. At the same time, the state of California's annual fire budget reached roughly the same figure—$1 billion—even as the state headed toward the threat of bankruptcy. That $1 billion figure is by no means the spending total for wildfire in California. Take one example: a year after the Esperanza Fire, in the extreme fire season of 2007, the Forest Service spent $1.4 billion on fire nationwide, half of that in California alone. The state of California spent an additional $1 billion for fire that year, bringing the total bill for California wildfire in 2007 to roughly $1.7 billion, a figure that is more than double what the Forest Service spent in the other forty-nine states combined. No wonder, then, that California firefighters regard themselves as the big time of the fire world. Simply put, they are.

During Bennett's brief drive along I-10, he noted that the fire was cooking up, as firefighters describe a fast-growing fire, and he put in a first call for reinforcements. He noted the flames at the base of Cabazon Peak, but what worried him most was a spot fire that had broken out midway up the peak; it already was bigger than the one at the base. He radioed the Perris dispatch center and ordered a second battalion chief and five more engines, all from the Forest Service, and several water tenders. Bennett made that call around 1:30 AM, and the order went out at 1:43 AM according to dispatch records.

The Forest Service maintains a string of fire stations in the mountains of the Banning Pass to protect national forest lands, but it has cooperative—and sometimes bafflingly complex— agreements with Cal Fire to share and allocate responsibilities and resources when jurisdictions overlap. Bennett wanted the five Forest Service engine crews of the San Jacinto District alerted and on the move immediately, in part because they had long distances to travel. Firefighters from state and municipal departments stationed along the floor of the Pass could reach the Esperanza Fire in minutes, and several did. The Forest Service crews would take an hour or more to assemble in the mountains and then to drive down State Highway 243, the twisting mountain road that links the San Jacinto Mountains and the floor of the Pass. At the time of the fire, the highway bore the picturesque name Palms to Pines Scenic Byway; its long hairpin turns and blind curves unite two worlds as separate culturally as they are geographically. Snow can cover the pines in the high country at the same time there's sunshine, shirtsleeve temperatures, and balmy breezes in the lower elevations. The highway name was changed afterward to the Esperanza Firefighters Memorial Highway.

Shortly after Bennett arrived at the base of Cabazon Peak, he had seen enough to make a bold prediction: he reported to the dispatch office that the fire's behavior was "abnormal," and he estimated it could grow to 25,000 acres, a guess that proved to be conservative. The fire was about 5 acres in size when he arrived, Bennett said, had established itself on the toe of a slope, and was moving swiftly upslope. "Very shortly it was 50 acres," he said, "and growing too fast to put firefighters on its perimeter."

Bennett, like virtually every firefighter in southern California, was aware that high winds were on their way. Forecasters had raised the possibility of a Santa Ana wind each day for the past five days. When the weather service had issued a red flag watch two days earlier, warning that winds *could* strike, the information had been distributed to the more than fifty fire agencies based from the Banning Pass to Los Angeles. At 10:23 the next morning, the day before the Esperanza Fire began, the red flag watch had been jacked up to a red flag warning, which meant high winds were imminent and fire behavior could become extreme. Red flags are the storm and gale warnings of the fire world, perhaps mind-numbing when repeated day after day but a crucial indicator of future extreme fire behavior. The mid-morning red flag warning was sent to Cal Fire's Riverside dispatch center but was not passed on to area stations and chief fire officers at that time, or even when it was updated at 2:00 PM. Much was later made of this oversight; John Hawkins, Cal Fire's Riverside Unit fire chief, who had the overall responsibility, blames himself for this failure. Hawkins was one of the supervisors who had telephoned Captain Chavez and heard his warning that the Santa Ana might be more intense than predicted. But one more broadcast of a wind warning would hardly have changed events.

During fire season, firefighters keep a weather eye and tune radios to National Weather Service broadcasts. Virtually every firefighter in the Banning Pass, and certainly every veteran, knew a Santa Ana wind was on its way. But winds and fires are not entirely predictable events, even for those whose lives depend on making judgments about them. Though no one successfully predicted the extreme effect of the Santa Ana wind on the Esperanza Fire, the result so exceeded the predictive powers of both science and practical judgment that it's difficult—and perhaps foolish—to say that the failure to disseminate the red flag warning made a decisive or even significant contribution to what was about to happen. Mistakes were made fighting the Esperanza Fire, to be sure, and underestimating the power of fire was a big one. But fire in the wild played the crucial role.

When Bennett assumed control of the fire at 1:34 AM, he became the first of many incident commanders, or ICs. Command of the Esperanza Fire changed hands repeatedly as it expanded from initial attack, under Bennett, to what is called a campaign fire, under the supervision of multiple agencies operating in unified command and finally under the supervision of a specialized, high-level team. The first firefighters to actually reach the flames were the three members of Cal Fire's Engine 24 crew, based at a station less than a mile from the fire's ignition point along Esperanza Avenue.

"We got dispatched just after 1:00 AM to a vegetation fire said to be about two and a half miles away," said Engine 24's Captain Martin Gill. "We were nearly there when one of the crew looked back out the window. She said, 'Oh, shit, the fire's back on Cabazon Peak and it's halfway up the hill.' And I looked back and said the same word."

A security officer at the Arrowhead Water bottling plant in Cabazon, Gill learned, had reported the fire, so Engine 24 had headed toward the plant. The misdirection to the vegetation fire caused almost no delay. "It took us four minutes to get there instead of two," he said. In fact, the official report says that Gill called in a size-up of the Esperanza Fire at 1:18 AM, barely six minutes after the fire was reported; given a minute or two for communications and the size-up, Gill's estimate of the swift response is no exaggeration. But the flames did not need time. They already were moving smartly up Cabazon Peak; the angle of the slope, even without a wind, drove flames uphill four times faster than they traveled on flat ground. Sensibly, Engine 24 stayed put on Esperanza Avenue, reporting to dispatch that the flames covered about 2 acres and were expanding very quickly.

"What caught my eye when we drove up was a large tree, the biggest one around," Gill said. "The leaves were all burned off and the bark was glowing orange. I'd never seen anything like that. The fire was burning *hot*."

Engine 24 never unrolled a hose line. After a few minutes, Bennett, the IC, drove up to the site and asked Gill what he could do to slow the spreading fire. Gill said his crew might hike up to an old trace called Hall's Grade, once used as an access road for the installation of underground water pipes but since then fallen into disuse, and start a fire on a nearby ridge to act as a firebreak. As they talked, they watched the spot fire farther up the slope expand in seconds to cover 5 acres. "That's when we knew we were not going to be able to take any stop actions on this fire," Gill said.

Gill and Bennett had been watching fires together since spring. Gill had been the first to arrive at the first fire in the Banning Pass arson series, on May 16, and Bennett had been one of the arson investigators there. "We knew it was arson," Gill said of the Esperanza Fire. "We'd been chasing those fires all summer long, sometimes three or four a day. It was like the arsonist was toying with us. We'd be on a fire for three or four hours, picking up hose and ready to go, and look up and there was another fire. It was like he was watching us and playing with us. Andy Bennett told me he thought the guy was trying to burn up Cabazon Peak on his shift."

At this point, another engine arrived at the scene and came up on the radio. "What's your pleasure?" they said. Bennett flicked his radio and there was a long pause. Then he said, "To be on vacation."

Bennett then drove to the fire's first incident command post, or ICP, located less than a mile from the base of the fire at the Engine 24 station, where he met with other arriving fire supervisors, who already knew they were in a losing race with time. They simply could not get personnel and equipment, and especially aircraft, to work fast enough to keep the fire small; at that time, almost all their aircraft were forbidden from fighting fire at night. "We were losing our window," one supervisor later remarked. Their best hope lay with the fire itself, which might climb Cabazon Peak and die out, as fires had done many times in the past. The Santa Ana wind could even help, several of the supervisors realized, if it arrived early enough. The wind, coming through the mouth of the Banning Pass from the east, could hold the flames low in the foothills, driving them west and keeping them away from the upper inhabited reaches of Twin Pines Ridge and beyond.

One firefighter who hoped for an early wind was Dan Felix, a battalion chief who supervised the Forest Service engine crews of the San Jacinto District, the five units requested by Bennett. Felix had been alerted to the fire at 1:30 AM by the buzz of a telephone next to his bed. As he pulled his gear together and listened to emergency radio traffic over a short-wave scanner, Felix realized he had a personal stake in this fire. The radio traffic indicated that the Esperanza Fire was big, growing, and headed up the mountains— right for his home.

Felix lived in the town of Idyllwild, located a mile high in the San Jacinto Mountains and a half century back in time. If the Esperanza Fire ran up and over Twin Pines Ridge, it could run into the pine forests that at higher elevations replaced the chaparral, the mix of chamise, scrub oak, and manzanita whose thick, waxy leaves can burn with white-hot intensity when dry. The fire could threaten communities including Idyllwild, which was home not only for Felix but also for several other Forest Service firefighters who fought the Esperanza Fire, including Captain Mark Loutzenhiser of Engine 57. Idyllwild, a woodsy oasis amid the fast life of urbanized California, drew Forest Service people and others with its small-town atmosphere and values. "Idyllwild is an old-fashioned Forest Service town," said Felix, who had lived there for over a decade. "It's a family up there on the hill."

The beautiful pine forest around Idyllwild paradoxically had become an extreme fire hazard. Wildland fire had been suppressed for so long that the woods had become overgrown and ripe for catastrophic fire, as elsewhere around the nation. The problem traced to the outmoded national policy of attempting to suppress all wildland fires, begun nearly a century before in response to the Big Burn of 1910, the most politically potent wildfire in U.S. history. The story is well-known but worth repeating.

In the early part of the twentieth century, the role of fire in keeping forests healthy, by turning mature timber into nutrient-rich ash, clearing brush and other understory vegetation, and in general helping forests replenish themselves, was not well understood. Native Americans had burned the western forests for centuries, resulting in a forest mosaic that was far more open than many remaining sections are today. The European settlers lived in fear that their permanent settlements, unlike the nomadic Native American villages, and possibly their lives, would fall victim to fire. Then came the Big Burn of 1910.

The conscience of the early Forest Service and other firefighters was born of the casualties of the Big Burn's massive forest destruction and heavy loss of life. Horrified over the loss of 3 million acres of forest and more than four score people killed, Forest Service leaders vowed that such a catastrophe would never happen again. The fire settled the dispute between proponents of Native American–style burning and those who favored full suppression. Fire was the enemy, period. The famous—today infamous—"10:00 am policy," which stated that all wildfires were to be controlled by mid-morning the day after they were spotted or, if not by then, by mid-morning the next day, grew out of the Big Burn experience and was formally adopted by the Forest Service in 1936. The full-suppression policy broke down in the 1970s and 1980s with the growing realization that fire plays a vital role in ecosystems. By then, however, the nation's population had greatly extended its reach into previously wild lands, and simply letting most fires go was no option. The Big Burn's legacy of overgrown forests impacts policy to this day, contributing significantly to the unresolved conflict between the needs of an expanding population and forest health. At the time of the Esperanza Fire, an ambitious burning and clearing project was under way throughout the San Jacinto Mountains, notably around Idyllwild, to make up for decades of fire suppression. The scope of the problem was daunting, however, even in this one forest, and the work was only partially complete. As a result, Idyllwild was in the middle of a potential inferno.

Felix's assignment on the Esperanza Fire was to represent the Forest Service at the ICP at Cabazon. The Banning Pass is a bewildering checkerboard of state, private, Indian tribal, and federal agency ownerships. By long-standing agreement, Cal Fire had responsibility for the ground where the Esperanza Fire started, which is why Bennett was the first IC, with overall control. The growing flames, however, threatened nearby Forest Service lands: the spectacular Black Mountain Scenic Area, which includes a section of the famed Pacific Crest National Scenic Trail, along with the San Jacinto Wilderness and the San Bernardino National Forest.

As Felix started the drive down Highway 243 to Cabazon, he heard the hubbub of radio messages that marks a major fire event. Like Bennett before him, he called for reinforcements while still on the road. "Tone out the district," Felix told the Forest Service dispatch office (a separate operation from the Perris emergency center). His order meant to call out the five engine crews of the San Jacinto District, in effect the same order Bennett gave the emergency center dispatcher in Perris at roughly the same time.

Felix drove down out of the pine woods across a broad open bench called McMullen Flat. He came to a spur road off Highway 243, Twin Pines Road, which provides access to the many homes along the ridge. Highway 243 was clear at this hour, though shortly it would jam with traffic as emergency personnel and evacuating citizens jockeyed for space on its narrow corkscrew lanes. From the intersection with Twin Pines Road, Highway 243 drops in a series of hairpin turns down the bare face of Twin Pines Ridge. As Felix began the descent, he saw the Esperanza Fire for the first time. The light from flames throbbing in darkness stirred an unhappy memory of another fire during another dry October on this same fire ground: the fatal Mount Edna Fire.

Mount Edna is a high bump in the foothills just over a mile west of Highway 243, about halfway down the ridge face. The day of the Mount Edna Fire, October 5, 1998, was another time of Santa Ana winds. On that day, observers in the air and on the ground watched with horror as the wind, gusting to more than forty miles an hour, struck pilot Gary Nagel's air tanker as it approached Mount Edna to drop a load of retardant. The S-2 tanker, buffeted by the wind, banked from 60 degrees to 90 degrees and plowed into the mountainside. Eight years later, the Mount Edna Fire remained a vivid memory for many a Banning Pass firefighter.

"I was driving a crew carrier toward the fire on a dirt road when one of the crew members called out, 'Hey, that S-2 just crashed!'" said Captain Richard Gearhart, one of the five San Jacinto engine captains called out for the Esperanza Fire. "The crew actually saw the crash, which let investigators know immediately the accident had been caused by a stall. They saw the plane rise up and nose over on one side. When I looked over, the plane had already hit the ground. There was a big ol' ball of fire, exactly like the movies. We drove over to put tape around the perimeter. We tried at first to keep the crew away from the plane because we didn't want them to see a mangled body. Finally, I told a couple of the guys, 'Look, we're not going to make fun of you and you don't have to go over there. But people die in this job. And we could use the help.'"

As Felix drove past Mount Edna on his way to the Esperanza Fire, the memory of the fatal fire had a double edge for him. The same Santa Ana wind that had sent Nagel's aircraft crashing into the side of the mountain had also kept flames low in the foothills and away from human habitation. Felix found himself hoping that the positive effect of the wind that day would repeat itself and that a Santa Ana wind would arrive early enough on this day to keep flames from the homes on Twin Pines Ridge—and not incidentally from his hometown, Idyllwild. The wind had a chance to redeem its fatal consequences, Felix thought, but it had better get started soon, because he could see flames already working their way up Twin Pines Ridge.

When Felix arrived at the ICP in Cabazon at about 2:30 am, he noted that the "fussin' and discussin'" of fire management was well under way. Felix went looking for the IC and found Bennett hunched over a map, puzzling over the crazy-quilt ownership of the fire ground. "It's going to be on you," Bennett told Felix, pointing on the map to six sections of Forest Service land on Twin Pines Ridge under threat by the fire. If flames reached those six Forest Service sections, it would trigger a unified command in which Bennett for Cal Fire and Felix for the Forest Service would be equals, sharing responsibilities and decision making—or that's what Bennett thought was about to happen.

No, Felix said, that's wrong. "It's not us; it's you guys," he told Bennett.

Those six sections of National Forest land are surrounded by land held by other government agencies and private owners. In expectation of the inevitable confusion over responsibilities during a fire in this area, an agreement existed for Cal Fire to take charge of firefighting on the six Forest Service sections and for the Forest

Service to pay Cal Fire for doing the work. Felix was correct. Cal Fire had sole overall responsibility for the Esperanza Fire at the outset and until well past daylight, though the question of just who was responsible when things went wrong caused a bitter controversy that lasted for years.

Bennett, though, faced a larger and more immediate problem than whether he shared responsibility with Felix. As IC, he had to get an army of firefighters, engines, bulldozers, helicopters, and air tankers ready to attack the fire at first light. And even more urgently, he had to decide whether to order a mass evacuation, in darkness and on narrow mountain roads, of hundreds of civilians from Twin Pines Ridge and other communities. The evacuation decision was a matter of life and death. Bennett remembered the stark lesson of only three years earlier, when most of the twenty-three civilian deaths in the southern California "fire siege" of 2003 occurred when wildfires spread faster than evacuation orders and flames trapped many people in their vehicles as they tried to flee. If an evacuation order was going to be necessary on the Esperanza Fire, it should come sooner rather than later. Bennett had considered ordering a general evacuation from the time he first arrived at the ICP and reported the fire's behavior as "abnormal" and its potential growth at 25,000 acres. An hour later, around 2:30 AM, when Felix joined Bennett at the ICP, the situation had grown worse: the fire was bigger, and no saving Santa Ana wind had arrived.

Evacuations along Twin Pines Ridge began at 2:40 or 2:45 AM, Bennett said later, though the official fire report puts the formal order at 4:00 AM. Many Twin Pines residents did not require the stimulus of an official order to recognize the peril. They packed up the four P's of wildfire evacuation—people, pets, papers, and photos—loaded them into vehicles of every description, and started down Highway 243, causing traffic problems with the fire vehicles trying to get up the road.

With the fire changing from an initial attack operation to a major campaign, a higher-ranking IC took over from Bennett, as a matter of normal procedure, at 3:07 AM. Cal Fire division chief Brenda Seabert became the second IC for the Esperanza Fire, a post she would occupy alone until well past daylight. Once Bennett had briefed Seabert, he was no longer needed at the ICP. Sensing that his further presence there perhaps would be distracting, Bennett left, and for the next few hours, until he was assigned as a branch director in charge of half the field operations, he found himself at loose ends. Bennett had been incident commander for less than two hours, but during that time he had put in orders for personnel and equipment as happens only in California.

The list was staggering; Bennett later said it was the biggest resource order he had ever placed for a fire in initial attack. For engines alone, Bennett ordered seven strike teams of five Type III engines, or thirty-five engines in all; ten similarly configured strike teams with bigger Type I and Type II engines, or fifty engines in all; and the five Forest Service engines of the San Jacinto District, all Type III. For hand crews, the order was for fifteen Type I hand crew strike teams, each team consisting of two twenty-person crews plus a supervisor, or 630 personnel in all. In addition, eight strike teams of two bulldozers each, or sixteen bulldozers, plus supervisors, were ordered. For aircraft, the order was for eight Type II helicopters, six air tankers, two Type I helicopters capable of carrying two thousand gallons each, and one Type III helicopter for reconnaissance. The order also included a communications unit and dozens of supervisors ranging from four division group supervisors to a staging area manager. More resources would be ordered as the day wore on.

With the coming of daylight, the fleet of helicopters and air tankers ordered by Bennett, backed by the fire engines, bulldozers, and hand crews, could hit the flames hard with water and retardant, the

familiar red mud that makes an air operation so photogenic. Under
normal conditions, air tankers and helicopters are often the first to
attack a fire, and ground crews finish the job, much the way infantry
follows an aerial and artillery assault in a military campaign. An air
show can cost many millions of dollars, but in California, a big bill
for aerial firefighting is considered preferable to lost lives and hundreds or thousands of destroyed homes. After the Esperanza Fire,
the policy restricting the use of firefighting aircraft at night would
be reexamined and changes made. But three years later, when the
Station Fire of 2009, which was started by an arsonist, turned into
the biggest fire in the history of Los Angeles County and cost two
firefighters their lives, a perceived delay by the Forest Service in
launching aircraft caused years of litigation, a congressional inquiry,
and a yearlong investigation by the U.S. Government Accountability Office, all of which still left many questions about night flying
and other issues about fighting fire unresolved. In the case of the
Esperanza Fire, virtually no one, except those engaged directly in
protecting a structure, fought the fire until after daylight, and by
that time what counted most had already come to pass.

Bennett, after being relieved by Seabert just after 3:00 AM,
roamed the fire ground over the next few hours and witnessed
many remarkable events: a panicked evacuation, flames that
rolled uphill "like waves curling and crashing," and eventually
a catastrophe of horrific magnitude. At one early point, he came
upon an abandoned Riverside County Animal Control truck and
worried that the missing driver had been killed or injured, until
the driver was discovered to have run a mile down the highway to
safety. One small incident would stick in his memory, however, as
a bearable stand-in for the many horrors of the day. As he drove
along Highway 243, the fire churned up the precipitous slope below
him "like a rototiller." A disoriented cottontail rabbit, caught in the
path of the fire, suddenly bounded forward—heading straight for

the flames. As rabbit and flame came together, the rabbit arose on its hind legs and frantically clawed at the wave of fire "like it was surfing." The flame wave drove the rabbit backward and for long moments the creature and its fate hung suspended, rabbit legs and fire madly churning at each other, until somehow the rabbit broke away, turned, and "got out of there," though precisely where the rabbit got to Bennett could never say.

♦ ♦ ♦

AT APPROXIMATELY 1:45 AM, James Carney Jr. pulled his gasoline delivery truck into a Shell Oil station just off I-10 in Cabazon. Carney unlimbered hoses and began pumping gasoline into the station's underground storage tanks. Looking up, he observed a glow in the sky back across I-10, a mile or so to the south. A brushfire was hardly a rare sight in the Banning Pass; there had been scores of fires in the Pass that year, and local news reports said a serial arsonist was at work. Carney noted that this fire, which illuminated a thick slice of the night sky, seemed to be off to a good start. Thankfully, though, the flames were headed up Cabazon Peak, away from the town of Cabazon and away from his gasoline truck.

As Carney bent to his work, he noticed a man walking in an agitated manner between the gas station's pumps. The man, who later came to be called the stranger, kept glancing over his shoulder in the direction of the fire and appeared excited by the sight. Well, why not? The station made a good observation platform, and the sight of a wildfire is always a thrill. But it was past 2:00 AM, and Carney wondered what business the stranger had at the station at such an hour. There was no vehicle parked at a pump to explain his presence. The stranger showed no sign of leaving. The man seemed fixated by the faraway glow. The fire made a natural conversation starter, and Carney asked the man what he thought of the sight.

"The fire's acting just how I thought it ought to, just the way I thought it would," the stranger replied. A sputtering line of flame advanced up the peak as though it were a tightening noose. Another long strand of flame spread in a jagged line across the low foothills as the fire moved west. The stranger seemed so confident and knowledgeable that Carney thought he probably was an off-duty firefighter, perhaps a volunteer firefighter. Carney had a job to do, however, and went back to his hoses and pumps, leaving the stranger to his curious vigil.

More than one observer took note of the stranger's odd behavior. For over a quarter hour, surveillance cameras placed in high spots around the gas station recorded images of the stranger's silhouette and body language. The images are jittery, as though from the age of silent films, but they show the shadowy figure of a man pacing back and forth while casting furtive glances over his shoulder. The figure is that of a white male of medium height, bulky of build, and with shoulders slightly hunched. The man has a brush haircut and the back of his head appears oddly flat, a memorable characteristic. The cameras took images only every few seconds and did not catch the man's every move.

Not once, for example, did any of the cameras capture a single clear image of the stranger's face.

3.

TELEPHONES RANG IN AND BEYOND Idyllwild shortly after 1:00 AM, their urgency magnified by the darkness and the ungodly hour. The five Forest Service engine captains of the San Jacinto District arose from their scattered beds with a mixture of fatigue, excitement, and heightened sense of duty. They phoned their crew members, starting with those who had the farthest to travel. The awakened crewmen headed for the five San Jacinto stations. Anna Dinkel's Engine 54 was based at the Cranston station at the foot of the mountains near the town of Hemet; the others were up in the mountains along Highway 243: Freddie Espinoza's Engine 56 at Keenwild, Chris Fogle's Engine 52 at Kenworthy, Richard Gearhart's Engine 51 at Vista Grande, and Mark Loutzenhiser's Engine 57 at Alandale.

Set in the jagged, precipitous San Jacinto Mountains, the town of Idyllwild is a one-time logging and mining community that never hit it big, to the relief of current residents. The miners found too little gold, the loggers overcut the forests, and both departed. There was too little snow and too few slopes for a major ski development and no big lakes for monster motorboats. Those drawbacks turned out to be nature's gift, sparing Idyllwild the overcrowding that has turned many a mountain town into a playground for urbanites. "It hasn't been polluted by fast-food joints and stoplights," said one longtime resident.

Highway 243 serves as Idyllwild's Main Street. The town has a central square with real estate offices, restaurants, retail stores, a good local coffee shop—and no stoplights. The residences are mostly hidden along winding roads in the surrounding forest. What first stands out to someone driving in from Banning Pass is the well-marked headquarters of the Forest Service's San Jacinto Ranger District. The plain but pleasant-looking one-story building is large by Idyllwild's standards. Inside is a roomy reception area with a welcoming feel, recalling the days when a ranger always had time to chat up visitors.

The Forest Service in Idyllwild, as in many small towns, is a major force in the community. The agency makes decisions with sweeping consequences for local inhabitants, from the use of the surrounding national forest lands to purchases of gasoline, food, and other supplies. "The firefighters make it so we can live in this beautiful paradise," said one of the town fathers. The Forest Service presence provides hope for kids who want to live and work where they grew up; in Idyllwild, one such generation of youngsters built their lives around the Forest Service. The kids went to school together, graduated, and became Forest Service firefighters together. Some joined the local Vista Grande Hotshots and San Jacinto District engine crews. They intermarried, started families, added members to the group, lost a few, formed adult sports teams, and hung out together. Those who stuck with the Forest Service won promotion. "Everybody knows about the San Jack, how tight they are up there on the hill," said one firefighter with a touch of envy.

Mark Allen "Lotzy" Loutzenhiser was the guiding spirit for the engine crews of the San Jacinto District. The 43-year-old had long experience and a reputation as a careful and reliable man, one who brought calm to a situation simply by showing up. Loutzenhiser held people together, whether it was as mentor and friend or as an organizer of down-home activities like Idyllwild's adult volleyball league. He was noted for sparking interstation volleyball matches, after which the losing team members had to paint their toenails pink. Somewhere along the line, Loutzenhiser had become a Pittsburgh Steelers fan, for which he took a lot of kidding. This year, though, the Steelers were on course for the Super Bowl and it looked like Loutzenhiser might have the last laugh.

Loutzenhiser had signed on with the Forest Service at the age of 18, four years after his family moved to Idyllwild. He'd grown up in San Diego, where he was born on November 2, 1962, the youngest of four children. As the baby brother, "Mark could have been a brat," his older brother Michael said. "But he always smiled, was always happy. Everybody thought they were Mark's best friend." In the nomadic world of southern California, Loutzenhiser lived a rooted existence centered on fire, family, the Forest Service, and Idyllwild. He met his wife Maria when she was a waitress at the Red Kettle, a town fixture that over the years had employed wives, mothers, and sweethearts of firefighters; some of those women had become firefighters themselves. Maria was a guest at Loutzenhiser's first wedding and then, before he and his first wife divorced, an occasional babysitter for his two children, Tesha and Jake. She took on an expanded role with the children after the divorce. Maria went from the Red Kettle to the Vista Grande Hotshots during the big push in the 1990s to bring more women into the ranks of wildland fire. Hotshots are highly trained, twenty-person crews called Type I, capable of taking on fire anywhere, and the Vista Grande Hotshots were based just a few miles from Idyllwild, at the same Vista Grande station as Engine 51. She joined up with two childhood friends, Anna Dinkel, who later made captain, and Janey Neu, who married a Forest Service engine captain, Freddie Espinoza, and went on to an administrative post at the ranger station in Idyllwild.

"Anna said, 'Hey, we can work for the Forest Service.' Everybody else was doing it," Maria said. The inclusion of women and the forced intimacy of a fire crew combined with predictable results. While Maria and Mark were dating, they were dispatched together on the Vista Grande Hotshot crew to a fire assignment in Oregon. As weeks passed in the close confines of fire camp, Mark and Maria found it difficult to keep their personal relationship private. "Mark didn't want to hold my hand because we weren't supposed to do that," Maria said. "But I made him kiss me." Maria was attracted by Loutzenhiser's steady presence and by his children, whom she adored. She longed for a big warm family of her own. Maria's mother had moved to Idyllwild with her seven children after her husband died, when Maria was a year and a half old. "She couldn't speak English; she couldn't drive," Maria said of her mother. "But the community rallied behind her. She got off welfare, got U.S. citizenship, and learned English from her children."

Maria was still a hotshot and Mark had moved to a Forest Service engine crew when they married in 1993. Maria willingly gave up her fire career for family life. She said of her fire experience, "I played because it's a game. Those guys play to kill." The couple produced three children of their own, a girl, Savannah, and twin boys, Kyle and Seth, for a total of five children. "If I didn't have children, I'd go back and be a firefighter," Maria said. "It's a dangerous job, but we know that."

The Vista Grande Hotshots proved to be a courting ground for others as well. Freddie Espinoza, a Vista Grande Hotshot before becoming captain of Engine 56, had known Janey Neu casually before she joined the hotshots. They began dating and then married in 1997, remaining close friends with the Loutzenhisers, a relationship that in time would bring a saving grace.

♦ ♦ ♦

THE NIGHT OF the Esperanza Fire, one of Loutzenhiser's first calls went to Daniel Najera, who had been a Forest Service firefighter for less than two weeks. At age 20, Najera was the youngest member of the Engine 57 crew. Daniel had spent the previous evening at the house of his girlfriend, Whitney Khrystine Lingafelter, playing parlor games with her and her family. The couple joked about the similarity between Whitney's tongue-twister last name and that of Daniel's new captain—both "real long, pretty German," as she remarked. Once, when Whitney picked up Daniel at the fire station, he pointed to a solid-looking older man of obvious northern European extraction, with fair hair, pale skin, and a sandy mustache.

"That's my Captain Loutzenhiser. He looks intimidating, doesn't he?"

"Is he German?" Whitney asked.

"Loutzenhiser? Well, duh," Daniel replied with a smile.

Daniel still had something of the boy about him. He was a wide-eyed youngster with an infectious smile, a skateboard fanatic who loved games of any kind, the sort of person who brightened an occasion with his presence. "He was someone everyone wanted to know," Whitney said. Though he had been on the Engine 57 crew only a matter of days, Daniel peppered his talk with fire jargon, spoke of firefighting as a lifetime career, and cheerfully bragged, "I'm a U.S. Forest Service firefighter!"

Daniel's life had taken a definite upswing. When he was an infant, his mother, Gloria, had put him in the care of his grandparents and an aunt. She'd left Daniel's birth father, Tim Hoover, while pregnant, ending an abusive relationship. Daniel developed a strong bond with his grandparents, Patrick Najera, a building contractor, and his wife, Linda. Patrick was a Seventh-Day Adventist who built churches across the country and abroad, and he often took Daniel with him and enrolled the boy in local church schools.

Daniel's aunt Vivian Najera became like a mother to him, though she was only a teenager. When Daniel was at home in California, Vivian took care of him and later her own son, Rikk, who was four years younger than Daniel. "Daniel was like a little doll for me," Vivian said. "I used to dress him up in the same kind of pants and jacket as Rikk; he was a plaything for me. It was a fun time." The fun stopped when the family matriarch, Daniel's grandmother Linda, died in 1999. Daniel was 13 years old, and the loss of his grandmother deeply affected him; he began having difficulties in school. About a year later, Daniel's mother, Gloria, reclaimed him in an ugly custody dispute with her sister Vivian. Daniel's world turned upside down and he became a sullen teenager: black clothes, long spiked hair dyed strange colors, problems with alcohol.

"Like many young people, he did experience some difficult times in his early high school years," said Richard Steadman, principal at Mountain View High School, a school for troubled adolescents in San Jacinto. "He began to hang out with the wrong kids, to fail in school, and to pull back from his family."

Daniel, though, had always wanted to be a firefighter. When he was a child, a toaster caught fire in the family kitchen and Daniel shouted, "Outside, outside, there's a fire!" As the entire family obeyed the little boy, he found a vocation. After high school, Daniel joined a volunteer firefighter company, with its demands for mental and physical discipline, and he took a giant step toward maturity.

"Danny had a dream. At a certain point, after high school, Danny was called to be a firefighter," said Max Copenhagen, deputy forest supervisor at the San Bernardino National Forest. After a year's experience as a volunteer firefighter, Daniel was hired by the Forest Service and was assigned, on October 15, 2006, to Engine 57 under Loutzenhiser, the most experienced captain in the district. Daniel called him Cap and from the first day made him his hero. "I think the captain likes me," he gleefully told his aunt Vivian. By this time, Daniel had again become the friendly-as-a-pup young man his family remembered. Many firefighters can testify that the discipline, comradeship, excitement, and physical challenge of fighting fire helped others in the fire service—and sometimes themselves—escape a troubled adolescence.

Another of Loutzenhiser's calls went to Pablo Cerda, 23, a second-year firefighter. Cerda had spent the previous weekend with his widowed father, Pablo Sr., at the elder Cerda's home in Fountain Valley, south of Los Angeles near the ocean. At the end of the weekend, Cerda returned to Engine 57's duty station at the fire barracks at Alandale, four miles north of Idyllwild on Highway 243. After his mother's death two years before, Pablo had become a pillar of strength for the family, his father said, a "best friend" to him and to Pablo's older sister, Claudia. "He was very protective of me. He was always my supporter," said Pablo Sr.

Pablo had shown an early talent for sports, which his father had encouraged, forging a bond between them. "He never gave me any trouble. I would take him everywhere to play soccer," Pablo Sr. said. "He was a very active young man; he told me when he was 14 he wanted to become a firefighter." Pablo had attended the Fire Academy at Riverside Community College and worked on a local hand crew before the Forest Service hired him. The Sunday before the fire, Pablo Sr. remembered, "We hung around together and it was obvious he loved me very much. We had breakfast together, and I went to watch him play soccer." Before leaving for the fire barracks Pablo told his father, "Dad, take care of yourself; I love you very much." Then, in a family tradition, they parted with a kiss and a hug.

The day of the fire was a regular day off for Engine 57's engineer and driver Jess "Gus" McLean, 27, who lived with his wife, Karen, in Beaumont, within sight of the fire. Day off or not, his name was on the call-out list, and when Loutzenhiser called, McLean volunteered to come to work anyway. "I'll be back when the fire's over," he told Karen as we went out the door. "I love you."

McLean, who was slight of build for a firefighter, had earned his place by being strong for his size, working hard, and being enthusiastic, including volunteering for extra duty. This day he replaced another crew member, Kyle Owen, who slept through his captain's call. A roommate, a Vista Grande Hotshot who got a separate call summoning him to the fire, eventually awakened Owen, who wound up driving a water tender on the fire—a providential switch for him.

McLean and Karen had delayed having children because Karen was a teaching certificate candidate at the University of Redlands. The youngest of three children, McLean had been "a handful" when he was a little boy, his mother, Cecilia, said. He loved sports and the outdoors to a fault. When his parents tried to pull him off playground equipment at the end of a long day, he would scream "Save me! Save me!" to make passersby think a kidnapping was under way. "He wrecked every car we ever owned," his mother said fondly. "If he had been my first, he would have been the last."

"When he was young he was just ornery," his older brother, Joshua, said, also fondly. "He was just bad all the time. He'd refuse to do his homework and sit at the table until dark." In about the fifth grade Jess "turned himself around" and stopped being a torment to his family, said his older sister, Jamie. He began instead to display a concern for others and became a support for the family. McLean was another firefighter who found his vocation in childhood. "By the time he was 6, he knew he was going to be a fireman," said Joshua. The young McLean would scan the newspaper for stories of local death and disaster and clip them out. He liked every sort of catastrophe, from car pileups on the freeway to earthquakes. But his favorite was fire.

Jess compensated for his small stature—5 feet 9 nine inches tall and 150 pounds—by competing hard at sports, usually against older players, and as a result developed both physical strength and a gritty attitude. After high school, he was a volunteer for the fire department in Banning, where he was raised. "He didn't try anything else; it was always fire," Joshua said. "He was the guy, if you broke down on the freeway, he'd stop and change your tire."

By the time he was 20, he was working for the Forest Service. Eager to become the best firefighter in the district, he applied to the Vista Grande Hotshots. When his application was accepted, McLean thought a miracle had happened. Once on the crew, he became a sawyer, running a chain saw at the head of the crew, a job normally filled by the biggest and strongest male.

He met Karen on a snowboarding trip and discovered they had a close connection: she had two brothers on the Vista Grande Hotshots, Jason and John. Jason was Jess's squad boss. "Jess was just a nice guy, he loved his parents, he cared about family," Karen said. "He'd call and say he was going to be late because something needed fixing at his parents' house, and that was fine." The couple had planned to marry in May 2004, but Jess's father, Bruce, became seriously ill, and Jess and Karen moved up the date and wed on December 24, 2003, with Bruce, who died a month later, in attendance. As a hotshot, Jess found he was spending too much time away from home, and he transferred to a more stable posting, Engine 57.

Already present at the Alandale fire barracks that night was Jason McKay, assistant engine operator and, at age 27, a veteran with five years of experience. A few months earlier, in August, McKay had helped deliver a baby and in doing so had discovered something new about himself. The mother was parked alongside Highway 243 in the final stage of labor; Engine 57, responding to a call of a motorist in distress, had arrived just in time. "The baby's coming!" said Claudia Posey, the mother. She, her husband, Jody, and two children had been driving from their home in Pine Cove, next to Idyllwild, to reach a midwife, hoping for a natural birth. McKay had never helped deliver a baby before, but as an infant boy emerged, McKay took it in his arms. After the ambulance departed,

McKay excitedly called his sister Crystal. "I can't wait to have a baby of my own," he told her.

At the time of the Esperanza Fire, McKay was making payments on a one-karat diamond engagement ring he planned to give his girlfriend, Staci Burger, who worked in the arson investigation unit of the Bureau of Land Management. McKay had already asked Crystal to be "best man" at the wedding, and she had agreed.

McKay, too, had had a childhood brush with the fire world that set him on a career path. At the age of 3, he had leaped off the kitchen table after stealing a hot dog from his sister's plate and jamming it into his mouth. When he hit the floor, the hot dog went down his windpipe and stuck like a cork. He stopped breathing. His mother, Bonnie, tried to dislodge the hot dog, but it wouldn't budge. Minutes passed. An ambulance with EMTs from the Antelope Valley Fire Protection District arrived, began emergency procedures, and sped away with the boy, leaving the family huddled over a radio scanner. Moments later they listened horror-struck as the ambulance driver announced: "That boy just went into cardiac arrest; we're pulling over."

After a strained silence came these words: "Okay, we got him going again."

At the hospital, doctors used forceps to successfully extract two inches of hot dog from Jason's throat. His career path was not sealed until two years later, however, when he burned himself playing with matches, blurted out "Fire hurts," and, putting the two experiences together, decided to become a firefighter.

The McKay family—Bob and Bonnie; three daughters, Brenda Lee, Jody Jean, and Crystal Jade; and Jason—had moved to southern California from Minnesota when Jason was a child. They'd settled near Victorville near the old Roy Rogers Ranch, a couple of hours north of the Banning Pass. Bob McKay, a truck driver with a "Good Buddy" patch on his jacket, left his family as Jason entered his teen years. "Bob was good at everything . . . except marriage," Bonnie said. "We had a rough time. We lost everything, the house, everything. I guess I was what they call a welfare mom. But Jason turned out to be a sweetheart. He appreciated life; he loved life."

As male head of a household that included four women—five including his grandmother Alberta "Penny" Reese—Jason developed a steady, quiet personality. One rookie firefighter at first thought McKay's careful ways were "nerdy" but in time came to regard him as "better than any of them." McKay took counsel with Crystal, who even guided his courtship of Staci. He joined the fire world at age 14, when he became a Fire Explorer with the nearby Adelanto Fire Department. He told his family he wanted to join the Forest Service because it fought more fires than municipal departments. "He loved being a firefighter," Staci said. "It was what he wanted to do since he was born."

After being roused at the fire barracks, McKay telephoned Staci, but he was not his usual upbeat self. "Sweetie, this one looks bad," he said, and then he signed off, "I love you."

In its first hours, though, nobody could be certain what the Esperanza Fire would do. When Captain Dinkel got her summoning call, she immediately telephoned a friend in the dispatch office to ask whether the Esperanza was another sputtering nuisance or the real thing. The terse answer came back: "Several acres, crossing roads, real fire." Dinkel's Engine 54 at Cranston had the shortest drive to the ICP at Cabazon, around the base of the mountains, and hers would be the first San Jacinto engine to arrive at the command post.

Civilians who saw the first flames that night also sensed that this fire could be different. Two of the Engine 51 crew, Eddie Harper and Mike Christian, rode together in Christian's pickup truck and stopped on the way to Vista Grande at an A&P supermarket to buy chocolate bars and bananas for quick energy. Noting their uniforms, the clerk rummaged in a cooler. "Looks like a bad one. Here, take these, you're going to need them," the clerk said, and he handed them Cokes. Harper gratefully packed the sodas with his extra gear, which included a digital camera. "They teach us the importance of capturing the moment in fire with pictures for training," Harper said. He subsequently took a remarkable set of images of the fire, providing a vital link to understanding what had happened, but many years would pass before he was willing to look at them.

Harper and Christian arrived at the Vista Grande station ahead of Captain Gearhart, who had a longer drive. As soon as Gearhart pulled in, Harper called out, "This is going to be a good one, right?"

"Oh, yeah!" said Gearhart, who had seen the flames while driving to the station. "Some of that stuff hasn't burned in thirty years."

When Engine 51's full crew was assembled—John Fakehany, Darrell Arrellano, and Shawn Evans had joined Gearhart, Harper, and Christian—Gearhart called everyone together for a stern warning. Gearhart had an aggressive, take-charge personality that some found abrasive; his crew, though, valued his firm direction. The predicted Santa Ana winds, Gearhart said, were going to fan the fire and push it hard. "Today's a Santa Ana day, so give yourselves three times the normal room for safety," he cautioned. "And, if I say 'Go' . . . *do it*."

The five engines of the San Jacinto District headed independently for the ICP at Cabazon. Loutzenhiser's Engine 57 gave a three-blast hello on its air horn as it passed by Engine 51's Vista Grande station, alarming Gearhart, who told his men to hurry up. If too many engines responded, Engine 51 could be ordered to stay back in reserve. "The crew would have been depressed for days," Gearhart said. "Young men and fire. They like to go."

The engines left the pines behind and moved onto the steep, eroded face of Twin Pines Ridge, with its panoramic view of the Banning Pass. The firelight made silhouettes of the foothills. Jagged zigzags of flame, slim as pencil lines, marked the rims of draws in the foothills and created a living graph line of the fire's advance. Firefighters recorded the scene in video snatches taken from cell phones and digital cameras. In the images, red-and-blue flashes from the lights of emergency vehicles mix with the Halloween colors of nighttime fire, orange and black. The spots of many headlights, sparkling like diamonds, accent the panorama. The overall effect is that of a canvas painted by an artist with an insanely heightened—and limited—sense of color.

The wind had not yet arrived. As the fire advanced slowly along the lower slopes of Twin Pines Ridge, a patch of chaparral flared here and there with sudden, white-hot intensity. There was no race of flame toward the top of the ridge, at least not yet, though history held a warning about this place and this time of year. On October 30, 1967, a nighttime fire in these same foothills had made a sudden rush up the face of the ridge, with fatal consequences. The Bailiff Fire, named for the ranch where it burned, was one of many big fires during that year's bad fire season. About two hundred Indian firefighters had been brought in from Arizona the day before to help fight the fire. One of these was Frank Rios, 21, a firefighter with the Bureau of Indian Affairs. Rios and his crew were told to take a break after a night of cutting hand line on a flank of the fire. Rios had settled down to rest in an unburned spot above the fire when the wind suddenly shifted and flames headed up the ridge. Rios's body was found in the morning. Nearly four decades later, flames once again advanced toward that spot.

The first of the five Forest Service engines, Engine 54, captained by Dinkel, pulled into the ICP at 3:36 AM, according to dispatch records, and the rest of the engines arrived over the next half hour. "The fire was right there in front of you," Gearhart said. "The street ends and boom, there's Cabazon Peak. It was like an amphitheater. We fight fires there all the time, and they're almost all man-made arson fires. We'd been fighting little fires around there all summer long."

Gearhart had a word with Fogle of Engine 52, who was skeptically watching the flames.

"It'll be lucky if it makes it up to the houses by morning."

"If it blows thirty-five miles an hour it will," Gearhart replied. "It'll go right through or around the old burns."

They bet a can of soda on it, "a bet of wits" as Gearhart called it, whether the flames would make the top of the ridge.

The overhead at the ICP handed out orders, and the Forest Service engine captains took theirs with a sigh: sure enough, they were to retrace their route back along Highway 243 up to Twin Pines Road and meet there with two Cal Fire supervisors, who would deploy them along the ridge.

"I told you we should have stayed up there," Loutzenhiser told Gearhart.

The Forest Service engines formed into a motorcade, led by Loutzenhiser's Engine 57, and headed back toward the interstate. They had driven barely more than a mile, through the town of Cabazon to the cloverleaf entrance to I-10, when Gearhart spotted a new fire right in front of them. The leading engines had begun to pull onto I-10 when Gearhart, the last in line in Engine 51, saw flames alongside a frontage road. He dutifully called dispatch and reported the fire, at 4:19 AM, but with a sinking heart.

"The new fire was popping in grass on the far side of the interstate," Gearhart said, "but we wanted to get up to the bigger fire; we didn't want to miss out. Everybody else was committed to the freeway. We were last in line, and so we took the fire." The new fire, about a quarter acre in size and burning in a fenced field, was named the Seminole Road Fire after the frontage road. "There was a wind blowing on the fire and pushing it onto the road, which stopped it," Gearhart said.

The engine parked along the road, and the crew began to pull hose off and haul it toward the flames. Gearhart hurried them along, shouting to be heard over highway noise from I-10, which had heavy truck traffic even at this hour. As the excited crew dragged the canvas hose over barbed wires, Gearhart yelled, "Pull the hose *under* the fence!"

Engine 51's four sister engines disappeared down I-10. The Seminole Road Fire was on Cal Fire's turf and a Cal Fire engine or two was bound to show up soon. The only thing worse than being delayed by fighting the small fire, however, would be to turn over a sloppy, half-finished job to the other fire agency. "It's a friendly competition," said Gearhart. "We always try to get a fire like this one out before Cal Fire gets there."

Engine 51's crew hit the leading edge of the fire with a stream of water from an inch-and-a-half hose. Gearhart yelled an order, but couldn't be heard and he strode through a blackened portion of the fire to get closer to his crew, not realizing that he was possibly stepping on and destroying evidence. "The ignition point was in the middle of the fire, which had been blown around by the wind, so it was hard to make out," Gearhart said, "and I walked right through it."

The Cal Fire engines arrived shortly, accompanied by an arson investigator from the state fire investigation unit in Perris. The Cal Fire crews helped knock down the last of the flames, and the job turned into a mop-up operation. The arson investigator, though, was not pleased at the way the site had been trampled. Engine captains had been told since spring to preserve points of origin to give investigators a chance to collect arson devices and other evidence. The cautioning had paid off: more than a score of ignition devices had been collected and stored in cardboard boxes and plastic bags at Fire Investigation headquarters. When a sympathetic Cal Fire captain told Gearhart to pack up and take off for the bigger fire, he did just that. The time was just past 5:00 AM and the sky was still dark.

As his crew loaded up, Gearhart took his first look in a while across the floor of the Pass at the Esperanza Fire. What he saw gave him pause. The Esperanza Fire had advanced from the lower reaches of Twin Pines Ridge to the midpoint. Flames blossomed along the ridgelines like flowers of the night. Visible across the floor of the Pass was the mouth of a wide gulch, marked by an alluvial fan of loose stones and boulders—the same gulch that later would be called the unnamed creek drainage—on the Bailiff Ranch, where Frank Rios had lost his life decades earlier. Gearhart knew that if the Esperanza Fire took off, it would run up gulches like this one to the top of the ridge. It then could roll on for miles, maybe as far as his home Vista Grande station, maybe all the way to Idyllwild. Everything depended on the wind. Once the Santa Ana wind arrived, the fire would sweep Twin Pines Ridge from bottom to top.

Gearhart took the captain's shotgun seat, and Engine 51 headed for the top of the ridge.

4.

A FTER LEAVING GEARHART AND HIS crew to handle the
Seminole Road Fire, the rest of the Forest Service engines
drove along I-10 to the turnoff onto Highway 243 and began the
climb up Twin Pines Ridge. From the floor of the Pass, the highway rises in a series of hairpin turns up steep, dry slopes made up
of loose boulders and stones that hikers call ball bearings for their
tendency to slide out from underfoot. Coming up from the floor of
the Pass, the engines passed a sadly familiar spot at the end of the
first and longest hairpin turn, where the downslope embankment
shears off at a steep angle into a boulder field. It's a hellish-looking
place to fight fire, which firefighters did on September 19, 1971.
Taking advantage of another bad fire season that year, an arsonist had touched off a blaze in the foothills of Twin Pines Ridge. It
became the Mack II Fire, named after a family that lived nearby.

Robert Maxwell Miller, 21, a foreman at the Vista Grande station, reported for work that morning complaining to coworkers
about exhaustion and a hangover following an all-night drinking
party. Miller, disheveled and unshaven, lay down on his bunk to
rest. He "had been gaining weight for the past several years," according to a later Forest Service report, and at 5 feet 10 inches tall
was "somewhat overweight" at two hundred pounds.

Miller's Vista Grande crew was called to the Mack II Fire at

10:18 AM, three minutes after it was reported. During the short drive down Highway 243 to the fire scene, there was a steady rattle on the outside of the engine. A Santa Ana wind was blowing hard enough to scoop pebbles from the ground and slap them against the engine. The crew parked alongside the highway, and Miller and two others, Ronald Courts and Bruce Mitchell, pulled a hose line down through the boulder field along a flank of the fire. The plan was to attack the fire from below and work up its flanks, eventually pinching it off at the head, using the road as a firebreak. Flames burned brightly in chaparral marked by blackened bushes from the fatal Bailiff Fire four years earlier. The three crewmen hosed hot spots while a fourth, Larry Smith, stood by at the engine to man the pump.

Mitchell and Courts made two trips back to the engine for more hose packs, laying out 300 feet of flexible "cotton jacket" hose and 250 feet of "hard line," or solid, rubbery hose from a reel on the engine. Returning from the second trip, Mitchell saw a flare-up on the slope just below him. He yelled at Miller and Courts, but the roar of the fire drowned out his voice. Mitchell turned and ran for the road. On the way, he glanced back and saw Miller and Courts scrambling up the slope behind him—with a wall of flame at their backs. Miller and Courts had seen the flare-up for themselves and had taken what looked to them like the safest escape route. Courts carried two heavy hose packs, confident that they would soon be back to fighting the fire. Unbeknown to the pair, however, they were headed straight for yet another flare-up, this one hidden behind a ridge.

When Courts at last saw the second flare-up, he threw off the hose packs and began a race for his life, up toward the road. Like Mitchell before him, Courts also took a backward glance—the need for a last look back seems to be embedded in the human psyche— and what he saw stopped him cold: the overweight and exhausted Miller was sitting on a rock taking a breather.

"Let's get out of here!" Courts yelled.

"I'm okay here," Miller replied.

"The hell you are!" Courts shouted. "Let's get out of here!"

Courts resumed his mad scramble up the slope. His legs burned and turned to rubber, his breath came in shallow gasps, his throat turned cotton-dry. He kept repeating to himself, as he later told fire investigators, "I'm going to make it! I'm going to make it no matter what."

Twice more he glanced back and saw Miller, on his feet at last, struggling less than twenty feet behind him. The line between life and death, as it often does in wildfire, came down to a few feet, a few seconds. Courts stumbled as he tried to lift a leg, nearly petrified by exhaustion, over the guardrail at the roadway. Never had anything so low seemed so insurmountably high. He managed to crawl over the guardrail, but his legs failed him and he collapsed in a heap. When he recovered enough to rise, he stumbled back to the guardrail and looked down for Miller. As Courts peered into the abyss, the fire roared "and a large mass of smoke, ashes, and heat" smacked him in the face. Barely able to breathe, he lurched across the highway to the partial protection of a cutbank and fell to the ground. He pulled his fire shirt over his head and put his face in the dirt, trying to suck life from the thin layer of oxygen at ground level. He stayed like that for long minutes, tucked against the cutbank, his lungs aching and his breath coming in snatches.

When the worst had passed, he got to his feet, walked back to the guardrail, and, eyes smarting, tried to see through the smoke. After a few seconds he made out a human form about ten yards below him. It was Miller, flat on his back, with his clothes on fire. By later estimates, Miller was a mere three to five seconds from safety. Courts made his way down to Miller, threw dirt on him to extinguish the flames, and then went for help. Miller survived long enough to be evacuated by helicopter, but his body was covered with burns and he expired at 6:39 PM. The Forest Service fire investigation report, in a judgment that for reasons of morale is traditionally reserved only for the most obvious cases, concluded that a firefighter had been responsible for his own death. "It is felt that Miller's physical condition played a major role in his being burned," the report stated. "It must be remembered that Miller almost made it to safety. It is probable that the extra few seconds Miller sat on the rock cost him his life."

Courts left the Forest Service shortly thereafter and eventually moved to New Mexico. The other crewman on the hose line, Mitchell, never escaped the pull of wildland fire. He went on to become a firefighter in Santa Barbara County, according to a coworker located by reporters Kimberly Trone and Lisa O'Neill Hill of Riverside's *Press-Enterprise*. One day while on duty there, he fought an arson blaze similar to the Mack II Fire that had killed Miller. Once the fire was under control, Mitchell returned to his station house, stacked his gear on his bunk, and walked out, never to return. He died several years later in an auto accident—by eerie coincidence, not far from the site of the Mack II Fire.

Smith, the engine's pump operator, retired as a Forest Service captain, lived on in the Banning Pass area, and by another coincidence was godfather to one of Loutzenhiser's daughters. On drives past the Mack II Fire site, Smith told Trone and Hill, "I've got this shield that comes up," raising his hand to mask his face to demonstrate. A marker with a brass plaque was placed at the fatality site, but after a passing vehicle struck the marker, the plaque was moved to the Vista Grande station, Miller's home station, and bolted to a rock away from the highway.

Though he had not fought the Mack II Fire himself, Fogle, the captain of Engine 52, kept the memory alive. "I never go by without remembering that fire," he said. The night of the Esperanza Fire, Fogle had more immediate concerns as he drove past the place. He and Loutzenhiser used the long drive up Highway 243 to confer by radio about the organized confusion they expected to face once they reached the top of the ridge.

The higher they went up Highway 243, the more chaotic the situation became. Fleeing civilians snaked down the hill in pickups, motor homes, and heavy rigs with horse trailers. One woman had her arm out of the cab window of a pickup holding the lead ropes of two horses trotting alongside her truck. Another motorist drove past while improbably grasping the halter of a trotting llama. By the time the Forest Service engines arrived at the intersection with Twin Pines Road at about 4:50 AM, traffic jammed the junction. Exiting civilians tried to work their vehicles around the incoming heavy engines, the pickups with pumpers, supervisors' SUVs, and water tenders. Red-and-blue lights flashed, headlights swept the area, engines idled or gunned, and backup alerts beeped in screechy pulses.

"We were not panicky," Fogle said later. "The evacuations were happening, but the situation was not hysterical. There was no livestock loose. For us, it was a normal fire scene."

Part of the scene was a temporary command post, set up in a broad pullout at the intersection. There, two fire supervisors huddled over a map spread out on the hood of a pickup truck. The map's red and green dots identified which homes and structures could be defended and which could not: green for defensible, red for indefensible. A red dot marked the Octagon House; green dots marked outbuildings at the homesite. One of the fire supervisors, Bob Toups, a Cal Fire battalion chief, had overseen the preparation of the map four years earlier, in 2002, as part of a fire risk study. The red and green dots were "snapshots in time," Toups said later, that were used to illustrate to county supervisors the threat to homes in their jurisdictions. "The dots were never intended to be used as a decision-making tool that was final," Toups said. "What was green back in 2002 could easily be red a few years later; the reds could have been modified and been green."

Nonetheless, the red-dot/green-dot map showed the topography of the area and the placement of houses and was used to develop the fire plan. As Toups huddled over the map with Mike Mata, the other fire supervisor and a fellow battalion chief, they realized that no one had gone down the face of Twin Pines Ridge to knock on doors and warn residents of the approaching danger. Residents along Twin Pines Road, alerted by sheriff's deputies and a volunteer telephone network, were leaving in a stream. But when Toups reached a sheriff's deputy by radio, he was told that none of the sheriff's vehicles could handle the narrow, rutted roads on the ridge face. The telephone network warning system functioned well, but not everyone on the ridge face had a telephone. Someone had to drive down to the scattered houses and give the warning in person. It was now past 4:30 AM, and time was growing short.

Toups and Mata split up duties. Though Toups's regular assignment was to an administrative post, he was proud of his twenty-five years of operational experience, most of it in the Banning Pass. "I wasn't some new guy," he said later. "Of all the people on the fire, I was perhaps one of the most knowledgeable and capable." He became Branch II director, responsible for half the fire, and Mata remained on the ridgetop as Twin Pines Structure Protection Group supervisor, giving overall direction to engines and other resources as they arrived. Higher-ups confirmed the assignments by radio, and Bennett, the initial IC, was named branch director for the other half of the fire, Branch I.

While these titles appear cumbersome, they are part of the Incident Command System or ICS that was developed by Firescope, a joint project of the Forest Service, which funded it, and six California governmental and fire agencies. Firescope was created after a series of disastrous fires in southern California in 1970. Those fires cost sixteen lives, destroyed 772 structures, and burned over 600,000 acres. ICS has proved so flexible and efficient that it has been adopted nationwide and beyond, and by many types of agencies, to handle disasters of every kind, from fire to flood to terrorist attack to spacecraft accident.

Toups decided he should be the one to drive down the ridge face to check houses and to see "if a viable place can be identified where we can put people in." Toups wanted to find a safety zone where he could pre-position engines so they would be ready in place to make a quick attack, and save structures, once the flame front passed by.

About this time, A.C. "Clem" Kunkel, the general manager of the local High Valleys Water District, contacted Toups and Mata and raised a disturbing issue. Kunkel reported that "homesteaders," or squatters, had camped and made temporary residences on the lower reaches of the ridge face. The report could have been true or not, but with human life at risk, it had to be checked out. "Okay, we've got to go find them," Toups said. The plan to pre-position engines to protect structures suddenly had been made more urgent by a higher priority: people in imminent danger.

As Toups started the drive shortly after 5:00 AM, he knew trouble lay ahead. "The fuel bed was forty to fifty years old, mature chamise and oak, and was ready to explode," he said. He could see flames to the east, lodging in gullies, forming a battle line along ridgetops, and creeping slowly his way. The flames were traveling east to west, but once the Santa Ana wind hit them, it would drive flames up the gulches and gullies on the ridge face. "The gullies are all in alignment," Toups said, meaning they all ran on a north–south axis up toward the top of Twin Pines Ridge. "Once the sun rose it was going to be a bad deal."

Toups drove a little more than a mile down Gorgonio View Road, one of the dirt traces leading down the ridge face, and came to a trailer house with a late-model vehicle parked in front. There was no sign of life, but someone might be sleeping inside. Toups turned on his emergency flashers and siren and let them run. When no one appeared, he figured it was safe to assume the trailer wasn't inhabited, which proved to be correct. He drove a few hundred yards farther along and came to a more substantial dwelling, a blue double-wide trailer on a cinder block foundation. It had a lived-in look. Nearby were a large motor home, several other vehicles, and a boat on a trailer. As he approached, siren blaring and lights flashing, a man and a woman came running out of the double-wide. They were Neil and Janet Garner, who operated a dog training and breeding concern at the site.

Neil Garner, in his bathrobe, cried out, "I hear your siren! What in the hell are you doing, buddy?"

"Turn around, sir," Toups said, directing Garner's attention to flames topping a nearby ridge.

Janet Garner screamed.

"You have a half hour to get everything you have and get out," Toups said.

"We can't do that!" Garner said. "We need more time."

"You've got to be out of here in a half hour," Toups replied.

The Garners disappeared back into the double-wide, where a third person, Mike Upton, had awakened. He was Janet's former husband and was acting as caretaker. The three of them began hurried preparations to leave.

Toups, meanwhile, made a quick survey of the place, which came to be identified as the double-wide. "They had corrals behind the trailer with a lot of clearing; there were some power lines which were of concern. But this was an area that initially I could safely put resources at," Toups later told fire investigators. Toups radioed Mata and asked him to send some engines down Gorgonio View Road "to be deployed at this location." The engines, he figured, could safely wait out the passage of the flame front and then put out any lingering flames.

At this point, Kunkel, the water company worker, drove up and joined Toups. Kunkel, still concerned about the possibility of squatters farther down the ridge face, volunteered to drive down and look for them. Toups decided to follow, and he almost immediately passed a driveway leading up to a knoll. He couldn't see a house from the road, but the driveway had a locked chain across it. He figured that meant nobody was there. Toups drove on for another half mile, to the intersection of Gorgonio View Road and Horse Trail Road. The roadway, which was deeply rutted and narrow higher up, all but gave out at this point. He could see no houses farther down the ridge face and figured his scouting mission had gone far enough. (There was a homesite farther down the ridge, and a modular home was supposed to have been installed there days earlier. But by a lucky chance, the delivery of the home had been delayed.) Toups turned his pickup and headed back the way he had come. Nobody, he decided, should be allowed this far down the ridge. "I was not going to allow anybody to go past what I deemed a safe area, that first house with the horse corrals," Toups said later.

The time was about 5:45 AM. The fire continued to sputter and flare, skipping from ridgeline to ridgeline, settling in the bottoms of gullies. Now and then it made a stunningly quick uphill advance. Once the sun arose and began to heat the slopes, the fire's behavior would change dramatically. "We had less than an hour to make preparations for a very extreme firefight," Toups said. "There was no question in anybody's mind that this was going to be the most extreme fire conditions imaginable. Everything a firefighter never wants to face, we were facing"—wind, slope, dry conditions, homes scattered in dense vegetation.

Meanwhile, the Forest Service engines had become separated by the traffic jam at the intersection of Twin Pines Road and Highway 243. All five Forest Service engines—including Gearhart's Engine 51, which was coming up from the Seminole Road Fire at this time—were assigned to go down the face of the ridge and check on homes and people. Loutzenhiser in Engine 57 and Fogle in Engine 52 arrived first at the intersection and were able to drive past and make their way along Twin Pines Road. Dinkel and Espinoza, in engines 54 and 56, were blocked by the traffic and told their drivers to pull over and wait for the jam to clear.

Loutzenhiser and Fogle soon met up with Toups on his scouting mission. Toups told them they were to go down the ridge face "and see what could be done," as Fogle remembered, but Toups also told them to check in first with Mata, who was supervising the engine assignments. Loutzenhiser and Fogle parked at the side of Twin Pines Road, radioed Dinkel and Espinoza, and told them to find Mata and get assignments for all the Forest Service engines.

Once traffic cleared, Dinkel and Espinoza had their engines pull into the temporary command post at the intersection. Espinoza walked over to Mata, who told him the engines were to perform "triage, rescue, and evacuation." He did not direct them to any specific house or road. "He wanted us to go down and see what needed to be done, as we saw fit," said Espinoza, who relayed the assignment by radio to Loutzenhiser and Fogle. Mata also asked Espinoza to wait before taking off until joined by a unit en route from March Air Reserve Base, March Brush 10, a pickup with a pumper and a two-man crew.

While the Forest Service crews waited, they got out of the engine cabs to stretch their legs. Paul Jacobs, a three-year veteran of Fogle's Engine 52, was a big man, once a pro baseball hopeful, who despite his bulk and athletic ability was feeling the desert chill. Jacobs had put on his turnout jacket, the heavy, protective coat worn by municipal firefighters. California is the only state in which Forest Service engines regularly carry turnout gear because it is the only state where Forest Service crews regularly defend homes. Jacobs, hunched into the jacket and stomping his feet for warmth, became an object of mirth for the rest of the crew. Jess "Gus" McLean, from Engine 57, rushed up to Jacobs and shouted with glee, "Let me in there. I'm cold too!" The much larger Jacobs opened his jacket flaps, engulfed McLean in a bear hug, and began to dance him around, much to everyone's amusement.

"That was the last interaction that ever happened between me and Gus," Jacobs said. "I looked up to that guy. We were about the same age, but he was farther along—he'd started fire right out of high school. When all is said and done, I remember that."

After talking with Mata, Dinkel and Espinoza quickly caught up with Loutzenhiser and Fogle, reuniting all the Forest Service engines except Gearhart's. But they had yet to set the fire frequencies on their radios. And they had to wait for the extra unit. March Brush 10 arrived in minutes with an experienced crew: Rod Rambayon, who had been a hotshot, and Gary Bicondova, who had more than fifteen years of fire experience. Neither man was familiar with the area, though, and they had to be briefed on topography and radio frequencies, which took several minutes. "I wanted a face-to-face meeting with them so they understood how serious the situation was," Espinoza said. By the time he'd finished, Fogle and Loutzenhiser had started down the ridge ahead of everyone else.

"They were ready to go—so they left," Espinoza said. This time the separation was final. The four Forest Service engines would never be together again.

5.

F OGLE'S AND LOUTZENHISER'S ENGINES HEADED down Wonderview Road, a dirt trace that forks off Twin Pines Road about two miles in from Highway 243. The wind was light and the darkness around them almost complete. Far below, in the bottom of the Pass, the wind picked up and whistled through dry chaparral, bending grasses double. The freshening winds held the fire mostly low in the foothills, by and large unseen by the engine crews. But the flames glowed with the intensity of an awakening volcano. The fire's leading edge bubbled and sputtered, forming a vanguard behind which arose a broad curtain of fire, white hot at the base, fading to yellow and orange-red at mid-height, and turning to black smoke that disappeared into the night sky. Probing fingers of fire slipped into gullies and crept upward toward the ridgetop.

Despite its cheery name, Wonderview Road is made up of fine particles of eroded granite that regularly wash out and leave the road impassable; in spots, high banks and enclosing chaparral make a narrow passage even tighter. Scattered dwellings, ranging from substantial homes to single-wide trailers, dot the landscape. Houses perched high on brush-cleared promontories look out on the promised wonder view of the Banning Pass and enjoy a degree of security against the inevitable passage of fire. Other dwellings tucked into gullies and surrounded by chaparral create a potentially fatal situation—for firefighters as well as residents. The scattered housing and wild terrain make the face of Twin Pines Ridge a classic example of wildland–urban interface. Fires are bound to occur in a setting of steep, dry slopes and nearly continuous chaparral, which burns about every twenty-five years or becomes overmature and prone to worse fires. Irreverent firefighters call such places the stupid zone.

Though they were Forest Service engines, the five units assigned to the Esperanza Fire were not there to save forest or vegetation, at least not initially. The job that first night was not to contain the fire but to protect lives and property. Though hundreds of firefighters and scores of engines and other equipment arrived in the hours before dawn, no aircraft dropped a load of water or retardant and no one put in line to flank the fire. Hoses were pulled and hand tools used, to be sure, but as part of a strictly defensive battle that did save lives and property. In the aftermath, none of the many official inquiries into the fire faulted the overall strategy of putting lives and homes first before fighting the fire. There would be time in the future to mourn the loss of tens of thousands of acres of chaparral and forest, especially if heavy rains arrived, loosened soil exposed by the passage of flame, and started avalanches of mud, a common aftermath of wildfire in the hills and mountains of California.

Fogle's and Loutzenhiser's engines lumbered down Wonderview Road until they came to a driveway leading to a large house on a thumb of land. The engines halted and the two captains got out for a look. The house had a metal roof, which offered protection from embers. A broad space around the house had been cleared of vegetation and other flammables. No one was home. The place "was going to be fine," Fogle determined, and needed no engine to defend it. Driving on, the two engines came to a faint track that disappeared off Wonderview Road into the chaparral. The engines stopped and Fogle walked over to Loutzenhiser's engine. "We're

behind you. We'll take it," Fogle said. And with that, Loutzenhiser's
Engine 57, with Cerda, Najera, McKay, and McLean on board,
drove ahead and disappeared down the road, separating from
Engine 52.

Fogle's Engine 52 headed up the narrow track, which in a few
dozen yards ended at an aluminum trailer surrounded by chaparral.
There was nothing to be done for the trailer, which in firefighter
lingo was a "loser," meaning if the fire came this way, the trailer
would be lost for sure. But a car was parked nearby, indicating a
human presence. A knock on the door raised Lili Arroyo, 76, who
lived alone except for a pet cockatiel. Flames by now were visible on
a nearby ridge, making the case for a quick getaway. Even so, when
the firefighters pleaded, "We need to go ma'am, the fire's coming,"
Arroyo became fearful and stubborn.

"She was eating, she had a parrot, and she said she was not going
to go," Fogle said. "She said it over and over, every time we told her
it was time to go. If there's a threat to life, you have to stop fighting
fire and protect lives. It's a little frustrating and irritating when they
won't go. Most people don't have any idea what wildfires will do."

Firefighters have no legal authority to evict civilians even when
fire is dangerously close, as it was here. Only law enforcement
officers can force an evacuation. "Loud voices don't work," Fogle
said. Riverside County sheriff's deputies were evacuating the more
populous community up along Twin Pines Road, but as Toups had
been told, they were unwilling to risk their vehicles on the ridge
face. As minutes dragged by, Fogle asked Josh Richardson, his most
experienced firefighter, to appraise the situation.

"If the wind changes, we absolutely cannot make a stand here,"
Richardson said. "We need to get out of here."

"That's my thought exactly," Fogle replied.

At about this time, Toups, who had finished scouting down the
ridge face for squatters, was driving up Wonderview Road and saw

the flashing lights of Fogle's engine. Toups drove in to the trailer site. He had just alerted other supervisors by radio that the fire had climbed the ridge to about this elevation, though it was still off to the east, and the situation was turning critical. "Estimate major structure threat within one hour," Toups wrote in a log note timed at 5:45 AM. As he stepped out of his vehicle at the trailer site, he was startled to see some of Fogle's crew walking around without the web belts that carry fire shelters and other line gear.

"You need to be in PPE; put your safety gear on," Toups said.

"We are in safety gear. What are you talking about?" a puzzled Fogle replied.

The initials PPE stand for personal protective equipment, which sometimes means turnouts, the heavy firefighting gear used inside burning buildings. Though Forest Service crews in southern California pack turnouts in their engines, they seldom use them. Wildland firefighting requires prolonged physical exertion next to but not in flames and thus demands lighter gear. Fogle's crew wore hard hats, gloves, and the fire-resistant Nomex yellow shirts and green pants that are normal dress for wildland fire. They did not have their web belts on because it was clumsy to wear them while jumping in and out of the engine to check one house after another and because they felt no immediate danger from flames. The web belts, though, carry fire shelters and the crew put them on before they engaged in structure protection. Confusion on the part of fire investigators over what Toups meant by PPE later made its way into the official fire report and caused much heartache because of the implication that the Forest Service crews had failed to wear required safety gear. In fact, later inquiry confirmed that all the Forest Service engine crewmen were in appropriate wildland fire gear, including carrying fire shelters, by the time they faced flames.

Toups turned his attention to the problem of Arroyo and tried his persuasive powers on her, as others had before him, with the same result: she would not budge. Toups put in a radio request for a sheriff's deputy to make a forced evacuation and told Fogle to remain at the trailer until one showed up. At that point Kunkel, the local water district manager who had alerted Toups about squatters, drove up to the trailer site. Kunkel reported to Toups that he had checked far down the ridge for the squatters and had found no one. But he knew Arroyo and offered to try his hand at persuading her to leave. Kunkel had a helper with him, and together they coaxed the woman out of the trailer and into her vehicle. With the helper driving that car and Kunkel driving the water district pickup, they headed up Wonderview Road. With the Arroyo evacuation accomplished, Toups got in his pickup and drove down Wonderview Road in the opposite direction, back the way he had come.

Fogle and his crew watched with relief as Arroyo departed with her cockatiel. Arroyo and the bird survived, but the same cannot be said for the aluminum trailer. Fifteen minutes after everyone had left the site, a run of fire reduced the trailer to a heap of ash and melted metal, making it virtually certain that Fogle's crew, Toups, and Kunkel and his helper had saved Arroyo's life.

Before he left the site, Fogle found a spot with a view down the ridge face and saw, several hundred yards below, flashes of illumination. The lights went around in a circle, and Fogle figured they must be the headlights of Engine 57, checking another homesite. Fogle tried to contact Loutzenhiser by radio, but the assigned frequencies were so overloaded with traffic that when Fogle tried to break in, he later said, "somebody would walk over on top of me." In frustration, he switched to the local Forest Service radio net, which was not authorized for use on the fire, and made contact that way.

From this point on, the Forest Service engines monitored the assigned frequencies with scanners but mostly used the Forest

Service net to communicate with each other. Afterward, the captains were blamed for using an unauthorized radio channel. But radio clutter is a major and unsolved problem on big fires: there simply are too many people using too few channels to talk about everything from high strategy to ordering Porta-Potties. While some supervisors—Toups for one—said they had no trouble getting through on the assigned channels, it would become unpleasantly clear in a short time that those channels were inadequate to handle a severe emergency.

Once Fogle made contact with Loutzenhiser, he asked, "Is that you guys coming back by that house?" referring to the circling headlights.

"Affirm," Loutzenhiser replied.

"How does that house look?" Fogle asked. "Is there room enough down there for two engines?"

"Yeah, come on down," Loutzenhiser replied. "I'll push down to the next driveway and see what's there." If he found no more homes needing protection, Loutzenhiser said, he would come back and join Fogle.

Loutzenhiser's voice, low and quiet, carried an authoritative quality that set it apart. The voice, even in scratchy video recordings, has a calming effect, which is exactly the effect that Loutzenhiser's family, friends, and coworkers say he had on them. His presence absorbed anxiety, brought calm, and carried certainty.

Engine 52 left the trailer site and drove down to the house Engine 57 had circled, which came to be called the Tile House. It was a handsome home under construction on a site overlooking the Banning Pass. The time was nearly 6:00 AM, more than an hour before sunrise and the unleashing of the full force of the Santa Ana wind. But strengthening winds at the eastern mouth of the Banning Pass had already set the long, graceful blades of the wind turbines there to spinning. The wind swept into the Pass and breathed fresh life into the fire burning on the ridge face. The bumps and ruts lining the ridge face were crisscrossed with flames that raced and halted, surged and settled, purposeful and predictable one moment and random and chaotic the next. The gusting wind whipped those flames into mad dancers who soared, tottered, and collapsed in wild extremes of revelry.

Toups reported by radio about this time that he had just seen the fire cover a half to three-quarters of a mile in fifteen minutes, the pace of a rapidly running fire. The flames had crossed Wonderview Road at one point, he said, and were headed toward Twin Pines Road with its many houses and inhabitants. Toups noted in his log at 6:00 AM, "Dramatic increase in fire activity and behavior. Advised of major fire run toward TPR," or Twin Pines Road.

When Engine 52's crew—Fogle, Jacobs, Richardson, and a fourth, Aaron Reyes—pulled up at the Tile House, they were relieved to discover that the house, being only partially built, was not occupied; there was no need for another troublesome evacuation. The Tile House was the dream home of Captain Ron Berry of the Riverside County Sheriff's Department and his family. It was a big, roomy house on cheap land with an extraordinary view in the middle of the wild. "Our family always wanted to live close to nature," Berry said later. "This was our chance, and we tried to do it right."

The Tile House was a dream place, too, for firefighters. Fogle did an immediate 360, walking around the place. The house, designed with fire in mind, was no loser. Plenty of defensible space had been cleared. There was a small motor home and a pile of construction debris nearby, but a safe distance from the house. The home was about 60 percent complete: cinder block walls were up and faced with fire-resistant stucco. Windows and doors had been installed, though they stood open. The tile roof, from which the building took its nickname, was closed over but only partially tiled. Ceramic, fire-resistant tiles were stacked on the roof awaiting installation.

The structure was single-storied and L shaped. The long side of the L, the living area, had an eagle's view of the Banning Pass. The shorter side of the L, on the east side nearest the fire, was a garage currently being used for storage. Engine 52 could be parked in the inner elbow of the L and would be protected from flames coming from below or the east, the directions from which the fire was advancing. It was Fogle's decision whether to commit Engine 52 and its crew.

"We were going to defend this house," Fogle said.

Fogle ordered the engine backed into the bend of the L, to give extra protection to the exposed hose lines stored at the rear of the engine. Richardson, Jacobs, and Reyes began pulling out and charging a hose line. The door to the garage had not yet been installed, and large containers, presumably filled with household goods, were stacked inside. In a few minutes, when flames drew closer, embers sparkling like fireflies would swirl inside the garage. Fogle then would order his men to pull hoses and wet the place down. But for now, the wind was light and the fire was distant. As they worked, they could see flames make a quick run above their location, back up at the elderly woman's trailer and then another, the event that destroyed the woman's trailer. Gusting winds whipped the Tile House site. With fire now enclosing them on three sides, the firefighters there knew it was their turn next to sustain a run of fire. They began shutting windows and doors but discovered that door locks and handles had not yet been installed. So they shoved bathroom and kitchen sinks and cabinets, some in unopened boxes, against the doors and tied wires through lock holes to help keep them shut. "We barricaded the house," one said.

During this time, Fogle and Loutzenhiser kept in contact over the Forest Service radio channel. After leaving the Tile House, Loutzenhiser had found another home about a half mile away on Gorgonio View Road, just below its intersection with Wonderview

Road. It was the eight-sided Octagon House, perched on a stubby promontory overlooking the Banning Pass.

The Octagon House was about a mile and a half up from the floor of the Pass, from where an observer could make it out on a clear day. It stood up like a turret or medieval outpost surrounded by a sea of chaparral, eroded gullies, and boulder fields. The Octagon House was constructed of fire-resistant materials, cinder blocks, and a tile roof and had considerable clearance to the front. The site had some fire protection from two cleared areas directly below the house that stuck out like terraces; the one right below the house had a large garage used to store aged trucks and cars, nine in all. Even the collector—Greg Koeller, the owner of the Octagon— described the vehicles as "vintage" rather than "classic"; they were in various degrees of repair. Koeller had cleared brush and hired a bulldozer operator to dig a fire line around the site; it was only partially completed. State fire inspectors had given the place a clean bill of health a few years earlier. "No violations—Thank you," was the comment on a 2002 fire hazard inspection notice. There also was a modest-sized pool to the rear of the house on the up-ridge side. The pool was a special bonus and could be put to use, as Loutzenhiser quickly realized.

"Are you coming back here?" Fogle asked. There was plenty of room back at the Tile House.

"No, we're good," said Loutzenhiser, an assessment he would repeat many times.

As Fogle and his crew began preparation work at the Tile House, Toups put in another appearance, making a final check on Engine 52. A video of this scene shot by a firefighter shows Toups's pickup in the clearing at the front of the house. Beyond the pickup on the edge of the clearing is a half circle of pulsing scarlet flame that forms a virtual moat. Yellow flames erupt from the glowing moat.

The camera imitates the drama of the moment as it bobs up and down in the hands of an excited firefighter. Blasting winds fan the fire and drown out voices. Flames pulse, emergency lights sweep the scene, cones of illumination from the headlights of Toups's pickup and Engine 52 penetrate the darkness. The camera pans to the dark silhouetted figures of three firefighters in a line, one behind the other, as they face the spurting flames at the edge of the site. One looks up and waves. The swirling chaos has the look of a world gone crazy, where dark and uncontrollable forces run amok. But fighting wildland fire in southern California means protecting structures. There is no reason for anyone to be there, so exposed, so nearly surrounded by flames, except to protect an unoccupied, half-finished house. As Toups drives away, flames form a halo above his pickup.

"The flame front was getting ready to hit us, but we weren't too worried," said Richardson. Even the arrival of a much-anticipated run of fire, however, has shock value, and this one had started to exceed expectations.

"*Look at that!*" Fogle said.

"Gee, the flame lengths . . ." someone said in a voice of awe.

"There's a little glow five minutes ago and now it's . . ."

"Yep."

The "it" was the cauldron of flames that had turned the Tile House into an island in a heaving sea of fire. A rising tide of yellow flame lapped up on the exposed side of the site. Firefighters scurried to make last-minute safety checks, but the siren call of the flames drew them from the protecting walls of the Tile House. This was the moment every young firefighter dreams of and remembers ever after, the ultimate adrenaline rush: men and flames in close contact, worthy of a photo posted on the fire barracks wall.

The camera panned the scene again: though only minutes have passed, the sky is much lighter and the flames are much higher. But now, Jacobs, the big athlete, marches stolidly toward the flames.

Richardson, unseen behind the camera, urges him onward, shouting excitedly, "That's what I'm talking about, Paul, huh?" Richardson suddenly appears in the video clip trotting to catch up with Jacobs.

"Still there," Richardson remarks with satisfaction as flames shoot up ahead of him. "Quick, quick," Richardson says as he and Jacobs, side by side, turn to face the camera. They look straight at the lens and hold the pose for a moment as the flames boil behind them. A voice of caution, probably Fogle's, finally breaks the spell: "Do a hot lap around that side and make sure . . ." the voice says before trailing off, ordering a last-second check around the house. In the final video image, Jacobs beats a hasty retreat away from the flames.

Richardson took the hot lap. As he rounded the house, he was disturbed to find a cluster of wild rabbits huddled in a nook of the building on the windward side. There was nothing he could do for them, and he watched the rabbits scurry and squirm as the heat intensified. Finally they broke from the house and scampered across the clearing, to an unknown but probably not happy fate.

A blast of wind picked up a Porta-Potty and sent it tumbling along the driveway. "We kept picking it up. We were trying to be nice, but a few minutes later it was down again," said Richardson. "The fire front hit and we ran a hose out there—the paint on the motor home was bubbling, the woodpile kept catching on fire. I thought, whoa, this is pretty impressive."

At the height of the fury, the wind drove a cascading wave of heat, grit, and smoke over the homesite. "We were getting sandblasted," Richardson said. "The stuff was getting into my eyes. There was smoke everywhere. We were getting embers down our backs. Enough's enough. It was almost unbearable to be outside."

"It felt like being in the middle of a tornado or hurricane," Reyes said. "I loved it. I was scared, but I loved the thrill of it. I think we all did."

Fogle hollered for everyone to get back to the engine, out of the smoke, and they piled into the cab.

"It was almost as bad inside the engine," Richardson said. "The smoke had settled in there. We were all coughing. Everyone said it was the most amazing thing they'd ever seen. I heard that from everyone—never seen a fire like this before."

Enclosed in the cab like submariners riding out a storm at sea, the firefighters watched the play of fire around them. Flames lapped over the edge of the clearing and embers swirled in the acrid haze. The engine's emergency lights reflected in flashes off the billowing smoke. As the fire growled, the engine radio, turned to high volume, carried fragmented messages from a distant, calmer universe, one voice overriding another: "Follow the driveway up . . . My bearings show we'll be heading south, away from Banning . . . Fred, you up on Tac II?"

Then the worst was past. The surging moat of flames around the Tile House died to a simmer. As the crew climbed out of the engine, the shroud of smoke lifted to disclose a lightening sky; it was just past 6:30 AM, and though sunrise would not officially occur until 7:07 AM, dawn was breaking. The debris pile flamed brightly, but the rest of the flames near the house had exhausted themselves, leaving behind smoking stubs of chaparral that minutes before had stood twelve to fourteen feet high. Fogle told one crewman to climb on top of the engine and check the roof of the house for embers; he told another to pull a hose line and start spraying water on the debris pile.

Adding everything up, Fogle figured the head of the fire moving low in the foothills had sent four definable runs up the ridge face. The first run had passed near the aluminum trailer; the second had burned the trailer to the ground; the third had passed between the Tile House and the trailer site. The fourth run had threatened Engine 52 at the Tile House; for sure it would not be the last run.

The Octagon House and Engine 57 likely would be next to take the heat. Loutzenhiser, who had seen the flames sweep past the Tile House, called over to see how his friend Fogle was doing.

"Everything okay over there?" Loutzenhiser asked.

"Yeah, we're fine. It just hit a little harder than I expected," Fogle replied.

Loutzenhiser had a plan for dealing with the fire when it reached the Octagon House, a plan that he related to Fogle in bits and pieces. Loutzenhiser intended to "fire out" around the site, he said, to protect the house from flames. The tactic involves the common practice of deliberately setting fire to fight fire. For this job, Engine 57 carried drip torches, large metal canisters with nozzles and wicks that use a three-to-one mix of oily diesel fuel and gasoline. Firefighters light the wick and dribble the flaming mixture onto brush or other fuel. If handled properly and conditions are right, this starts a fire that is drawn into approaching flames. The two fires meet and flare up, consume the available fuel, and then, with nothing more to burn, die down. That's the theory, and it often works. There were plenty of places around the Octagon to launch a burnout, though the homeowner had cleared much of the vegetation. A partially completed bulldozer line, intended as a firebreak, ran through the chaparral on the east slope of the site, where some additional thinning had been done. But the battle with the brush was a losing proposition. The east slope had plenty of chaparral to carry a burnout, or any other kind of fire.

"Lotzy was saying over the radio that he was in a good place and that he planned to do a burnout," Fogle said. "I told him a second time that there was plenty of time to come back to the Tile House. His response was, 'No, everything's fine. I'm just doing this to keep the heat away from the house.' He wasn't trying to create a safety zone for his crew. He wouldn't have stayed there if he didn't think it was safe.

"You wait to light a burnout, though, until the fire front is moving toward you, so you don't light it early and draw the front in. You want your fire to move out smartly to meet the oncoming flames. He had plenty of time. The burn line had to be around at least the front and side of the site."

Loutzenhiser also remarked on the swimming pool at the rear of the house, a reassuring oasis in the midst of fire and desert. Loutzenhiser said he was putting a portable pump in the pool and running out hose from there. If other engines needed to refill their water tanks—the Forest Service engines held five hundred gallons each—they could come by when the conditions had calmed down.

Loutzenhiser and Fogle could see each other's general locations, but the Tile and Octagon houses were separated by the unnamed creek drainage. The drainage, after running narrow, deep, and nearly straight up from the floor of the Pass, split at the foot of the Octagon House into two smaller gullies that went around the sides of the Octagon site. Viewed from below, in the creek drainage, the Octagon looked like a medieval fortress perched atop the slope above.

Looking over at the scene from the high vantage point of the Tile House, Fogle could see down into the unnamed creek drainage to its narrowest point, several hundred yards below the Octagon House, marked by an outcropping of rocks. At that spot, the gulch takes a slight turn, the only one of consequence in its entire mile and a half length. As Fogle watched, a golden button of flame popped up at the rock outcropping, filling the narrow gap. The golden button glowed and began to pulse with an almost sexual energy.

"Hey, I just want to let you know the fire is picking up in the drainage, and it looks like it will make a good push toward you guys," Fogle radioed. "It's coming, and it's going to hit you hard."

"Yeah, I see it," Loutzenhiser replied in his low, calm voice.

And then, right on schedule, minutes after 7:00 AM, the Santa

Ana wind in all its strength and fury arrived at the eastern mouth of the Banning Pass.

Santa Ana winds unsettle life in California as surely as an earthquake or giant mudslide, sometimes with catastrophic results. The winds develop in the vast, heart-shaped Great Basin desert to the east, which extends from southern Oregon, Idaho, and Wyoming down through Nevada and Utah to southern California. Layers of cold air pile up during the fall in a massive high-pressure area above the basin. The heavy cold air—and it is the cold, not the heat of the desert, that causes a Santa Ana—descends and presses against the mountain front that runs north–south in California until it finds an opening through which it can vent. The Banning Pass is a perfect escape route. As winds blow through narrow passes and down mountain slopes, the air is compressed and accelerated, which dries and heats it. In the extreme, and a Santa Ana is by definition an extreme event, the air can heat by as much as twenty-nine degrees per mile and the wind can reach speeds of over one hundred miles an hour. (If a Santa Ana blows during the cold months, in late fall or winter, it can be a cold wind, at least by southern California standards.)

In this instance, only one weather station operated reliably to record the Santa Ana, and it was at Beaumont, eleven miles west of Cabazon. The station there logged a steady increase in wind speeds through the dark hours, from seven miles an hour gusting to twenty-five shortly after midnight, to thirteen miles an hour gusting to thirty-one just after 7:00 AM. An hour later, just after 8:00 AM, the gauge hit one hundred miles an hour, but that is a default reading indicating an equipment failure. As a result, the exact wind speeds are not known for the crucial time period from 7:00 AM to 8:00 AM. During the hours from midnight to 7:00 AM, the humidity hovered between 5 and 8 percent and the temperature remained around sixty.

"The humidity was low, but that's normal for this time of year in chaparral in southern California," Fogle said afterward. "People who live in timber don't understand this. They think these low levels are special. We plan on humidity levels like that."

The Santa Ana wind, blowing along the floor of the Banning Pass, quickly covered the distance of about nine miles from the mouth of the Pass to the mouth of the unnamed creek drainage. On the way, offshoots of wind angled up the face of Twin Pines Ridge in an uneven pattern, driving a fast run of fire here or a slow one there, depending on terrain. But the wind encountered special circumstances just before it reached the unnamed creek drainage; it entered a kind of mixing bowl, a protected and cleared area formed behind a massive tailings pile that extended like a dike out from the foot of the ridge, where an old quarry is located. The mixing bowl effect caused the wind to eddy and swirl, making it easier for it to change direction from east to northeast, head into the mouth of the unnamed creek drainage, and from there ascend the ridge.

Martin Gill, the Cal Fire captain who had been the first to arrive at the fire, watched from the floor of the Pass as this happened. With him was Tim Chavez, the Cal Fire captain and weather sage who had warned that the Santa Ana wind would be more intense than predicted. The two captains and their engines had followed the fire's progression through the foothills, prepared to do something—anything—if flames made a run toward the town of Banning. Maybe they could use Highway 243 as a firebreak and make a stand there, though the narrow road would offer little protection. Gill and Chavez wound up directly opposite the unnamed creek drainage at the ultimate moment.

"We were there just as the sun came up," Gill said. "There are two drainages, and the fire had gotten in there and quieted down—there's a kind of bowl at the mouth of those drainages. There's water in those drainages in the winter, and a lot of vegetation grows there.

The place hadn't burned for twelve or fifteen years. As the sun came up there was a massive, spontaneous ignition in the two drainages. The amount of energy released was incredible. It looked like a nuclear bomb went off. Tim turned to me and said, 'Thank you for not sending me up there and keeping me down here.'"

The fire exploded up both drainages, but only the unnamed creek drainage was both perfectly aligned, northeast to southwest, and long and straight enough to carry fire very far up the ridge face. The unnamed creek drainage never veered in its course, as did other nearby gulches, including the neighboring drainage observed by Gill and Chavez. When the Santa Ana wind surged into the gaping, boulder-strewn mouth of the drainage and thrust upward, there was nothing to stop it.

At that time, scattered pockets of fire smoldered in the drainage, from its mouth up to the rock outcropping where Fogle had observed the golden button of flame. A shroud of smoke covered the drainage like a layer of fog, dense in one place, light enough in another to allow the flames underneath to be seen—and photographed—from above. Images of the smoke shroud were taken from an early arriving aircraft around 7:14 AM. The smoke was held almost flat on the ground by what fire weather scientists later said was a temperature inversion. The effect was not that difficult to achieve, considering the drainage was a deep one. According to this theory, as the Santa Ana wind arrived in the Pass, a layer of warmer air arrived far above it, at about 6,000 feet, much higher than the 3,400-foot level of the Octagon House. The layer of warmer air held down the cooler air below it, along with the smoke and heat of the fire. As the Santa Ana wind climbed the face of the ridge, the inversion layer at 6,000 feet did not elevate, so there was a compressing effect on the air close to the ground, which under this pressure further accelerated. The opposing pressures from the wind, speeding up the drainages on the ridge face and seeking escape, and from the inversion, which held down wind, heat, and smoke, created an unsustainable situation. Something had to give, and it did: the area ignition.

At least that was the theory outlined in the official fire report. Later, others observed that an area ignition does not require wind: in fact, area ignitions usually occur in calm air and depend on other factors for their intensity. In any case, the compressed pockets of fire and hot gases in the unnamed creek drainage could not vent, which caused them to explode, the effect enhanced when a massive supply of oxygen suddenly rushed in from below. Just prior to the area ignition, the fire had grown to about 2,200 acres. Some flames already had spread up and over Twin Pines Road, to the east and above the Tile and Octagon houses. Those flames, plus the enormous fresh energy once the area ignition occurred, generated enough heat to pierce the shrouding layer of smoke at a spot above and to the south of the Tile and Octagon houses; the official fire report gives the location of the rising plume variously as a mile to the south and two miles to the southwest, one of many factual discrepancies in that document. In any case, once the plume formed, the effect was that of a giant vacuum cleaner suddenly pulling the fire up through a narrow vent. When this happened, a towering plume of smoke, the "nuclear explosion" observed by Gill and Chavez, rose to a height of over 18,000 feet, visible from more than one hundred miles away. From his vantage point at the Tile House, Fogle had a bird's-eye view of the entire event, from the explosion of fire that swept the Octagon House to the development of the plume. As it began, he watched the golden button of flame at the rock outcropping suddenly burst and let loose a torrent of fire, which raged forward, engulfing a quarter-acre bowl below the Octagon House, where the unnamed drainage split into the two arms that forked around the base of the house.

The burst of heat and flame moved at near-miraculous speed, covering three-quarters of a mile and sweeping over the Octagon House within five to seven seconds, by Fogle's later calculation. The official fire report more conservatively estimated that the flames ran "in excess of 30 miles an hour" and that wind speeds exceeded fifty miles an hour, so fast and powerful in fact that at the Octagon House the blasting wind did not allow flames to rise more than fifteen feet above ground, as indicated by burn patterns on still-standing scorched trees. Curiously, the sound the fire made was not explosive—more a rip than a bang.

The sight, however, was shattering.

Angry coils of gray smoke streaked with scarlet flames boiled out of the unnamed creek drainage and obliterated from sight the drainage, the Octagon House, and the knoll on which the house was sited. The flames raged on up Twin Pines Ridge, advancing for several minutes before the mushroom-shaped plume became visible to Fogle and others.

Area ignitions require slope, flame, compression, and an injection of oxygen, along with other incendiary conditions, but the exact combination of elements required to trigger one eludes fire scientists. The phenomenon, which is also called simultaneous ignition, is not predictable, though it happens with some regularity. "I've seen those conditions a hundred times," Fogle said afterward, "but they did not result in area ignitions." Fogle had seen something like the one at the Octagon House, however, on a fire about a decade earlier. "That was a cauldron of fire," Fogle said. "There was no measurable fire progression. There was a solid churning, as though someone had laid down a flamethrower in the drainage. There was a simultaneous ignition over a large area—it lit up the whole place. And that's what Esperanza did."

At the Tile House, where the sky was now clear and growing lighter by the minute, the spectacle of the unnamed creek drainage filled with boiling fire proved an irresistible lure. Richardson stepped to the edge of the clearing in front of the house, gripping his hard hat to keep it from blowing off. He handed his camera to Reyes and told him to take a photo of him with the fire in the background.

"Hurry up, man, this is killing me," Richardson said, bending away from the whip of wind and grit as the camera recorded the scene. In the video clip, the fire behind Richardson churns like a lava flow played in fast-reverse, one that spills uphill at an incredibly accelerated rate. "It's just boiling right there," Richardson says excitedly as the camera pans over the site of the Octagon House, now obliterated from sight by flames and smoke. Radios on high volume blare fragments of speech, clear and calm, about matters of ordinary concern: "Whatever we don't need . . . I'm going to try and get out." Then in the background, a young, agitated voice, barely audible, cries out a brief exclamation. The transmission lasts barely a second and is hurried and faint. A guess would be, "Engine 57, we have emergency traffic," which makes sense, but none of the words except "Engine 57" can be made out with any certainty. The passion in the voice, however, is unmistakable. It is the cry of a young man in desperate fear of his life beseeching the universe for deliverance.

"We all said, 'Oh my God,'" Richardson said later. "The smoke was so thick you couldn't see over there. Jacobs and I heard a scream on the radio. It was a cry for help, a quick yell, like screaming out at the end of their lungs. Then the radio had a different noise, a long static—a creepy sound. We all looked at each other and we were thinking this can't have happened. We were all thinking the same thing."

Jacobs walked over to Fogle, who was standing near the wall of the Tile House. "Hey, I just heard a scream on Tac II," Jacobs said. "Did you hear that?"

Fogle tried to raise Loutzenhiser on the radio. He called "Captain 57, Captain 52" three times without answer and then tried one last time, "Anybody on 57?" When that call too went unanswered, he told his crew to load up; it was time to get over there. They piled into the engine and started the drive to the Octagon House.

6.

The evacuation along Highway 243 was in full swing when Captain Gearhart's Engine 51 left behind the dregs of the Seminole Road Fire at about 5:30 AM and began the climb from the floor of the Banning Pass to the top of Twin Pines Ridge. Gearhart's crew was keyed up from working the little Seminole Road Fire and eager to get to the bigger Esperanza Fire. "Everybody was jazzed," said Mike Christian, a crewman in his first season. As Engine 51 headed up the highway, it passed civilian vehicles headed down, with occupants nervously twisting their heads, on the lookout for advancing flames. More than two miles to the east, in the direction of the desert, a slow tide of orange flame moved across the ridge face toward Highway 243. The orange glow illuminated clouds of smoke that rose and twisted into fantastic shapes before they disappeared into the blackness above. "I heard somebody on the radio say, 'The fire should get here in about two hours,'" said John Fakehany, another crewman. Someone answered, "This fire isn't going to hit us in two hours. It's going to hit us in two minutes!"

Engine 51 took one of the road's many sharp curves and suddenly confronted a horse galloping pell-mell on a lead rope held by a man driving a pickup. "It took us off guard," Gearhart said with understatement. A squeal of brakes and an athletic move by the horse avoided a collision. Engine 51 had been "going stealth," without red lights or siren, because civilian vehicles pulling over on twisting roads like this one invite rear-end collisions. An engine–horse smashup was no alternative, and Gearhart ordered red lights turned on but not the siren, in a compromise he hoped would keep any other horses from startling.

Highway 243, after twisting up the face of Twin Pines Ridge to the intersection with Twin Pines Road, continues south on a winding course into the mountains and past the town of Idyllwild. Twin Pines Road branches off due east and runs about three miles, serving the residential community along the ridgetop, and comes to an end at the Twin Pines Ranch, a boot camp run by the county for probation-referred youth. The several dirt roads that head down the ridge from Twin Pines Road, including Wonderview and Gorgonio View, peter out before reaching the floor of the Pass. In other words, if you drive downhill from the top of the ridge, the only way out is back up.

Gearhart's Engine 51 finished the drive up the ridge face and rejoined Dinkel and Espinoza, who had just concluded an unsuccessful effort to drive down Wonderview Road to catch up with Fogle and Loutzenhiser. Dinkel and Espinoza had waited along Twin Pines Road until they were joined by March Brush 10, the two-man air force crew in a pickup. By the time March Brush 10 showed up, Loutzenhiser and Fogle were long gone down Wonderview Road, and conditions on the road had changed for the worse: smoke and heat were driving other units up and out of the lower reaches of the ridge. "I could hear Lotzy and Fogle talking on the radio; they already were engaged in their assignment," Espinoza said. As the Forest Service and air force vehicles started down the road, they found their way blocked by a pair of Type I Cal Fire heavies, much larger than the Type III Forest Service engines. The heavies couldn't handle the narrow, rutted road; unable to find space to turn around, they were backing out. That created enough of a jam. But coming up behind the heavies was another vehicle, a Forest Service pickup with two Vista Grande Hotshots: the crew supervisor, Jesse Estrada, and his driver, B.J. Scott. Estrada and Scott had been scouting the lower reaches of the ridge face for a safe spot to commit the hotshots but had become alarmed by the reach of the fire and had decided to pull out. Estrada hailed the Forest Service engine captains, who were familiar faces. "I told those guys not to go down there; it was no place to be," Estrada said later.

Scott worked the pickup around the Forest Service engines and back up to Twin Pines Road, where a personal matter needed his immediate attention: his parents' house on Twin Pines Road was in the path of the fire. "The fire was almost to us," Scott said. "I called my parents on my cell phone and said, 'The fire's one hill away; it's time to go.' But they were already on their way out the door. Then Jess said, 'Let's go to the house and verify that they're gone.' We got there, and I ran down the driveway and yelled, but they were gone by then. Fire was engulfing the hill behind the house about two hundred feet away, and Jess said, 'Let's haul!'"

Estrada and Scott rode out the fire in their pickup at a wide spot along Twin Pines Road. Later that morning they were able to return to the parents' home, which was still standing. But Scott's classic 1960 Chevrolet Apache pickup, for which he had just paid $3,000, was on fire. A Cal Fire engine crew appeared and doused the vehicle, which was a total loss, but the hosing kept flames from reaching a nearby shed.

Meanwhile, Espinoza, Dinkel, and the March Brush 10 crew, blocked by the Cal Fire engines and warned by Estrada against going farther downhill, made their way back up to Twin Pines Road. As they retreated, Espinoza radioed to Loutzenhiser and Fogle. "I told them we couldn't make access and wouldn't be able to help them," Espinoza said. As he and Dinkel reemerged onto Twin Pines Road, they had a welcome reunion with Gearhart and the crew of Engine 51, who had driven in to meet them. The three Forest Service engines, plus March Brush 10, stopped at the side of the road to confer.

Gearhart had received instructions by radio to go with Dinkel and Espinoza and meet Branch Director Toups, who was waiting for them along Gorgonio View Road, which was not immediately threatened by the fire. Toups would lead them down the ridge to do structure protection at the double-wide, it would turn out, where Toups earlier had roused the owners and warned them to evacuate. As Gearhart described the assignment to the others, he was the only one who had a map of the vicinity. It was a hand-drawn sketch made by a patrol unit several years earlier, but it showed in a general way the roads that branched off Twin Pines Road. Possession of the map made Gearhart the navigator.

The official fire report would make the excellent criticism that existing topographic maps of the area had not been distributed or used to brief the captains. George Solverson, the chief Forest Service investigator on the report staff, said that fire crews have come to rely far too much on global positioning devices rather than map-reading skills. An irony of the fire is that Cal Fire vehicles had computers with maps that showed the location of the agency's vehicles but not the Forest Service vehicles, which had no such computers.

Gearhart climbed back in his engine and led the others back along Twin Pines Road to the turnoff for Gorgonio View Road. They quickly found Toups, and Gearhart went over for a talk. The time was about 6:15 AM.

"You're Branch?" Gearhart said.

"Yes," Toups replied. "Are all the engines here?"

"Where are we going?" Gearhart asked, with some apprehension.

"It's safe," Toups said reassuringly, and he promised to lead the way down.

Gearhart relayed the news to Dinkel and Espinoza. "He said it's safe," Gearhart said. "If we don't like it, we'll leave."

Toups started ahead in his pickup but had not gone far before a caravan of vehicles appeared in the road ahead, coming up from below. Leading the caravan was a forty-foot motor home, its extension doors flapping in wild disorder. Inside were Neil and Janet Garner, the couple Toups had roused at the double-wide, and following them in an SUV was their caretaker, Upton.

"Hey guys, save the blue house, save the blue house with the white top!" the Garners shouted out the window.

Man, you just hit the fire truck jackpot, thought one of the engine crewmen. *Three big engines are about to park at your door.*

Toups had met the Garners for a second time only a few minutes earlier near the Tile House as they had tried to escape the fire by driving up Wonderview Road, which Toups knew was engulfed by flames higher up the ridge face; he had seen it for himself. If they kept going that way, they would run right into the fire. He flagged them down and told them to turn around, go back past the double-wide, and use Gorgonio View Road as an escape route instead. Garner at first complained that he couldn't back or turn the motor home around on the narrow road. When Toups told him his choice was to do that or face a burnover, Garner managed to back the big vehicle into a driveway and make the turn. If Toups hadn't already saved their lives by waking them, he probably did it this time.

Afterward, Garner gave a jittery account of his close call to a television news reporter: "I ran out right ahead of the flames. I was worried that I wasn't going to get out because I was driving a forty-foot motor home, which I was backing down a twisty dirt road, because I couldn't get around where I needed to because of the flames."

The meeting between the Garners and Upton in their vehicles going up Gorgonio View Road and Toups and the others coming down luckily occurred at one of the few wide spots in the road, and the civilian vehicles managed to squeeze past the fire vehicles and move on to safety. As the fire vehicles continued down the road, the glow from the fire and the first traces of coming dawn lightened the sky. Gorgonio View Road climbs a slight rise before heading down the ridge face, and at the crest of the rise, a shadowy panorama came into view: the broad, open sweep of the Banning Pass; the mostly barren, rutted face of Twin Pines Ridge; and the approaching flames. From this vantage point, the situation did not appear overly alarming. The flames were distant; the breeze a gentle three to five miles an hour. "The fire was not threatening at all, and it looked to be an hour away. At this point, I thought time was on our side," Gearhart said.

On the floor of the Banning Pass, however, the vanguard of the Santa Ana wind had arrived with gusts of twenty-five miles an hour, strong enough to stir up the fire, though nothing like the sixty-plus-mile-an-hour winds that would follow. When the full strength of the Santa Ana arrived, anyone caught out on the ridge face had to be prepared to withstand a major blast of fire. As Hotshot superintendent Estrada had warned, it was "no place to be."

As the firefighters descended Gorgonio View Road, the panoramic view was lost and the convoy became almost blind to the outer world. Toups was in the lead, followed by Engine 51 with Gearhart and his crew: Shawn Evans, John Fakehany, Eddie Harper, Darrell Arrellano, and Mike Christian. Next came Engine 56 with Espinoza and his crew: David Goldstein, Doug Donahoo, Ryan Henninger, and Chris Matthews. Next was Engine 54 with Dinkel and her crew: Josh Spoon, Jarod Baker, Adan Castro, and Ian Governale. Last in line was March Brush 10 with Rod Rambayon and Gary Bicondova.

The road twisted down the ridge through a tunnel of chaparral that rose a dozen or more feet on either side. For the first mile, the road trended west, directly away from the approaching fire, an effect that was not lost on the fire crews. "As long as we were headed away, everything was fine," one firefighter remarked. "What was going through my mind, being fairly new, I really didn't like the looks of it. I knew it was going to be a good one. But I was a little scared."

At the start of the descent, Toups saw a troubling sight halfway down the ridge face: the flashing lights of an engine in a place where no engine should be. Wondering who this could be, and what they were doing there, he decided to investigate as soon as he dropped off the engines at the double-wide.

Gorgonio View made a severe hairpin turn about a mile and a quarter down from Twin Pines Road, and as the engines took the curve, they wound up headed straight for the fire; this effect was not lost on them either. "When we hooked right, the whole complexion of the fire changed," Gearhart said. The flames were still a ridgeline or two away, but the freshening wind had kicked them into life. The engines now headed directly toward a very active fire that had the potential to spot or make a run that could easily engulf them.

"Oh, no," Gearhart said under his breath. *I can't believe it*, he thought, *I'm going to burn to death tonight*. His leg started to shimmy, and he put his hand on it to keep it quiet.

In the glow of firelight, the engine crews saw that they were headed into a deep basin, a perfect mixing bowl for flames. "Are we getting close?" Gearhart asked Toups by radio. "Is this place coming up? We have to have time to set up." The radio frequency was swamped with traffic and nobody answered.

Gearhart ordered his driver, Evans, to step on it.

"Everybody was pretty pumped up. It was the biggest homeboy fire of the season," Evans said.

Nervous laughter broke out in the backseat of the engine. "Two guys in the back of 51 were getting excited and saying, 'Hey, hey, great. Look at that. We've got fire!'" Fakehany related. "As we turned

that corner, all of a sudden the brush was taller than the engine. I
said, 'Wow, we're committed.' We couldn't outrun the fire uphill in
that old engine. Captain Gearhart is normally a steady hand, but
he was becoming very agitated and he started talking to himself. I
could see his leg shimmy up and down. He was saying, 'I've seen
this before, I've seen this before.' But he never said *what* he'd seen
before."

When the laughter started, Gearhart felt a surge of frustration.
They had to be sharp; they needed every second to get ready for
what was coming. And he snapped at the crew, "No! This is fucking
serious. We've got to get in there!" The laughter died out as Engine
51 accelerated and opened a gap with the other engines.

Dinkel and Espinoza, hearing the worry in Gearhart's voice on
the radio and seeing his engine suddenly speed up, became worried
themselves. "As we continued down the road, driving into a bowl,
all the guys in the engine went dead quiet," Dinkel said. When
one member of Espinoza's crew, Henninger, said he didn't like the
situation, Espinoza ordered the engine stopped. The crew talked it
over, calmed down, and agreed to keep going. "You always get fear
on a fire," said another crewman, Donahoo. "The day you don't get
fear is the day you need to quit. Give me butterflies any time."

Dinkel and Espinoza ordered their drivers to catch up with
Gearhart, and the engines slewed over deep ruts and swung heavily
around curves in a bouncing, anxious dash to the bottom of the
bowl. The road made a final turn at the bottom of the bowl, and
there, off to the left, was a narrow driveway that led to a small
mobile home, the same place where Toups had stopped earlier and
sounded his siren without raising anyone.

"The trailer was sitting on the edge of a drainage and had mature
brush almost touching the eaves," Gearhart said later. "There was
no clearance whatsoever. That's when I wondered how much
pain there would be when I died, how long the pain would last. I

wondered how my wife and kids would handle the knock on the door." He and his wife, Cindy, had a son and a daughter—Alek, 16, and Gloria, 12.

"This can't be it. Move on," Gearhart told Evans.

With much relief, the engine crews saw the lights of Toups's pickup continue past the small mobile home, and they gladly followed, leaving that place to its fate—flames eventually took it. The engines had gone only a few dozen more yards when Toups stopped next to the double-wide. It was the main structure in a sprawling 25-acre compound that owner Neil Garner himself described as "out in the sticks." In addition to the double-wide and the mobile home there was a horse corral, dog kennels, and storage sheds. Nearby were several vehicles, a boat on a trailer, and a riding mower. Horses stomped and snorted inside the corral and banged their chests against the rails. The Garners had taken some of the dogs with them but left behind in an outdoor run what looked like dozens more—miniature pinschers and toy fox terriers, both high-strung breeds. The dogs yapped and leaped up against the enclosure's wire fencing.

"This isn't where we're supposed to be, is it?" exclaimed an unbelieving Espinoza. The place looked to him like a junkyard, littered with paint cans, lumber, and banged-up vehicles. "And there were power lines overhead—I really didn't like the power lines," he said. "The only place we could park was under the lines. No place was going to be safe when the winds started."

Gearhart looked at the brush-covered slope on the side of the road opposite the double-wide. *That has to go. If the wind hits, it will drive the fire onto our engines like a blowtorch.* The moment the engine stopped, Gearhart told the crewmen in the backseat to set up drip torches, intending to fight fire with fire. He walked over to Toups's pickup, testing the leg that had begun to shimmy from tension on the drive down the ridge face.

"Is this the place?" he said.

"This is it," Toups replied.

Gearhart asked Toups if the power lines were live, but Toups didn't know. He said he had to get going to investigate the flashing engine lights he had seen farther down the road, and with that he left. The clearing under the power lines was the only place that looked big enough to accommodate the engines, but two autos were already parked there. The brush had been cleared on the high bank on the opposite side of the road, but enough fuel remained to carry fire. "The space around the double-wide wasn't big enough for a safety zone, but it was a place where you could work," Gearhart said.

Gearhart, Dinkel, and Espinoza gathered for a quick conference.

"Looks like you're as pissed off as I am," Gearhart said to an assembly of sullen faces. Unhappy or not, the captains agreed there was no time to make a retreat back up the ridge face: they'd have to stay and fight it out.

"We need to burn this," Dinkel said, indicating the brush on the high bank.

"Oh, yeah, we're going to burn," Gearhart said.

The captains' first concern was to clear the area around the power poles, to keep them from catching fire and falling down, wires and all. The parked civilian vehicles had to be shoved out of the way, hoses had to be pulled and lines charged, and debris had to be cleared away from structures, especially the double-wide. And what to do about the riled-up horses and the yapping dogs?

What about letting the horses loose? someone suggested.

"They die where they stand," Gearhart announced abruptly.

Gearhart had had a previous run-in with horses on another fire, eight years earlier, and had no intention of repeating the experience. He had been on a hotshot crew fighting a fire on the Fort Apache reservation in Arizona and in an effort to be humane had let horses loose from a corral threatened by flames. The freed horses had run amok through thick smoke, almost colliding with the firefighters and creating a general uproar at a critical time. Afterward, the hotshots, including Gearhart, swore they would never do such a thing again. The horses at the double-wide were left where they were, in the corral.

The approaching fire seemed to have quieted for the moment, and Dinkel started to supervise preparations for the burnout. She put some firefighters to work clearing brush and told others to move the cars from under the power lines. Several crewmen were about to shove the cars into a gully when Donahoo found keys on the dashes of both vehicles and drove them out. Fakehany hefted a chain saw with a heavy-duty twenty-eight-inch bar and began trimming back brush with what others judged to be excessive care. "It doesn't matter if it's pretty. Cut the shit!" Evans barked at him. Someone found a garden hose and put it with a sprinkler on the roof of the double-wide; others pulled a hose line and made it ready. Still others piled propane bottles and other combustibles away from the double-wide. Dinkel also asked Rambayon and Bicondova from March Brush 10 to do something about the dogs; they pulled a hose line and put a stream of water on the dog run.

Leaving those preparations in Dinkel's hands, Gearhart and Espinoza walked down the road to scout ahead. All five Forest Service engines now were in their final positions—three at the double-wide, one each at the Octagon House and the Tile House. The positions formed a rough triangle, with no one location more than a half mile from the others. As Gearhart and Espinoza set out, they could not see any of the others. They could hear Fogle and Loutzenhiser on the radio, however, and realized they must be close. "Give me a flash," Espinoza radioed, and when Loutzenhiser blinked his engine lights, Espinoza was surprised to discover that Engine 57 was just a few hundred yards below the double-wide.

"When I looked down in the dark and saw the Octagon House where Lotzy was, I was trying to get my bearings, and my first impression was that it was two houses, and I thought I was talking to Fogle but it was Lotzy," Espinoza said.

Once again, Loutzenhiser reported that he was in a "good spot," and he repeated the good news about the existence of a swimming pool. But Loutzenhiser added a warning for the others, telling them to steer clear of a house nearby his location. "Don't do anything with that one because it's a loser," Loutzenhiser cautioned. He meant a mother-in-law house belonging to Greg Koeller, the owner of the Octagon. The little place was tucked into the upper end of a dead-end gulch—one of the forks of the unnamed creek drainage—on the far, east side of the ridge opposite the double-wide. The house exemplified the term *loser*: surrounded by propane tanks and paint cans, it looked certain to burn if any fire went that way. But appearances can deceive even experienced fire captains, as happened more than once that day. Flames eventually came straight for the "loser" house, but in a random act of sparing, left the place, just a few hundred yards from the Octagon House, virtually untouched.

7.

WHAT HAPPENED NEXT WAS CERTAINLY the most disputed conversation to occur on the Esperanza Fire. After Toups drove away from the double-wide he stopped briefly at the Octagon House and met face-to-face with Loutzenhiser. Toups's account of what was said, while it cannot be corroborated, should not be ignored—as it mostly was afterward. Toups says that he and Loutzenhiser came to an agreement that the captain would pull his crew back from the Octagon House and ride out the coming run of fire at the double-wide, where the corral and other open ground made a good safety zone. Further, Loutzenhiser understood this plan and agreed to it. But for some unknown reason, the captain remained at the Octagon House with his crew.

Toups says he told Gearhart and Espinoza about the agreement when he drove back to the double-wide a few minutes later and instructed them, or at least Gearhart, to "make it happen." What follows is Toups's version of events, pieced together from the written records, from telephone talks, and from a day he spent with me retracing events on foot and by truck at locations where they occurred.

After guiding the three Forest Service engines and March Brush 10 to the double-wide and telling the three captains there, "It's safe," Toups drove ahead to investigate the engine lights he had seen farther down the ridge face where he thought no engine lights should be. When he came to the driveway to the Octagon House, he saw that the chain across the driveway had been cut since the last time he had driven past, which meant an engine crew had passed that way. As he started up the driveway, he saw several firefighters standing about in fire shirts and pants but without fire shelters or hard hats. It was the same situation he had encountered earlier at the Tile House with Fogle's crew, and the sight made the hair on the back of his neck stand up: How could the crew be so complacent? He leaned out the pickup window and told the firefighters to get into proper gear.

"Where's your company officer?" he asked.

"He's up looking at the house," said one.

That was the first Toups knew there was a house on the site; the Octagon House, being on top of a knob, is almost invisible from the lower driveway. The owner, Koeller, was away, the house was unlighted, and dawn was just a hint in the sky. As Toups pulled up in front of the garage, Loutzenhiser came walking out from behind Engine 57, which was parked in front of the garage. Toups introduced himself and asked Loutzenhiser to step away from his crew for a private word. The two men walked to the edge of the clearing. From there they could see down to the unnamed creek drainage, its outlines now partially illuminated by firelight and the approaching dawn. The time was about 6:25 AM.

"It was an affable discussion; we were both on the same page," Toups said. "I got him away from his crew and said, 'Hey, I'm really concerned here. Who assigned you to come down here?'"

Loutzenhiser replied that he thought he was in a "great place" and was acting as lookout for the other engines. "I can see what's going on," he said.

"You're right. You're in a good position to be a lookout," Toups said. But he had other, larger concerns. "Here's the plan," he told Loutzenhiser.

Most of the other engines were only a few hundred yards away at the double-wide, Toups said, which was a safety zone not only for them but also for Engine 57. He told Loutzenhiser to take his crew and join the others at the double-wide before the flame front arrived, which was expected in the next forty-five minutes to an hour.

"This blue structure back here is where I want all you guys," Toups said.

Once the fire had passed, he said, Engine 57 could return to the Octagon House and "places like this" and see whether they could put out lingering flames and save structures. But more important, Toups said, would be a search for squatters who might be farther down the road.

"We're told there's people down here at the end of the road, but we just don't know," Toups told Loutzenhiser. "You need to go down these roads and see if there's people down here. But only after the fire front passes. Let everything go through first. If they're not down here, that's great. But you're not to be protecting these structures; that's not the intent." Toups told Loutzenhiser he expected that when the flames reached the bottom of the drainage in front of them, "it's all going to be in alignment, and it's all going to go up—I told him exactly what was going to happen here." Toups says he specifically used the words "area ignition" as one possible outcome.

And Loutzenhiser replied, "Got it. I understand."

The conversation lasted no more than five minutes. Toups and Loutzenhiser shook hands, and Loutzenhiser said in farewell, "Be safe." Toups made a note of the conversation in his unit log soon after the event: "We discussed state of weather, reviewed topography of structure location, other resources at structures just above this location, the safety zone at that location and assigned TAC frequencies. 57 acknowledged these concerns and direction."

The main points of Toups's story, then, are that he told

Loutzenhiser to pull back to the double-wide before the fire arrived, he specifically warned about the possibility of an area ignition, and he believed Loutzenhiser agreed to pull back to the double-wide and ride out the fire there. "The captain and I came to agreement that nobody should be at this house because it was indefensible," Toups told me. "Something caused him to disregard those instructions that he said he understood."

Loutzenhiser cannot speak for himself, but his friend Fogle is in a position to speak for him on several of these points. Fogle was close by, in sight of the Octagon House, and in regular radio communication with Loutzenhiser. Most of those radio exchanges were overheard and attested to by others. Fogle says that Toups's account sounds to him suspiciously like an overdetailed attempt to cover himself on all the main points that fire investigators look for after a fatal occurrence. Fogle called these points the "big five" of fire safety investigations: lookouts, escape routes, safety zones, communications, and personal protective gear. Specifically, Fogle makes these arguments:

In his radio transmissions, Loutzenhiser never wavered from his intention to ride out the fire at the Octagon House. If he had agreed to come back to the double-wide, he would have said so. He never departed from his rationale for staying where he was, repeatedly calling it a "good place." Everyone who heard the radio traffic agrees that was what he said.

Loutzenhiser never described himself to the other engine captains as a lookout. Anyone who formally takes on the role of lookout is required to identify themselves to the people they are looking out for, and then to remain at the lookout spot until further notice. Fogle, not Loutzenhiser, was actually in the best position to be a pair of eyes. It was he, after all, who warned that the fire was about to explode in the unnamed creek drainage. In fact, none of the Forest Service captains formally took on the role of lookout.

While Fogle does not challenge Toups's account that he and Loutzenhiser discussed potential fire behavior—that's what firefighters talk about—he doubts Toups used the term "area ignition" even as a possibility. "If Toups thought the fire was going to move up the gulch real fast, he would have said that. We don't talk 'area ignition' on the line. Area ignitions are not predictable. He would have had to be a fire god to predict that."

On the subject of character, Fogle said that Loutzenhiser was the last person in the world who would have refused a direct order. If he had been told to leave, he would have smiled and packed up. "They had some kind of conversation, but I have serious doubts Toups said half of what he said he did," Fogle stated. "If he had told Lotzy he didn't want him there, I guarantee Lotzy would have loaded up his folks and driven back to the double-wide. He was laid back about things like that. They didn't matter to him."

There is no way to either affirm or deny Toups's assertion that Loutzenhiser agreed to a pullback and then reneged. What can be said with assurance is that the two men discussed Engine 57's situation and there was a communications malfunction between them. Toups readily acknowledged that he behaved in a deferential manner toward Loutzenhiser, and perhaps he overdid it. Toups, however, went to the Octagon House because he didn't think an engine should be there. It would have been natural and proper for him to take Loutzenhiser aside for a private talk and discuss options for Engine 57 other than staying put; the nearby double-wide site, which Toups had identified as a safety zone for others, was one obvious option. That discussion took place in some form. But a polite exchange of views about options was not likely to change Loutzenhiser's commitment to a plan he had had in mind for over an hour.

Loutzenhiser, too, has a voice in this debate, though it is an indirect one. He repeatedly declared on the radio that he was in a good place. The Octagon House, he said, had good clearance and was "a block house with a tile roof," meaning it was built of fire-resistant materials. He reported finding a swimming pool full of water and signaled that he was putting in a portable pump to charge lines, and in fact that's what he did. He invited the other engine crews to come by to replenish their water tanks as necessary. He never wavered from any of those declarations. He also said, in less clear terms, that he planned to burn out around the Octagon House when the fire got closer, and in fact preparations were undertaken to do that.

The bottom line is that the encounter between Toups and Loutzenhiser, the last real chance to change plans, changed nothing. It was as though the two men had talked past each other, each convinced he had communicated something that was clear in his mind but was never clear in the mind of the other—and that may be the truest explanation of what actually happened.

As Toups started the drive back toward the double-wide, at 6:30 AM according to his log, he saw the crew of Engine 57 putting on hard hats and web gear as he had told them to do. There appeared to Toups, however, to be little sense of alarm or urgency among the crewmen; this observation can be corroborated by evidence on the ground and may have contributed to the fatal outcome. When Toups got back to the double-wide, he pulled up next to Gearhart, who was standing at the side of the road. Espinoza was standing within listening distance.

Toups is the only living witness to the exchange with Loutzenhiser, but the same is not true for this subsequent meeting with Gearhart and Espinoza. The two captains flatly contradict Toups's account of what was said there. Toups's exchange with the two captains took place under chaotic conditions, with Toups in his pickup talking out the window. Gearhart was close by, with Espinoza steps away. The fire was getting close and the captains were hurriedly preparing to meet it, including by lighting a burnout. With all that going on, conflicting versions of what was said are not surprising, but in this case they defy reconciliation. What follows is based on accounts from Gearhart and Espinoza as well as Toups.

"Were staying here," Gearhart told Toups as soon as he stopped. Gearhart wanted to end the conversation quickly.

"You're staying here?" Toups said to Gearhart out the pickup window.

"Yeah, we're staying," Gearhart repeated, his voice edging toward sarcasm.

What choice do I have? Gearhart thought. The Forest Service engines could never lumber up to the ridgetop ahead of flames that were edging ever closer to Gorgonio View Road. The double-wide site was no safety zone as far as Gearhart was concerned: it was a flammable junkyard with power lines overhead and barely enough room to park four engines. The corral was more open, but it was at the top of a drainage funnel that could fill with fire.

"This wasn't structure protection; it was turning into crew protection," Gearhart said later. "We were under the gun, and I did not believe Toups understood that. But I wasn't going to fight about it."

In Toups's telling, he and Gearhart talked extensively about safety and other matters. He said he told Gearhart that Engine 57 was parked at a homesite farther down the road, where Loutzenhiser was acting as lookout. The two then went over a standard safety checklist, LCES, which stands for lookouts, communications, escape routes, and safety zones. "We discussed the area of the corrals, the fuel types," Toups said. "I pointed out the power lines. The last thing I said to Gearhart is, 'Engine 57 needs to be back here. Make it happen.'" At the conclusion of their talk, Toups said that Gearhart appeared reassured. He quoted Gearhart as saying, "Chief, when we came down here I was very concerned. Now that I see this, I'm comfortable doing what we're going to do."

Gearhart said the exchange with Toups, to the contrary, amounted to a few quick sentences and was anything but reassuring; he called parts of Toups's version a "fabrication." Gearhart agreed that Toups said Engine 57 was stationed down the road. But Toups never told him that Engine 57 was supposed to come to the double-wide. Nor did Toups tell him to "make it happen." Further, Gearhart said he never told Toups he was comfortable with the situation; in fact, he was the opposite. "Our remarks were brief; I just wanted him to leave," Gearhart said.

The high tension of the situation and the different perspectives of the men may explain some but certainly not all the discrepancies. On the key question of whether Toups told Gearhart and Espinoza that Engine 57 was supposed to retreat to the double-wide, the difference is stark. Espinoza was within listening distance, and he, like Gearhart, says he did not hear Toups make any such remark. These flat denials also cast some doubt on Toups's claims about his earlier conversation with Loutzenhiser.

In fairness to Toups, from his initial log sheet to what he later told me, the broad outline of his account does not differ. It certainly gains in detail; the passage of time and formats more open and conversational than a log sheet should elicit expanded accounts, though the level of added detail raised eyebrows on more than one official fire investigation team. But Toups's claim that he told Gearhart to make certain Loutzenhiser came back to the double-wide—to "make it happen"—does not appear in his formal statements. He did say it to friends, however, before he said it to me.

On a few points, Gearhart and Toups agree on what happened during their final encounter. "Toups did mention to me that the wind was starting and it wasn't even daylight yet," Gearhart said. Both men took this as a warning. "I acknowledged that the wind was present, and I believe we both expected the wind to increase once the sun rose in the sky."

Gearhart says that before leaving, Toups asked him if he had checked "the other houses." "What?" Gearhart answered, unable to conceal his disbelief. The only other houses he knew about were the unoccupied mobile home they had passed just before reaching the double-wide and the "loser" in the nearby gully—and he thought neither of those was worth a second look. Toups let the matter drop; he had more pressing concerns. Flames visible on the ridge face above were threatening Gorgonio View Road, Toups's only escape route.

"I'm going to try to get out of here," Toups said.

"You're not going back out of here the way we came in? I wouldn't do that if I were you," Espinoza said.

"Well, I have to try," Toups said, and he started up the road.

Gearhart, watching Toups's pickup snake back up the ridge, raised the middle fingers of both hands in salute. "One for each of the two houses he was worried about," Gearhart said later.

As Toups negotiated Gorgonio View Road, he watched in alarm as approaching flames to the east ran up toward Twin Pines Road and its many homes. "It's now become very apparent the worst possible thing is happening," Toups told fire investigators afterward. "The fire behavior is extreme. There was no chance of doing anything but protecting life and property." At 6:40 AM, according to his log, Toups radioed a warning to fire supervisors that it was time to consider evacuating the Poppet Flats area, which lies beyond Twin Pines Road to the south. "OK, Mike, your resources along Wondering View [sic] and Gorgonio are really going to get hammered here," said a voice on the radio, which Toups believes could have been his, in a transmission picked up by a firefighter's video camera. "So get 'em on the radio, get 'em heads up."

Whatever had happened between Toups and Loutzenhiser at the Octagon House, whatever had been said or left unsaid or ignored or misunderstood or was later embellished, the tide of events on Twin Pines Ridge swept forward and passed the point of no return.

8.

A CUNNING ARSONIST COULD NOT have chosen a better spot to set his torch than the place the engine crews at the double-wide started their burnout: in chaparral on the steep slope of the cutbank opposite the double-wide. Conditions for burning were perfect. Months of hot, rain-free weather had cured the chaparral until fuel moistures (the measure of water held by vegetation) had reached the season's usual incendiary low. The humidity had dropped to the single digits, and the air carried an anticipatory tingle. The wind picked up. The slope of the cutbank would accelerate the fire's spread by a factor of four to five. All the necessary things were in alignment. But when the firefighters put flame to brush, the fire sputtered, fizzled, and refused to take. And the mounting wave of wildfire appeared over a ridge, coming straight for them.

Gearhart had tried to report his burn plan to the command staff but couldn't make contact using the assigned radio frequencies. Switching to the Forest Service frequency, he called Loutzenhiser and Fogle to alert them.

"We're in a bad spot and we need to fire out," Gearhart said. "The trucks are twenty feet off the brush line, and we're not going to burn too much; it shouldn't affect you."

"It won't bother us," Loutzenhiser replied. "We're in a good spot. Go ahead."

Loutzenhiser remarked that he could see the headlights of the engines at the double-wide and that he, too, planned to do a burnout. Several firefighters remember hearing Loutzenhiser say something like, "We might need some help from you guys a little bit later; it's getting hot up here. We might lay down some fire, too."

After their scouting trip and the talk with Toups, Gearhart and Espinoza had called the others around for a quick briefing before starting the burnout.

"I don't care about that fucking house," Gearhart said, pointing toward the "loser" home, the mother-in-law house on the other side of the ridge. "Or that fucking house," he added, nodding toward the unoccupied home that they had passed on the way in. "But that one has got to stand," he said, indicating the double-wide. When he asked for volunteers to ignite the burn, many hands shot up.

"Not you. I don't know you," Gearhart said to Donahoo, at age 20 the youngest firefighter at the double-wide, leaving him crushed. "Hey, Goldstein," Gearhart said to a more familiar figure. "Get that firing stuff and let's go."

Goldstein started to load a Very pistol, the modern version of a flare-launching device invented in the nineteenth century, often used by firefighters to start a burnout. "My knees are banging together, my hands are shaking, and I'm trying to load the gun. It takes .22 blanks," Goldstein said. "My body was telling me this was no good. Every other time, a burnout operation has been fun. It's planned, you've got dozers cutting line, you're with a lot of people, and it's fun. This time it was burn out or possibly get burned up."

Gearhart picked Henninger to handle the drip torch. Henninger took the metal canister out of its compartment on the engine and assembled it. He ignited the torch, fed by gasoline and diesel from the canister. Then he tipped the canister at shoulder height, and flaming goo spilled into dry brush next to the road. The goo started a fire about the size of a hard hat in one of the most incendiary spots on the planet, but nothing much happened. The tiny patch of fire would not grow.

"Just before we fired, we looked up and could see the fire above us on the hillside, Gearhart said. "The fire had gotten exposed to the wind. I was relieved because I now needed to burn only a few acres and the fire would go around me, and there would be less heat for Lotzy. But we lit the brush, and then the fire wasn't doing anything! It was burning in little circles. There was no wind at that spot. The slope wasn't taking it up the hill. If the main fire worked over to the knob in front of us, it could come right down on the engines. I walked over to Anna and said, 'Goddamn, we've got to get this show going.'"

The coming fire appeared over the ridge like a blood-red dawn, a searing, halo-shaped terror that swelled into the lightening sky and threatened to sweep down on the burn crew in a fiery wave. The failing burnout was the only thing that stood between them and the inferno. Captains and crew began throwing everything they could grab into the chaparral—broken-up fusees, handfuls of brush. Goldstein fired his Very pistol point-blank at the chaparral. Another hopeful firefighter stood by with a charged hose line in case the burnout became too successful, but for long minutes he was an idle spectator.

The scene became theatrical. The burn crew succeeded in starting a row of spot fires, much like footlights, in the brush next to the road. Behind the little lights, a curtain of scarlet flame arose from the main fire and formed a backdrop for the drama, a seemingly unfair contest between the overmatched spot fires and the huge curtain of flame. But the spot fires grew together into a continuous line that sent tongues of yellow flame lapping up the hillside, drawn by the approaching curtain of fire as it sucked in oxygen to sustain itself. The two fires—the burnout and the approaching fire—met in a soaring pyramid of flame, consumed all available fuel, and collapsed together in a smoldering, flaming heap.

"The fire went up the knob in front of us and over the power lines," Gearhart said. "And suddenly the fire went down to the ground. The flames went down and the power lines were still up. That was victory."

After stopping the fire from sweeping the roadway, firefighters turned their attention to the vicinity of the double-wide, where wind-cast embers had started numerous small spot fires. One ember ignited a hose line; firefighters quickly doused it and replaced the burned section. The horse corral was free of fire and the horses were safe, but the dog kennel was threatened and the frenzied dogs inside were raising a racket, yapping, leaping into the air, and banging against their wire cages. "As long as we're here, we might as well save the dogs," Gearhart said, and a crewman pulled a hose to the kennels. Things were looking up, Gearhart thought. "Great job!" he said, but any celebration was premature.

Gearhart had started to walk over the site, checking for spot fires, when he was stopped by a mass of hot air surging up from the direction of the Octagon House. The blast turned spot fires into lashing pinwheels of flame. "It made a whooshing, venting noise that made you stop and look," Gearhart said. What he saw was a jet of flame, "like someone had laid down a flamethrower," which sent a glittering shaft of light into the surrounding darkness. "There was nothing subtle about it," Gearhart said. "It was the hammer of God!"

The blast of fire lit up the scene with eerie noontime brightness, as though someone had set off a pile of flash powder; in a moment, visibility stretched to one thousand feet and more. The brilliant intensity did not last long. A swirling cloud of gritty smoke followed close behind the jet of flame, enveloped the double-wide site, and turned light to darkness. "You could see the particles," one firefighter said. "You took a breath and it came out ashy."

Waves of heat followed one after the other. The motorboat

caught fire, adding toxic fumes to the mix. The air was so thick with debris that firefighters held their breaths in fear they would suck in living embers. "It was *Star Wars*," Goldstein said. "We started taking a lot of heat. All you could see was embers flying past your head." Even so, the worst of the blast was deflected from the double-wide site by the thumb of land with the Octagon House.

Donahoo, having been denied the Very pistol, was manning a hose near the double-wide when he saw the fire take off. "It looked like a sea of flames, choppy and uneven," he said. "The winds hit me in the face, forty to fifty miles an hour, and a shower of embers the size of golf balls. I remember seeing the flames come over the engines in a wave, curling like a tsunami. Everything we had burned started to reburn, like we'd never burned it. The fire was moving up the hillside and out of the bowl. If it got worse, I knew we'd have to deploy right there in the driveway. The March Brush 10 guys were behind their vehicle, and I saw the embers hit it and go over the top. I stopped for a second and said a prayer, and a eucalyptus tree lost a branch and came down ahead of me. If I hadn't stopped for the prayer, I would have been right under it."

"Back to the trucks!" someone shouted, and an air horn blared the signal to rally at the engines.

"Where's Darrell?" Gearhart tried to shout, but he barely managed a whisper.

"Right here!" replied Arrellano, who was invisible in smoke just a foot or two away.

"You could feel the particles in the air, and I held my breath as long as I could," Gearhart said. "I remember feeling big embers bouncing off my back. But you had to take a breath." He bent double, trying to get below the smoke, and headed for the engines.

Goldstein had traded his flare pistol for a hose and was trying to cool the edges of the fire. "The fire grew so fast there was no chasing it," he said. He switched to a fog nozzle and began spraying a cloud of water near the vehicles to cool the air and keep heat from scorching the engines. As others, too, pulled out hose lines, the doors to the empty hose compartments flapped and slammed in the wind. The spaghetti pile of hose atop Gearhart's Engine 51, tossed there after the Seminole Road Fire, began to smoke; Goldstein hosed it down.

"I got on the radio and said, 'Firefighters 56, back to the engine, now!'" Goldstein said. "And you could hear that same thing over the radio from 56, 51, 54—everybody saying, 'Everybody back to the engines, hunker down, get accountability for personnel!' I knew it was bad. I could see people running in toward the engines, coming from all directions."

Some followed hose lays back to the engines. One firefighter, with smoke coming out of his hard hat, took off the hat and snatched off a superheated bandanna that he had wrapped around his head. Exposed to oxygen, the bandanna burst into flames. Another firefighter ran up to the engines, dove to the ground, and vomited. A panicked call blared over the radio: "I don't know where everybody is!"

Dinkel, recognizing the voice as one of her crewmen, ran back to her engine. When the caller said he couldn't account for everyone and could barely breathe himself, Dinkel looked at him hard and said, "I know where everybody is," and he calmed down. In a moment, however, his cry of alarm proved prophetic. The point of calling everyone to the engines was to make certain that all personnel were accounted for, but as the captains made the count, Dinkel realized one of her crew had not responded: Jarod Baker. Alarmingly, just as she realized Baker was missing, she saw another firefighter carrying Baker's radio.

"Where did you get that?" she demanded. The firefighter replied that he had found it lying on the ground.

Dinkel and Gearhart set off in different directions to search for

Baker. In a few steps, Dinkel found another bad sign: Baker's hard hat, lying on the ground.

"Jarod!" she shouted, "Jarod, where are you?"

She felt a tap on her shoulder.

"I'm right here," Baker said. He had lost his gear while running to the engines and in his exposed condition, with no hard hat, had taken refuge inside the engine cab, where he had been invisible to the others because of the smoke.

At some point during the retreat to the engines, Loutzenhiser made a radio call to Espinoza, called him by his nickname, Fuman, and said it was getting hot where he was and he needed help. This probably was a later call than the one in which he said he planned to do a burnout and might need some help later on. "It was just a real brief click," Espinoza said. "I told him it would be some time before we could get down there, and I went back to getting people back to the engines." Others, too, heard the transmission. "It was a broken transmission," said Goldstein, with a "gagging noise" at the end.

The driving head of the fire swept past the double-wide site and up the ridge toward Twin Pines Road, Poppet Flats, and beyond. All hands at the double-wide were now accounted for; most of them were huddled on the leeward side of the engines. Only three had climbed inside engine cabs to escape the smoke. The situation had been hectic and confused, but no one had suffered serious injury, though several had pounding headaches from the bad air. Everyone had trouble breathing. Gearhart told Evans to pull out an oxygen bottle in case someone needed a whiff to clear his head. Conditions were still too extreme to allow the firefighters to get far from the engines. A few of them, however, managed to stretch hose to the double-wide and wet it down.

The smoke turned from black to gray to a thin whitish haze. The dogs quieted down, and the horses stopped their restless stomping.

The time had come to complete the chain of accountability and check in with Fogle at the Tile House and Loutzenhiser at the Octagon House.

"Hey, Fogle, the fire made it to the ridge; what about our bet for a soda?" Gearhart called over the radio, trying to ease tension by reminding Fogle of their bet. "I can't get 57," Fogle called back.

The Santa Ana wind, howling in full fury on the upper ridge face, had scrubbed the sky over the Tile House to a harsh clarity. It was now 7:30 AM and full daylight. When Fogle had tried to reach Loutzenhiser—the thrice-repeated call "Captain 57, Captain 52," and then, "Anyone on 57!"—and no one had answered, he told himself that Loutzenhiser must be engaged with that extraordinary rush of fire from the unnamed creek drainage and too busy to answer.

"Okay, I'll try to get him," Gearhart said. At the double-wide, conditions were still severe. The wind pelted grit and charred brush into the faces of firefighters already half-blinded by smoke and heat. Espinoza pulled a pair of swim goggles out of his pack and put them on for protection.

"Lotz, how you doing over there?" Gearhart called. Engine 57's crew had several radios; somebody had to be on the right channel. But volume knobs get turned down and communications breakdowns happen. Gearhart tried again, "Engine 57 . . . Engine 57 . . . Engine 57."

Then he heard explosions, one after another, coming from the direction of the Octagon House. *Explosions and engines do not belong in the same place,* he thought. The worst of the area ignition may have been over, but slow fire, churning smoke, and twisting currents of intense heat continued to sweep the shattered landscape.

"We started to get the idea this was a big deal, something out of the ordinary," Gearhart said.

The Octagon House was only a few hundred yards away, down Gorgonio View Road. He and Espinoza started off in that direction but had stumbled forward only a few yards in the smoky darkness when they realized they could be walking into a death trap. The fire had shown an eager willingness to spring back to life, and there was plenty of unburned fuel left between them and the Octagon House.

"I could feel the road, but it was gritty and smoky, and I thought, *If I walk into an unburned island of fuel and it takes off, I'm going to be down too*," Gearhart said.

Gearhart called Fogle, "Chris, I can't get 57 on the radio, and I can't make it down there. There are a lot of explosions over there, and I think the engine and house are on fire. You want to make a call here? You want to tell them we're missing an engine?"

There was a long pause.

"No, not yet," Fogle said. "We'll wait a few more minutes."

As the minutes went by, the heat lessened and the smoke cleared, and after a time Gearhart and Espinoza figured it was safe to go on. They had walked only a few dozen yards more when the curtain of darkness around them suddenly lifted, night turned to day, and they found themselves looking at blue sky. The pair walked past the intersection with Wonderview Road, which was about halfway to the Octagon House, and on to the driveway that leads up to the house.

Ahead on the driveway lay a single firefighter, motionless on his back. He wore the scorched remnants of a yellow shirt and green pants and no hard hat. His arms were raised in the curled, pugilist position that can result from exposure to extreme heat. Gearhart approached the figure but could not tell who it was. Espinoza, who was trailing behind Gearhart, had no view of what lay ahead.

"Fred, there's a body here," Gearhart said. And then he made a radio transmission that froze everyone who heard it.

"Hey, I found one. He's dead," he said. "They're all dead."

As Gearhart said those words, the stiffened body in front of him moved its right arm.

"Cancel that," Gearhart said. And then, "They're alive. Get us some medical equipment. Get the engines up here now."

9.

THE JET OF FLAME THAT had swept over the Octagon House exhausted itself, leaving behind an after-battle scene of blackened desolation. A milky fug of smoke blurred the wrecked landscape with a soft-focus filter and muffled sound. Partly shrouded by the smoke, tiny flames danced and jigged in the skeletons of trees, whose stiff, blackened branches reached out, frozen in supplication. A few remaining clumps of chaparral burned as brightly as cheery campfires. But men were down and missing.

The Octagon House itself was gutted, though its sturdy namesake sides remained standing. Outbuildings had collapsed into piles of twisted metal roofing. The extreme heat had stripped and dismantled—as effectively as a chop shop—some of the owner's collection of vintage vehicles and had reduced flammable parts to ash. In another random act of sparing, a military pickup was left virtually intact. The fire had also performed one useful act: it had scorched the ground, creating a waxy crust that helped preserve for later study telltale signs of the firefighters' passing, namely boot prints.

Fogle, who had been frustrated and alarmed by his failed attempts to raise Loutzenhiser, rallied his crew at the Tile House and told them they were going over to the Octagon House to see what was wrong. Everyone piled into the engine and started down

Wonderview Road. They had driven only a few hundred yards, into the gully that separated the Tile and Octagon houses and contained the "loser" mother-in-law home, when Fogle ordered a halt, spooked by an island of unburned brush along the road ahead, where the fire had a chance to reignite and take off again. Fogle stepped out of the cab and told Jacobs, a certified emergency medical technician, to come with him. The others should stay with the engine. "Don't move until the smoke clears," he said. Setting off across the gully on foot, Fogle and Jacobs had a view of the "loser" house at the head of the gully: brush and debris were on fire around it, but amazingly the house was untouched by flames. The blast of fire they had witnessed from the Tile House had appeared to consume everything in this direction, yet here was evidence of sparing; and if the "loser" house had been spared, why not the crew of Engine 57?

Fogle and Jacobs had just climbed up the opposite side of the gully onto Wonderview Road, where it ran after making a switchback turn behind the "loser" house at the gully's head, when they heard Gearhart's electrifying transmission, "They're all dead," followed by the reprieve, "They're alive." Switching to the main tactical radio frequency, Fogle called, "Branch Two, emergency traffic," but could not break through the chatter.

"Nobody stopped talking," Fogle said with exasperation. "They are supposed to stop when there's an emergency call, but there was an inordinate amount of radio traffic. It's a constant problem on fires. So I walked on top of traffic and called again, but still nobody answered. I switched to the command channel and again said, 'Branch Two, emergency traffic.'"

When no one answered on that frequency either, Fogle switched to the Forest Service network and immediately reached the San Bernardino National Forest dispatch office. In a call logged at the hauntingly coincidental time of fifty-seven minutes past 7:00 AM, Fogle made his own alarming report, and to his later regret used the engine number: Engine 57 had been burned over, he said, and emergency medical help was needed immediately. At the Idyllwild Health Center, Tammy Wright, a licensed practical nurse, heard within minutes from a volunteer fireman who happened by, who had picked it up from a radio scanner, that an engine had been burned over, and she thought at first it could be Fogle's. Wright, who was dating Fogle at the time, later became his wife. The news, in various forms, spread from firehouse and scanner to the general community: Engine 57, the heart and soul of Idyllwild, had been burned over.

After Fogle made his report, he and Jacobs sprinted the last few yards to the driveway of the Octagon House. Ahead they saw the downed figure of Cerda with Espinoza bent over him. Espinoza kept repeating, "Hey, Pablo. Don't worry. Some guys are coming to help out." But he thought, *How are we going to get him out of here?* Cerda couldn't speak, and his skin was leathery and without expression, but Espinoza saw a look in his eyes that showed he understood what was being said to him. No sooner had Fogle taken in the sight than he heard Gearhart again on the radio.

"I found Mark," Gearhart said. "He's hurt bad, but he's alive."

After finding Cerda and realizing that he was alive, Gearhart had headed alone up the driveway looking for others. He kept a watch along the way in hopes of catching a flash of silver to indicate that Loutzenhiser or a crewman had been able to deploy a fire shelter. There was no bright metal flash, but Gearhart noted bits of gear and clothing, suggesting that Cerda—or someone—had staggered along the driveway. The driveway took a gentle curve, and there, about twenty yards above Cerda, Gearhart saw Loutzenhiser lying crosswise on his back in the driveway, rocking back and forth. His arms were moving, but they appeared as stiff as heat-hardened tree branches. Gearhart squatted on his haunches, avoiding the hot ground, next to Loutzenhiser.

"Mark, it's Richard," Gearhart said.

"I know," Loutzenhiser said with surprising calm.

He must have heard my voice when I called Chris, Gearhart thought. He grasped Loutzenhiser's hand to establish contact, but it was so stiff that he had to wrap both his hands around to hold it. He touched Loutzenhiser's thigh, and it too was hard as wood. Loutzenhiser rocked back and forth, gasping, "Air, air," and Gearhart could see that heat had penetrated and damaged the interior of his mouth. He realized that his friend was dying, but he also knew that oxygen would help ease him. He had been friends with Loutzenhiser all his adult life, but Fogle loved the captain like family. It was Fogle who most needed to be here. Gearhart called on the radio to the men working on Cerda, "If Pablo's breathing, I need John," he said, meaning John Fakehany, an experienced EMT, and he immediately regretted making the call. He was standing close enough to Loutzenhiser for him to hear; now Loutzenhiser knew for certain that a crewman of his had been badly injured too.

Gearhart didn't wait for an answer: he started down the driveway to get help but immediately saw Fogle coming up toward him. He touched Fogle's arm as they passed, making no effort to stop him.

"When you get there, it's bad," Gearhart said. "I just want you to know it's bad."

Fogle did not rush. Ahead, Loutzenhiser lay amid a litter of scorched and ruined gear, clothing, a pack of his brand of menthol cigarettes; the stuff was widely scattered, as though the captain had been able to move or crawl directly after the fire struck him. Something had partially protected him from the worst of the heat, though he obviously had taken a severe blast. His boots were intact, but what was left of his clothing was tattered and scorched.

Fogle took one of Loutzenhiser's hands.

"He looked at me and I was talking to him," Fogle said. "I told him everything was going to be okay. He tried talking back, but I couldn't understand what he said."

The moment of deep friendship could not last for long. The desolate scene was coming alive as firefighters from the double-wide site rushed up the driveway with oxygen tanks, trauma kits, and other medical supplies—and with hope and fear. Fogle stepped back and let the rescuers do their work; he had his own duties to perform.

Fogle again called the Forest Service's San Bernardino dispatcher, in a transmission logged at 7:58 AM and forty-eight seconds, a minute and a half after his report that Engine 57 had been burned over, and said he needed two ambulances. The ambulances would have a daunting drive if they could even get to the Octagon House, and it would be a nightmarish ride out for the injured. When told by the dispatcher that a helicopter was nearby and available, Fogle replied that visibility was too poor to risk landing a chopper.

Gearhart overheard the exchange and figured two ambulances weren't going to be enough. "Better bump it to four," Gearhart said, and Fogle called in the additional request.

Minutes ticked by as Fogle watched the feverish efforts to get oxygen into Loutzenhiser's lungs and to protect the open burns on his body. As the rescuers clipped away fragments of Loutzenhiser's clothing, it became evident that he was burned over nearly his entire body. Searchers many yards away began to shout, and Fogle knew what that had to mean. So, in his final transmission of the day to the San Bernardino dispatch office, in a call logged at one second before 8:05 AM, he said:

"Captain 52. Requesting coroner respond."

10.

AN EMERGENCY DRAWS PEOPLE THE way a magnet draws metal filings, but this one was special: this one was family. The firefighters at the double-wide listened in alarm to cries over the radio of "Firefighter down! Lotzy needs oxygen! Get up here!" Then the call came through, "We're going after Engine 57!" and they ran for their engines. As one crewman tried to step into an engine cab, his leg froze from shock and a comrade had to shove him up and into a seat. Those who were EMTs pulled together oxygen bottles, aid kits, burn blankets, and other trauma gear. As the wind cleared the heaviest smoke, it also stirred up an ashy dust storm that made it difficult to see and breathe. Goldstein told a crew pulling hose back to an engine to stay calm, muttering to himself, "They're all dead ... They're all dead ... This is no good," until someone told *him* to calm down. The ride from the double-wide down to the Octagon took mere seconds. The engines drew up at the foot of the driveway, and as the crews spilled out, Espinoza met them with a pale face and a blank stare.

"Something very bad has happened," Espinoza said. "Engine 57 has burned up. We don't know where three people are. Lotzy and Pablo are in bad shape. We can't make access to the engine. We can't make access to the house. I need some of you guys to walk down this drainage and look for bodies."

Bodies? Many had suspected the worst, but few had really believed it. "Firefighters aren't meant to go down," said Fakehany. "They have experience; this isn't supposed to happen to them. I felt like I was standing next to myself looking at what was going on. Then I popped back in and I cocked my head like a puppy. Is that Pablo? He put his arm in the air and rolled onto his side, and I could see how bad it was."

Yellow-shirted firefighters swarmed up the driveway and converged around Cerda. Fakehany and Harper, along with March Brush 10's Rambayon and Bicondova, all of them EMTs, went down on their knees and fitted an oxygen mask to Cerda's face. "You hear *firefighter down*, and it's one of those things; you don't hear that except in a drill," Rambayon said later. "I was thinking, *Who's down?* I thought we had everyone accounted for." They had barely started working on Cerda when they heard Gearhart shouting to bring up oxygen for Loutzenhiser. Harper grabbed an oxygen mask and bottle. Tucking the bottle under his arm like a football, he sprinted up the driveway, leaving the others to tend to Cerda.

"It's me, it's me, Lotzy," Harper said as he dropped to his knees next to Loutzenhiser. "It's all right, buddy, I'm going to get you some oxygen."

"Eddie, what are *you* doing here?" Gearhart said. "Where's John?" For this job, Gearhart had asked specifically for Fakehany, who worked as an emergency room technician in the off-season and was the most experienced EMT available. Fakehany could be excitable, but he settled down when things became hectic, and the emergency room staff, like Gearhart, had come to count on him in times of trouble.

"I've got the oxygen," Harper replied, matter-of-factly.

"Okay, go to work," Gearhart said, "but be careful with that stuff. It can catch fire."

Loutzenhiser, his breathing labored and his tongue swollen, started to fight Harper's efforts to place an oxygen mask over his face. *Fakehany should be doing this*, Gearhart thought. *Why didn't he come when I called?* Gearhart started down the driveway to fetch Fakehany but stopped short in his haste and instead yelled, "If Pablo's breathing, I need Fakehany!" Fakehany raised his head from tending Cerda, and Gearhart shouted at him, "Goddamn it, John! Get your fucking ass up here right now!"

A startled Fakehany jumped to his feet. "I turned around, and it was Rich in the middle of the driveway yelling and swearing, which is something he doesn't do," Fakehany said. With no idea what was wanted of him, Fakehany trotted up the driveway empty-handed and took in the scene: Loutzenhiser, prone in the driveway; the ruined clothing and intact boots; Harper having no luck with the oxygen; and Gearhart, pointing to his nose and asking Fakehany where his gear was.

"Give me a second," Fakehany said, and he ran back to where Cerda was being tended. He grabbed his equipment and sprinted back. Kneeling beside Loutzenhiser, Fakehany inserted a nasal trumpet, a device that fits into a nostril and has a flared end to keep it from going in too far, and forced open an air passage. "As soon as I put it in, you could hear him start to relax, because he was getting air," Fakehany said.

Harper backed away and let Fakehany take over; this was no time for jealousy. Then quietly but out loud, Harper began to pray: "Jesus, have mercy. Help us, Jesus. Jesus, have mercy." When he had finished, he heard Gearhart ask if anyone had a camera. Harper had one, a digital camera he already had used to take images of the firefight back at the double-wide.

Gearhart, a military history buff, realized that a vital but perishable history was unfolding before him, just as had happened countless times before on a confused battlefield or fire ground. He knew that if there were no accurate record of this scene, it could wind up like many battles and fires before it, a source of everlasting, never-resolved myth, supposition, conspiracy theory, and blame that could blunt the lessons that needed to be learned to save lives in the future. This was a chance for all the hours he had spent under a reading lamp, and for lessons taught at the cost of brave lives, to gain an afterlife that would change things for the better. And he knew that multiple investigations of the Esperanza Fire were sure to follow.

Like every seasoned wildland firefighter, Gearhart was familiar with the South Canyon Fire and its troubled aftermath. The 1994 fire, on Storm King Mountain in Colorado, had killed nine hotshots, three smoke jumpers, and two helicopter crewmen, and the investigations that followed deeply unsettled the wildland fire community. The fourteen deaths were the greatest loss of wildland firefighters since fifteen firefighters had been killed on the 1953 Rattlesnake Fire in northern California. The South Canyon Fire had branded the conscience of the wildland fire community. How could such a thing have happened in modern-day firefighting, it was asked, with its trained workforce, technical proficiency, and emphasis on safety? The South Canyon Fire investigation report, and spin-leaks connected to it, placed much responsibility for the catastrophe on the dead; in fact, fourteen deaths were a good indicator that somebody that day had lost sight of what a wildland fire can do. The event could be partly explained away, though, if it were accepted that the firefighters who died, and who could not speak for themselves, had caused their own deaths. Further inquiry, however, showed that fire supervisors who should have backed up the crews on Storm King Mountain had failed to do so and had later very publicly ducked any responsibility whatsoever for what went wrong.

With the South Canyon Fire as a goad, the fire community made and continues to make improvements in the way fire is fought and safety is taught. Fire, though, did not give up its ancient powers of surprise and destruction. The next major catastrophe for wildland firefighters came seven years later. On the Thirtymile Fire of 2001, four members of a Forest Service hand crew—two women, aged 18 and 19, and two men, aged 21 and 30—were killed when a small blaze in a narrow canyon in north-central Washington unexpectedly roared to life, raged up the canyon, and turned a laser-like jet of fire onto the small rectangle of scree where they were huddled. The fire had started from an abandoned campfire. DNA was recovered from a partially eaten hot dog in the campfire, but as of this writing, it has not been traced to an individual; the case remains open. This time, the official investigation outright blamed the dead for ignoring an order that might have saved their lives. That charge did not last even a week; when the survivors held a press conference and denied that anything like that had happened, the Forest Service ordered a reinvestigation, which produced a new set of possible conclusions, watering down but not entirely disowning the accusation of orders given and ignored.

After that, several of the families of the Thirtymile firefighters, enraged by the clumsy charges against their children, demanded remedial action bordering on vengeance. In response, Congress passed Public Law 107-203, which requires an independent investigation of every Forest Service death from wildfire, to be conducted by the Office of Inspector General of the Department of Agriculture, the parent agency of the Forest Service. The OIG had no previous experience with wildland fire management when it began its investigation of the Thirtymile Fire. And it showed.

PL 107-203 may have been passed with good intentions, but the results brought confusion and alarm to the wildland fire community; the bill proved to be a license to criminalize wildland fire management. Prompted by the bill, the U.S. attorney in Spokane, James McDermott, who previously had declined to take any legal action regarding the Thirtymile Fire, brought involuntary manslaughter and other charges against the fire's incident commander, Ellreese Daniels. The case was so unpopular in the prosecutor's own office that Tina Hunt, Daniels's public defender, said several of McDermott's assistants called her, risking their jobs, to offer her help. The involuntary manslaughter charges eventually were dropped, and Daniels was let off with a wrist slap, but a precedent had been set. From that point on, Forest Service firefighters would be exposed to the possibility of criminal charges for nonmalicious mistakes, or perceived mistakes, that led to fatalities.

By the time of the Esperanza Fire inquiry, participants in a fatal fire knew, or should have known, that when investigators interviewed them, their testimony could be used to support criminal charges against them and their fellow workers. Hundreds of firefighters had bought liability insurance. Many who had been incident commanders no longer accepted those assignments. Firefighters were cautioned to "lawyer up" after such incidents, and it became common for them to demand "use immunity," so that their testimony could not be used against them, before relating their accounts to fire investigators. One result has been to make official fire investigations, which are supposed to extract lifesaving lessons from fatal fires, into adversarial proceedings hampered by delays and guarded testimony. The Esperanza Fire would provide another test of the effect of PL 107-203, with mixed results.

♦ ♦ ♦

THE FIRST STEP in the investigation of the Esperanza Fire got under way at the Octagon House when Gearhart told Harper, "Start taking pictures of everything." Harper took forty-one photos, including some at the double-wide, providing an extraordinary record of unfolding events. When Harper had finished, he handed the memory card to Gearhart and told him he never wanted to see what was on it. Gearhart passed the card along to his superiors, also without looking. Those photos, combined with a rich trove of still and moving images recorded by others who were there, make a significant contribution to an understanding of what happened. They do not, however, answer all the important questions, especially ones concerning motivation, some of which may never be answered.

I obtained Harper's photos, a selection of which had been used in the murder trial. I then contacted Harper, whom I had interviewed previously, to ask whether he would be willing to look at the photos and describe what they showed. Curiously, no official fire investigator or court authority had asked him to do this. Three years had passed since the event and time had had an effect; Harper agreed to the request. When we had finished, I asked for his overall reaction and he said, sadly, "It brings it all back."

Harper's first photo at the Octagon House shows Loutzenhiser covered by a blue burn blanket that hides his body and nearly all of his face. Though Harper showed restraint in choice of subject matter when he could, the images are straightforward, and many of them make difficult viewing. As Harper moved on, taking more photos, more people and vehicles showed up at the site, and fresh faces joined the search for the missing.

"Hey, we found another one!" somebody shouted.

"Is he alive?"

"No, he's dead."

Fakehany, at Loutzenhiser's side, heard the shout and thought it was wrong to be talking like that within earshot of the captain. He radioed Gearhart and told him they had better evacuate Loutzenhiser immediately, even if it meant putting him on one of the engines and driving him out. Someone had brought up a backboard, but getting Loutzenhiser onto it was going to be a challenge.

"I leaned over and said in his ear, 'Lotzy, I'm so sorry, I'm going to have to roll you over,'" Fakehany said. "'And it's going to hurt.'" Careful hands slid Loutzenhiser onto the backboard and secured him with straps. His comrades bore him down the driveway to what surely would have been an excruciating if not fatal journey to the outside world. His arms were frozen in a half push-up position, but he was conscious and managed to say something that sounded like, "Arms tired, arms tired." Halfway down the driveway, the stretcher bearers heard another sound: the familiar—and welcome—metallic rotor chop and engine whine of a helicopter.

"We stopped," Fakehany said. "I called on a radio to Gearhart, 'Rich, can we use the helicopter?'"

The wind was clearing away the smoke. A skilled pilot might be able to land a helicopter below the house at one or another of the small cleared sites. At that moment a mighty explosion came from that direction: the gas tank on a vintage military truck had caught fire and blown up. Landing a helicopter anywhere nearby appeared to be out of the question.

◆ ◆ ◆

THE HELITACK CREW of Forest Service Helicopter 535 had assembled before dawn at their duty station, the Keenwild Helibase along Highway 243, about six miles south of Twin Pines Ridge. The crew included Captain Daniel "Sepe" Sepulveda; Daniel Diaz, squad boss; and Randy Ruiz and Ryan Gonzalez, crewmen, along with Chris Templeton, the pilot of Helicopter 535. The helicopter lifted off the pad at Keenwild at about 7:00 AM as dawn's light began to penetrate the fire's smoke cloud. First light also brought out a full-scale air show: a fleet of helicopters, air tankers, and an air attack supervisor.

"It's amazing what southern California can put on a fire," one of the fire's top supervisors said later. "We can put more resources on a wildfire than anywhere else in the world. We had ordered about two thousand personnel, and one thousand were expected to be present by daylight." The surge of manpower and aircraft added to the overburden on the radio frequencies; Sepulveda had trouble that morning finding out what the crew's assignment was supposed to be. Once airborne, though, he was told by the air attack supervisor to link up with Forest Service engines 52 and 57 and help with structure protection.

Helicopter 535 was over Twin Pines Ridge moments after takeoff, but dense smoke covered the ridge, and the helicopter crew could not establish radio contact with the engine captains. They saw a spot of open ground, however, at Twin Pines Ranch, sometimes called Last Chance Ranch, a facility for delinquent boys at the eastern end of Twin Pines Road. Overnight, sheriff's deputies had evacuated more than fifty youths and staff from the 1,200-acre ranch and had moved the youths to another juvenile facility in Indio. Though the main fire had passed by the ranch to the north and west, an arm of flame was moving toward the ranch buildings on a southwesterly course that, if continued, would take the flames straight to Idyllwild. The crew made a plan to land at the ranch and conduct a burnout ahead of the fire to protect the ranch buildings. Templeton set Helicopter 535 down on a baseball diamond on the ranch grounds. After dropping off the crew, he took off again to make water drops elsewhere on the fire from the chopper's 270-gallon water tank.

The crewmen checked out the ranch buildings—a handful of administrative offices, barracks, and other structures—and found that much clearing work had been done to provide the defensible space needed around buildings in the wildland–urban interface. After the Cerro Grande Fire of 2000 destroyed more than two hundred homes at Los Alamos, New Mexico, a Forest Service fire scientist, Jack Cohen, visited the site. He determined that most of the homes were lost because homeowners had failed to clear the ground around their dwelling places. "My examination suggests that the abundance and ubiquity of pine needles, dead leaves, cured vegetation, flammable shrubs, wood piles, etc. adjacent to, touching, and or covering the homes principally contributed to the residential losses," Cohen concluded. Colleagues began calling Cohen "Mr. Nooks and Crannies" because of the emphasis he put on fire getting ahold in clutter. Nonetheless, his study proved influential. At Twin Pines Ranch, the nooks and crannies were free of brush, and that helped save the buildings.

While the crewmen scouted the place, a Cal Fire air tanker appeared overhead and dropped a load of retardant on a ridge above the ranch.

"The drop helped, and I told air attack we were going to fire out from the baseball diamond," Sepulveda said. "But by the time we got mounted up and ready, we could see the column of smoke from the fire being pulled to the west, away from us." A burn operation might not be necessary after all. As the crew talked it over, they heard a familiar voice over the radio, in an unfamiliar state of distress.

"I heard Chris Fogle. I recognized the voice, but it was a different tone than I had ever heard him use before," said Diaz. He and the others listened in shock to Fogle's string of reports: Engine 57 was burned over; two men were down and required immediate evacuation; others were missing. And then the call for the coroner. Like virtually everyone else on the San Bernardino National Forest, they were well acquainted with the crew of Engine 57, especially Loutzenhiser. Diaz had worked with Loutzenhiser when both were Vista Grande Hotshots, and later with Fogle, before switching to the helicopter. In addition to his fire job, Diaz was also a sergeant in the Marine Corps Reserve, with two combat tours in the Middle

East. He didn't like the blank, staring expressions, like combat shock, he now saw on the faces his fellow crewmen.

"What are we going to do?" Diaz demanded to focus their attention. "What are we going to do?"

Sepulveda figured that if there were burned firefighters, they had better go looking for them. He told Diaz to radio Templeton and see if the pilot could fly back and pick them up. Luckily, Templeton was nearby and had just made a water drop, emptying his tank and lightening his ship. He was back at the baseball diamond in minutes.

"Let's go, let's find these guys," Diaz said, and the crew loaded up and took off. The smoke was so thick that Templeton tried using an old dirt road leading down the ridge face as a guide, but the road petered out and disappeared into smoke. As Templeton circled the helicopter, searching for an opening in the smoke cover, the thump of the rotor blades caused a universal wave of relief at the Octagon House, where efforts were under way to start the injured on the long, rough drive off the ridge face. Templeton flew the helicopter round and round until, after the third or fourth circle, the smoke cleared, swept away by the wind. There was no mistaking the site of the burnover, directly below the helicopter. The Octagon House had become a ring of dancing fire, a flaming punctuation mark in a seemingly endless expanse of scorched desert and blackened chaparral. The roof of the house had collapsed, but flames shot up from standing sides marked by vacant gaps, like missing teeth, where windows had been. The garage below the house was on fire. And there in the clearing in front of the garage stood the smoking hulk of Engine 57.

"As the smoke opened up, the first thing I saw was the engine," Diaz said. "I don't remember if I could tell if the engine was burned out—there was the house, another Forest Service engine, down the road. I said, 'There it is, there's the engine. Let's get down there.'"

"I think we can fit, but it's going to be tight," Templeton replied.

Templeton decided to try to land in the small clearing farthest down from the Octagon House because it had fewer vehicles and less debris than the upper clearing, where Engine 57 was parked in front of the garage. In a laconic report about an air operation that was later hailed as "Vietnam-like" and heroic, Templeton wrote, "It was obvious from the way the smoke was laying over that the wind was blowing very hard out of the east." Templeton continued, "From the air, it looked like the only suitable landing area was on the north end of the property in a clearing. I set up a landing approach to the clearing and still had 60kt [sixty knots, or just over sixty-nine miles per hour] showing on the airspeed indicator as I was on short final to the clearing, even though I was moving at a brisk walking pace over the ground." In other words, Templeton came in for a landing on a tiny lip of land, dotted with vehicles and debris, while heading into a Santa Ana wind blowing at over sixty miles an hour. He did not mention in his report the cutbank on the upper end of the clearing that threatened his rotor blades.

The crew jumped out of the chopper before the skids touched the ground. Sepulveda saw a familiar face. It was Gearhart, who looked dazed but functional.

"What the fuck happened?" Sepulveda asked.

"They're dead; there's Danny right there," replied Gearhart, pointing to Najera.

Gearhart asked Sepulveda if the helicopter could handle a backboard, and he said yes.

"Get the injured out of here," Gearhart said.

As Diaz moved away from the ship, he too saw someone familiar, Richardson, from Fogle's crew. "We're here," Diaz said. "What do you need?"

"I don't know; I'm not sure," Richardson replied. "They're working on Lotzy and Pablo, trying to get them packaged and up here." Diaz ran back to the helicopter and told Templeton that two firefighters were being prepared for evacuation. The crew was trained to convert the chopper from its water-dropping configuration with a tank to a configuration with a Stokes litter for evacuation, but even under ideal conditions, the changeover took eight to ten minutes.

"If the crew hasn't practiced this a couple of times recently, it could take even longer," Templeton said in his report. "I told my crew to hold off on tearing my helicopter apart while I tried to contact a medium helicopter on the radio to see if they could come and pick up the patient, as this would save a lot of time. A friend of mine, Dave Patrick, was flying Helicopter 301, a Cal Fire Huey that could easily accommodate a patient on a backboard without any reconfiguring."

Templeton radioed Patrick, who agreed to give it a try. Templeton lifted off in Helicopter 535 and hovered overhead, ready to talk the larger ship down onto the miniscule landing spot. Men on the ground, meanwhile, worked at clearing the site. "We didn't want those guys to say they couldn't get in," Diaz said. They shoved a heavy drag sled, used for brush removal, over the edge of the clearing, and then a trailer with a generator; the military pickup the fire had left nearly undamaged was pushed out of the way along the driveway.

Helicopter 301 appeared and began to make its descent, its powerful rotor blades kicking up stinging clouds of dust laced with pea-sized gravel. By this time, Loutzenhiser had been carried on the backboard to the edge of the landing zone, ready for evacuation. The burn blanket had been pulled down to allow his body to cool, and dressings had been applied, but more than 90 percent of his body was burned, and there weren't enough dressings to cover him, leaving third-degree burns exposed to the dust and gravel storm.

Without orders or instructions, a circle of firefighters drew close around Loutzenhiser as he lay on the stretcher. They bent to their knees and turned their faces from the wind. Castro, Christian, Diaz, Fakehany, Governale, and Jacobs put their arms over each other's shoulders and leaned in to form a human shield over Loutzenhiser, a protecting brotherhood of yellow shirts, green pants, hard hats, and humanity. One said, "Hang in there buddy, we're almost out of here." Another thought, *Now I know why I'm a firefighter. Now I know why I joined in the first place: when it's tough, we hang together.* Another would remember this moment as he lay on a couch at home in the days ahead, wondering why he ever became a firefighter, and the memory would set him back on his course for life.

Templeton talked Helicopter 301 down until it settled in the skid marks he had left behind. "They would not have been able to land without those marks there," Sepulveda said.

With Loutzenhiser loaded aboard, tended by Fakehany, Jacobs, and Castro, Helicopter 301 took off and headed for the Banning Municipal Airport, located almost directly below on the floor of the Banning Pass. The takeoff time was 8:22 AM, just over an hour after the area ignition had swept the Octagon House. A medical evacuation helicopter waited on the tarmac at the Banning Airport to take Loutzenhiser to Arrowhead Regional Medical Center, the lone burn unit in a four-county area, about thirty miles away in Colton. The flight down to the Banning Airport took only a couple of minutes, but it combined terror and a near miracle.

"It was a roller-coaster ride down—drop, turn, drop, turn," said Fakehany. "We were running low on oxygen, and I asked the pilot for some, but he said, 'We don't carry that.'" The oxygen bottle ran lower still, and Loutzenhiser showed signs of being unable to breathe on his own. Something had to be done, and Castro stuck a finger down the captain's throat and probed to open an air passage.

When the helicopter arrived over the airport, the wind blew it off track, and Patrick had to go around for a second approach run. At this point, Fakehany lost Loutzenhiser's pulse: the captain's heart had stopped beating. Fakehany knew from experience that while Loutzenhiser was clinically dead, he was not yet biologically dead and there was a chance he could be brought back to life. Once before, Fakehany had revived a man with no pulse, in the Eisenhower Medical Center near Palm Springs, where he worked in the off-season as an emergency department technician. The nurses had called on Fakehany to start chest compressions because they knew he was strong and could keep pumping for long periods, an hour or more if necessary; he had done that once before with another patient, who had not survived. The second time around, Fakehany pulled on a rubber glove and started pumping the man's chest with the gloved hand while using his teeth to pull a glove onto the other hand. After four or five pumps, a nurse said, "Hey, we got a pulse!" Feeling cocky, Fakehany blew on his fingertips like a gunslinger blowing smoke from his pistols and walked away.

Now, in the helicopter with Loutzenhiser, Fakehany felt anything but cocky. This patient was no stranger, and the helicopter was no emergency room with a ring of admiring nurses. This was the brotherhood and this was the ultimate test. Fakehany leaned directly over Loutzenhiser's chest and placed the heels of both hands, one over the other, on Loutzenhiser's breastbone. He pumped down hard, compressing Loutzenhiser's chest, then drew back to allow the chest to fully recoil, and with that first pump Loutzenhiser's heart started beating again. Fakehany took a deep breath in relief. For Jacobs, however, huddled close by in the confines of the helicopter, the clinical death and near-miraculous resuscitation, coming on top of everything else, was shattering. Fakehany had to tell him to pull himself together.

When Helicopter 301 landed after circling the Banning Airport, it was discovered that the waiting medevac helicopter had been parked facing into the Santa Ana wind, and its engine had been damaged by grit. There was no backup helicopter, Helicopter

301 was low on fuel, and the thirty-mile drive to Arrowhead Regional Medical Center was no option. Loutzenhiser would have to wait at the airport while transport was arranged. Medical personnel transferred him from the helicopter to an ambulance, where they started an IV and attached monitors to check his vital signs. Fakehany climbed into the ambulance and continued chest compressions, because the drugs now being fed into Loutzenhiser slowed his breathing. The solution of the transportation problem was to refuel Helicopter 301. The helicopter then flew the captain on the last leg of his journey, arriving at Arrowhead Regional Medical Center at 9:09 AM, forty-seven minutes after takeoff from the Octagon House.

At the Octagon House, Templeton had talked in a second Huey to evacuate Cerda. A photo taken from the air shows pilot George Karcher's Huey, Helicopter 305, on the chosen spot about to pick up Cerda. Karcher, who worked for the San Bernardino County Sheriff's Department and often landed in tight places, later described the landing zone as "typical." Even so, the ship's red-and-white-striped rotor blades appear to be perilously close to the cutbank. Karcher flew Cerda directly to the Arrowhead burn center after briefly landing at the Banning Airport and discovering the difficulties with the damaged medevac helicopter. Doctors at the burn center placed Cerda in an induced coma to stabilize his condition. They scheduled surgery to remove burned tissue, though the prognosis at the time was that he would not live more than a few hours.

♦ ♦ ♦

THE SEARCH FOR the still-missing crewmen at the site had resumed immediately after Loutzenhiser and Cerda were found. Espinoza walked on up the driveway looking for a place where someone might have survived. "I started up toward the engine, but Gearhart said not to go there; there was stuff still exploding. The house was still burning. That's when I started looking where somebody could run to and survive. That's when I found Danny."

"Hey, Josh, hook up a hose so I can put out that stob," Espinoza called to Spoon, not wanting to draw everyone's attention.

As Spoon dragged the hose over toward Espinoza, he saw on a slope below the driveway what looked like a smoldering log with sputtering flames wedged against a burning stob, or tree stump, which had stopped it from rolling over the bank and onto the road directly below. Spoon had never seen a burned dead body before. It looked unreal to him, like a charcoaled mannequin.

"Let me do this," he told Espinoza. "You go be with the guys."

"Are you sure?" Espinoza said.

"Yeah, yeah. I'll do this."

"Okay. Thank you."

A three-man crew from Cal Fire Engine 3176, the first state unit to arrive, walked toward Spoon, down the slope from the driveway where they had helped attend to Cerda. The captain, Jeff Veik, saw what was going on and told a crewman, Frank Ebner, to go back to the engine and get the banjos—canteens shaped like the round head of a banjo—and a tarpaulin. As Ebner came down the slope with the equipment, he noticed what he thought was a burning log.

"I'm so sorry about your friends," Ebner said to Spoon. Then Ebner took a closer look at what Spoon was doing with the hose.

"Oh, my God," Ebner said. "Do you want something to cover him?"

"Yes," Spoon said.

Quickly, helping hands appeared from every direction.

"We all did it," Spoon said, "six or seven of us."

They poured the water from the banjos on Daniel Najera as gently as human hands could manage. Ebner, with tears welling in his eyes, asked if it was okay to say something. It was. The group recited the Lord's Prayer, and then they covered Najera's body with the tarp.

The crew of Engine 3176, suppressing shock and bewilderment, returned to firefighting duties. The men—Veik, Ebner, and Craig Roberts—had just endured an experience similar in everything but outcome and degree of intensity to what had happened at the Octagon House: they had been swept by the same wave of superheated air that had engulfed the men of Engine 57. When the area ignition occurred, Engine 3176 was stationed at a home just off Twin Pines Road. The home was on a direct line above the unnamed creek drainage; by later measurement, it was 835 feet higher in elevation and two-thirds of a mile as the crow flies from the Octagon House. "We experienced exactly what they experienced at Engine 57, except we were at the top of the ridge and they were mid-slope," Ebner said five years later. "It's a story of camaraderie, survival, and situational awareness."

By the time Engine 3176 had arrived at that ridgetop house, the smoke was so heavy that the crew could hardly see. They drove around the house several times in the darkness, doing "triage from the engine cab." The house was in the middle of a wide clearing and appeared to be defensible. Ebner and Roberts got out of the engine and unrolled hoses, Ebner manning one at the rear of the engine and Roberts one at the front. Veik, the driver, remained in the cab.

They barely had time to charge the hose lines before the inversion layer that had been holding down flames blew out and a jet of superheated air blasted the homesite, catching Ebner and Roberts in the open. "When the inversion broke, the wind was immense," Ebner said. "I saw flames at the edge of the clearing, and I opened the nozzle, but the wind blew the stream at a ninety-degree angle. I shut down the nozzle and turned my back to the fire—I couldn't stand—and crouched down."

Though a protective shroud and a separate mask covered Ebner's nose and mouth, he felt his airways dry and start to stiffen. Heat invaded the face coverings and scorched the inside of the shroud and the outside of the mask. Ebner, feeling a burning sensation deep in his chest, let out a scream. "I thought I had burned out my airways," he said. But the combination of the scream plus the protective gear kept the superheated air out of his nose and mouth.

"Get in the fuckin' truck!" Veik yelled from the engine.

Ebner staggered to the engine and stood on the running board. He and Veik called out to Roberts, who was in an exposed position close to the edge of the clearing. Wind and fire filled the air with a thunder that swallowed up their shouts. Veik put the engine in reverse and used the hose line that Roberts was holding to pull him away from the flames. Roberts and Ebner clambered inside the engine cab, but it was no sanctuary. The crew could hear the engine creak as the wind flexed the metal body. Veik began driving around the site to keep the brakes' air lines, which are under the engine, from catching fire. If that happened, the brakes would seize up and leave the engine immobile in the face of advancing fire. He finally parked in the lee of the house for protection. The crew heard heavy thuds that sounded like bodies hitting the side of the engine. Veik opened the cab door to investigate, inhaled a mouthful of hot air, and slumped back in the cab, clutching his chest and coughing. When Ebner asked if he was okay, the captain couldn't speak.

Oh God, he's injured. Now what do I do? thought Ebner.

The thudding they heard was roofing tiles blown from the house.

Ebner quickly made a plan: he jumped out of the cab and retrieved the heavy breathing apparatus and turnout gear carried in compartments toward the rear of the engine; he tossed them into the cab. If the inside of the cab became unbearable, the crew could take the equipment into the house and shelter there. "We can go into that house and stay on air until we push the limits of our gear," he told Roberts. Luckily, the crew did not have to implement the plan, which depended on everyone following Ebner's direction and the house remaining intact. The heat wave subsided, the house did not catch fire, and the crew settled in to ride out the firestorm inside the engine cab. For a while, during the worst of it, the radio was silent. Then, after a few minutes, the crew heard battalion chiefs calling for engine captains to report in.

"I'm in the fight of my life," one captain responded. "I'm doing everything I can to save my crew and the engine."

"I know, hang in there," came the reply.

When the first radio reports of an engine burnover came through, Veik decided the house where they were stationed was no longer under threat—he was right, it was not badly damaged then or later—and they should go and do what they could to help. They headed down the ridge face until they found the Octagon House. After assisting with the dead and injured, the crew of Engine 3176 wrapped up a thirty-six-hour shift engaged in home protection at Poppet Flats. They did not seek medical aid, and the rush of events gave them no time for reflection until several weeks later, when they discussed the experience with other firefighters who had fought the fire.

The lessons he learned, Ebner said, are to prepare for the worst, have a contingency plan, and never get complacent.

◆ ◆ ◆

THE GROUND HAD cooled enough for Espinoza and others to walk up to the clearing at the front of the garage where Engine 57 was parked. Darts of flame shot up from the gutted engine. The remains of another body had been found on the ground beside the engine by two firefighters, Baker and Reyes, who had needed breathing apparatus to get there because the smoke, laced with poisonous fumes from the burning machines and building materials, was so thick. Espinoza figured that the body must be Jess

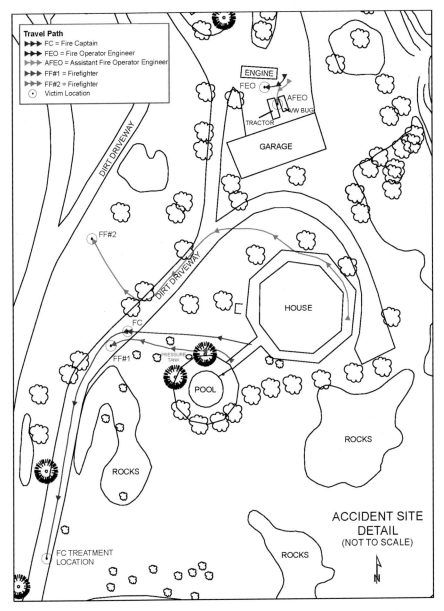

This map, taken from the Esperanza Fire Accident Investigation Factual Report, shows fire struck them. The travel paths of Capt. Mark Loutzenhiser (FC or Fire Captain) and Pablo Cerda (FF#1 or firefighter) were mistakenly transposed in the report. FF#2 is Daniel Najera, FEO (Fire Operator Engineer) is Jess McLean, and AFEO (Assistant Fire Operator Engineer) is Jason McKay.

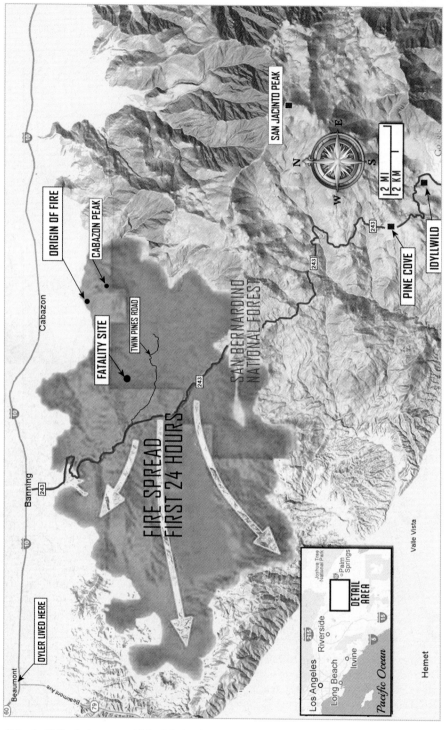

(Map by Kelly Andersson and John Maclean)

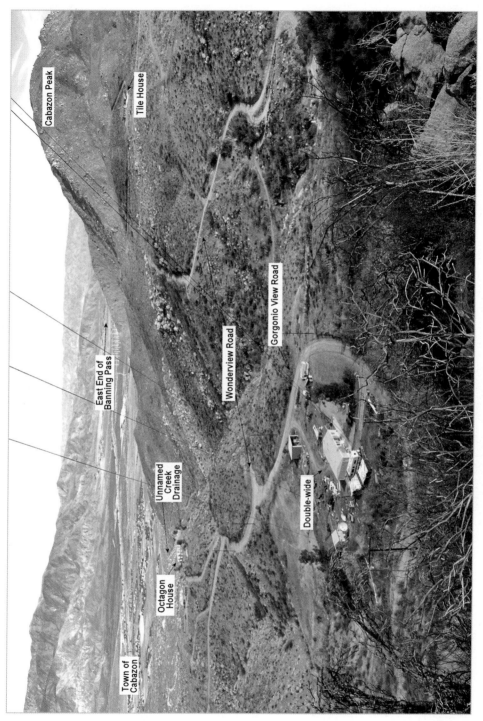

Looking northeast across Twin Pines ridge; Forest Service engines were stationed at the Octagon House, the Tile House and the doublewide. Five power lines descend the ridge. *(Map by Kelly Andersson and John Maclean; photo by Maclean)*

Daniel Najera's aunt Vivian Najera points to the spot just off Esperanza Avenue where the Esperanza Fire arson device was discovered. Note the steep terrain that gave the fire a fast start.

The cigarette-match device that started the fire. *(Photo by John Maclean; device photo by Cal Fire.)*

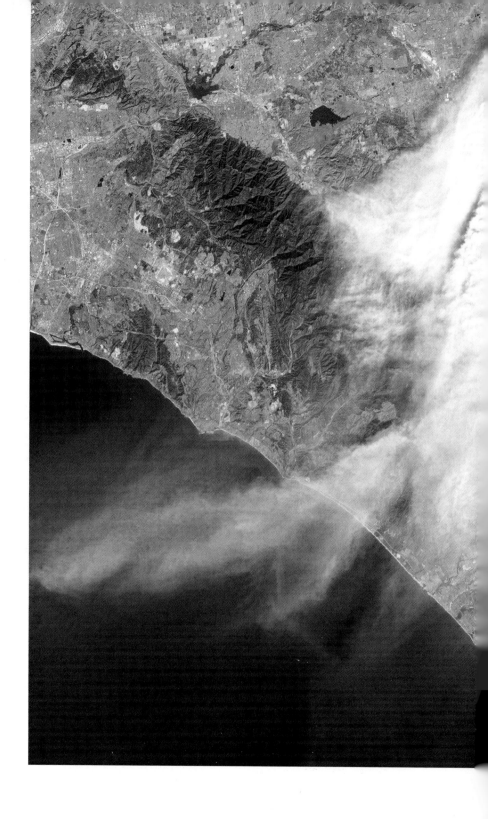

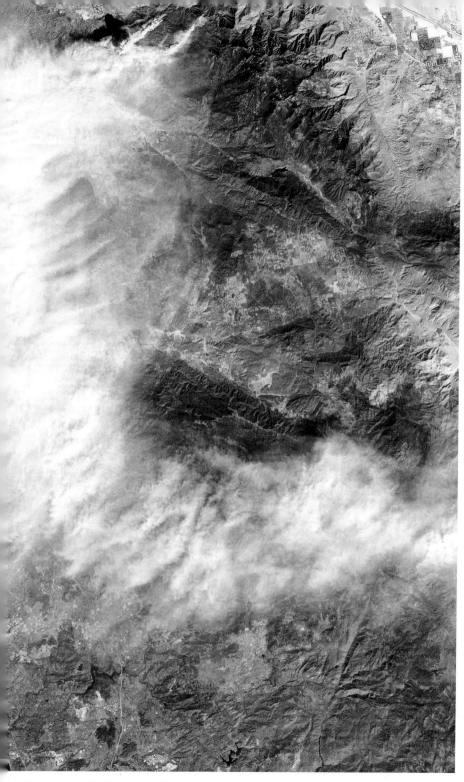

Smoke from the Esperanza Fire extends from the Banning Pass to the Pacific Ocean just to the south of Los Angeles in this NASA satellite photo.

TOP: Two crewmen from Forest Service Engine 52, (left to right) Paul Jacobs and Aaron Reyes, pose in front of flames at the Tile House. *(Photo by Josh Richardson, USFS.)*

BOTTOM: Paul Jacobs stands atop Engine 52 looking out at a smoldering landscape after the fire has passed the Tile House. *(Photo by Josh Richardson, USFS.)*

Crewmen pull hose to wet down the doublewide and dog kennels as flames burn close by. *(Photo by John Fakehany, USFS.)*

Mike Upton, caretaker, at the doublewide after the fire. Firefighters encountered a jumble of machinery and livestock around the home. *(Photo by John Maclean.)*

The Octagon House directly after the fire. INSET: the Octagon House before the fire.
(Fire photo by Eddie Harper, USFS; earlier photo courtesy of Greg Koeller.)

ABOVE: Fireighters Jarod Baker and Aaron Reyes, wearing breathing equipment, head up the driveway of the Octagon House toward Engine 57's position at the garage area. Others tend Capt. Mark Loutzenhiser in the driveway. *(Photo by Eddie Harper, USFS.)* BELOW: The Octagon House continues to burn as rescuers carry a badly injured Pablo Cerda to Pilot George Karcher's Helicopter 305, waiting at a tiny helispot. *(USFS photo.)*

TOP: Engine 57 directly after the fire. BOTTOM: Two drip torches (A), one with the cap still on, were found next to the engine. The presence of a wand (B) from a drip torch indicates that the cap from the second torch, which is not visible, was unscrewed and the wand taken out in preparation for a burnout. *(Photos by Eddie Harper, USFS.)*

ABOVE: The Forest Service captains assigned to the Esperanza Fire with Engine 57 stand outside the Riverside County courthouse where they testified during Raymond Oyler's arson-murder trial. (Left to right) Freddie Espinoza, Anna Dinkle, Richard Gearhart and Chris Fogle. *(Photo by John Maclean.)*

LEFT: Raymond Oyler casts a stricken look: his family as he leaves the courtroom in shackles following his conviction on five counts of murder and other charges for setting the Esperanza Fire. *(Photo by Press-Enterprise newspaper.)*

OPPOSITE TOP: The Banning Pass as seen from inside the Octagon House at 7:15 AM, the approximate time of the area ignition, on the fifth anniversary of the fire, October 26, 2011. *(Photo by John Maclean.)*

OPPOSITE BOTTOM: On the fire's fifth anniversary, Maria Loutzenhiser places a flower at her husband Capt. Mark Loutzenhiser's marker beside the driveway of the Octagon House. *(Photo by John Maclean.)*

At noon on the fifth anniversary of the fire, family, friends and supporters of the men of Engine 57 stand in front of a memorial to the fire at the Octagon House for a minute of silence. *(Photo by John Maclean.)*

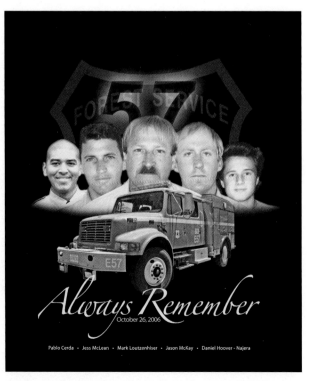

A Memorial to Engine 57.

McLean because as an engineer he might well have been standing at the engine, handling fittings and gauges. The clearing had been exposed to the full fury of the area ignition; McLean apparently had moved only a step or two. The others already found—Loutzenhiser, Cerda, and Najera—had been partially protected from the firestorm when it hit, either by the knoll or by the Octagon House itself. The three of them had been able to run or stumble some distance before dropping to the ground.

"I looked inside and under the engine and walked around until I didn't want to look anymore," Espinoza said. "I went back to my engine crew and let them know what had happened. I had to give them something to do, so I told them to grid the area and see if they could find anybody else. They spread out and walked, ten feet apart, down by the road to make sure nobody else was down there."

No birds flew. No insects scuttled across the blackened ground or rustled in the scorched remains of chaparral. Snakes were deep in their holes. The music of the living earth had been replaced by the dry crackle of lingering flames. "Surreal . . . dreamlike . . . standing outside myself and watching," were words the searchers used to describe this time. More people showed up needing to be briefed. The superintendent of the Vista Grande Hotshots, Jesse Estrada, was one of the first to arrive; he'd been on the top of Twin Pines Ridge with his driver, B.J. Scott, checking on Scott's parents' house, which had barely survived the fire. Estrada met Gearhart in the clearing near Engine 57, and together they looked down at the gaping mouth of the unnamed creek drainage.

"Mark's going to die, you know," Gearhart said.

"Yeah, I know," Estrada said. "What the fuck were you guys doing down here?"

Gearhart paused.

"Engine stuff," he said, and he thought, *They're not going to believe where we are. I'm either getting a medal or I'm getting fired.*

Echoing Gearhart's silent thoughts, Dinkel, who was standing nearby, said out loud, "They're not going to believe where we're at; we're in trouble." She used a cell phone to call the division chief, Norm Walker. Walker had a steady, calming presence; he was someone to count on. If anyone could bring stability to this situation, he could.

"I talked to Norm until I couldn't talk anymore, and I handed the phone to Richard," Dinkel said. Walker said he was driving in from Twin Pines Road, but after the passage of the fire, everything looked different, and he was having trouble finding the site.

"I'm lost, Rich," he told Gearhart.

"You're on the right road. Keep coming," Gearhart said.

Lost isn't the word for it, Walker thought as he approached. *What in the world were we doing down in this hole?* He located the driveway to the Octagon House and put on his yellow shirt and hard hat. As he started up the driveway, he saw Gearhart and Fogle. They looked drained and exhausted, down to white flesh covered by gray ash. It was time to get everyone out of there.

There were things Walker needed to see first, and the briefing task fell to Gearhart and Fogle. They started with the place where Cerda had been found, just a few steps up the drive, and then moved on to Loutzenhiser's spot. Medical and other gear marked the places where the two men had been. Next came Najera, whose body had not yet been moved, and then McLean, next to Engine 57.

Walker got a cell phone call, and after listening for a moment he told those gathered around, "Okay, they want us to leave." People were reaching emotional and physical limits, but the job wasn't finished yet. "It got kind of corny," Gearhart said. "I said, 'I'm not going to leave. I'm still missing a man.' And other captains chimed and said the same thing: 'We're not leaving until everyone's accounted for.'"

In the meantime, Dinkel and one of the fresh arrivals, Chris

Hardy, a Forest Service patrol officer, had made a grim discovery. Hardy had found the fifth body, McKay, still flaming. McKay was lying between two burned-out vehicles, a Volkswagen and a small tractor, in the clearing in front of the garage, just a few steps from Engine 57. Searchers had walked by him several times without realizing what they were looking at. Dinkel and Hardy were joined by Gearhart and Fogle, who had heard a shout, "We found him!" and had hurried over. The four of them wordlessly performed a last rite for McKay, pouring water from their canteens to quench the flames on his body.

At long last the survivors were free to leave. "We're done," one captain said with finality. Everyone went back and loaded into the engines, which formed into a column and moved slowly up to Twin Pines Road, then along Highway 243 and south to the Vista Grande station, where everyone got out, safe at last on familiar ground. In moments, the enormity of what had happened swept the gathering, in a wave that brought tears, hugs, or stoic expressions; most of the latter quickly broke down. Supervisors tried to stop people from using cell phones to call home and spread the news before formal notification of families who had lost loved ones, but they soon realized the news was already out via Forest Service radio. Everyone was free to call home and say they were okay, but nothing more.

Walker, meanwhile, remained at the fatality site, standing next to Engine 57 with his hands in his pockets. He tried to imagine how such a catastrophe could have happened to such a seasoned crew. Engine 57 had three qualified engine bosses, Loutzenhiser, McLean, and McKay, making it perhaps the most experienced engine crew on the San Bernardino National Forest. Yet they had been taken by surprise. The evidence was overwhelming that McLean and McKay had had only a couple of seconds to react before the fire had brought them down. Walker noted a telltale sign: the trunks of ornamental trees near the engine bore the deepest fire scars on the lee side, or back, facing away from the direction from which the fire had come. Big fires often did that, whipping past trees too fast to burn the front side and then igniting a slower-burning fire that crept back and scorched the tree's lee side. In this case, the trees were charred to a height of no more than three feet from the ground. Their upper branches, while covered with soot, retained twigs and even a few leaves, indicating that flames had been blown forward with such ferocity that they had hardly risen but stayed close to the ground. Walker had seen something just like this once before. Early in his fire career, during his first year as a hotshot, Walker had experienced an area ignition that had exploded a quarter of a mile away. The heat had been so intense that the hotshots had had to shield their faces with their hard hats.

I think we've had an area ignition, Walker thought, and a shiver went up his back.

11.

O N THE MORNING OF THE first day of the Esperanza Fire,
October 26, as flames burned out of control and the Santa Ana
wind gusted to sixty miles an hour and more, southern California
residents awakened to the sight of a smoke cloud moving across the
sky like a heavy storm front, visible from more than one hundred
miles away. Mike Mayman, the Riverside County assistant district
attorney who had been tracking the Banning Pass arson series ever
since it began in May, was scheduled to make an early morning
appearance in an outlying courthouse south of Riverside. When
his alarm went off at 5:30 AM, he rolled out of bed and turned
on the TV to catch the latest weather and traffic report. Even at
that hour, commuting in southern California can be a challenge,
and indeed the TV announcer reported that heavy smoke from a
large wildland fire was expected to delay traffic in the vicinity of the
Banning Pass. It was too early to know for certain, but Mayman
thought this sounded like yet another Banning Pass arson fire. The
blaze already had covered several thousand acres, far more than any
of the previous fires.

Mayman reached for the telephone and called Matt Gilbert, one
of the Cal Fire investigators on the Banning Pass series. Mayman
was an ex–police officer and marine, and both he and Gilbert were
competition-level pistol shots, often attending shooting matches

together. Gilbert answered his cell phone so quickly that Mayman knew he had guessed right: Gilbert already was at the fire scene.

"Matt, is this our guy?" Mayman asked.

"Yeah," Gilbert replied, not wasting words.

Gilbert had been dispatched to the fire at 1:30 AM, less than twenty minutes after it was reported. The location was in the same general area of the Banning Pass as the other arson fires. There was no obvious cause such as lightning or a downed power line to explain how it had started. Gilbert already had identified the likely point of origin, which like the other fires in the Banning Pass series was alongside a lonely stretch of roadway. Gilbert hadn't found an ignition device and thought it could be a "hot start," lit by hand with a single match.

When Gilbert had pulled up at the base of the fire along Esperanza Avenue about 2:30 AM, he had been gratified to discover that the first responding engine, Martin Gill's Engine 24, had taken no suppression action, thus preserving any evidence that may have survived the flames. The ground was hot, the sky was dark, and Gilbert knew he shouldn't disturb the site by walking over it. The arson devices recovered so far, made up of wooden matches and a cigarette, could be crushed by a single misstep. Gilbert stretched flagging tape along Esperanza Avenue to keep out fire units and settled down in his vehicle to wait for daylight. Just after 4:00 AM, however, he heard a radio report of a second fire—the Seminole Road Fire—and decided to drive over to check on it, which left the Esperanza Avenue site unguarded, as it would remain for more than twenty-four hours. Investigators who arrived after that time said they found the site apparently intact, or at least there were no obvious marks of intrusion, and no one ever made a public issue of the time it was left unprotected.

After his phone conversation with Gilbert, Mayman decided to go ahead and make his morning court appearance. But as he pulled into the parking lot of the courthouse, at about 8:00 AM, he called Gilbert for an update.

"What's happening? Mayman asked.

"We've just got an engine crew in a rollover," Gilbert said, leaving Mayman confused as well as alarmed. Had a fire engine rolled over in the heavy smoke? Gilbert translated the fire lingo. An engine had not *rolled over*, he said, it had been *burned over*, and it sounded like there were fatalities. Mayman was sitting in his car, digesting the disturbing news, when his cell phone rang with a message from the DA's main office in Riverside.

Forget the court appearance, he was told. The Esperanza Fire has just turned into a murder investigation. Detectives from the Riverside County Sheriff's Central Homicide Unit are on the way to the scene. Someone named Gilbert from the Cal Fire arson squad is there and will give a briefing shortly at the incident command post. Get over there and find out what's going on.

When Mayman arrived at the incident command post at Cabazon just after 9:00 AM, the place was in an uproar. Incoming sheriff's detectives, arson investigators—and now an assistant DA—mingled with the fire supervisors and arriving engine and hand crews, the vanguard of a force of more than one thousand firefighters who would arrive in the next few hours. The fire supervisors had been stunned by Fogle's broadcast about the Engine 57 burnover. One of the Forest Service supervisors, Dan Felix, had just stepped outside the ICP for a cigarette, taking a break from putting together a fire map for the day shift, when he heard someone say, "We think there's been a burnover." A minute later, Fogle's voice came over a loudspeaker at the ICP connected to the fire radio. Engine 57 was burned over. Two ambulances were needed; no, make that four. Send the coroner.

"After that, it became a bit of a blur," Felix said.

As the loudspeaker reverberated with Fogle's shocking reports,

Norm Walker and Mike Dietrich, the other Forest Service supervisors assigned to the ICP, returned from making a quick run up Highway 243 to check on the fire. "I heard Fogle's last words while I was still in my rig," Walker said. "And I turned around and went screaming back up there."

◆ ◆ ◆

MORNING ALSO BROUGHT an answer to a question that caused much trouble after the fire: Who was in charge at the time of the fatalities? The *Esperanza Fire Accident Investigation Factual Report* says the Forest Service and Cal Fire were in unified command at that time, meaning they shared the top management responsibilities, including for the fatalities. That is not the case. Shortly after daylight, the Forest Service dispatched Mike Wakoski, a fire management officer at a nearby district, to assume the role of incident commander jointly with Cal Fire's Brenda Seabert. Wakoski arrived at the ICP at 8:30 AM and was briefed by Seabert. "When I got there, most of the people at the command post were pretty shaken," Wakoski said. At precisely 9:00 AM, according to Wakoski's written record, he assumed the role of IC for the Forest Service in joint or unified command with Seabert. In other words, Cal Fire alone was in charge at the time of the fatalities. The later dispute about the issue was a nasty one, pitting one agency against another, but it had limits: the argument was always about who at the top level was accountable and never about who might have saved the day. The claim was never made, at least by anyone in a responsible position, that the addition of a Forest Service IC would have prevented the fatalities.

John Hawkins, Cal Fire's Riverside Unit fire chief, arrived at the ICP between 5:00 and 5:30 AM and later offered a vivid description of how the fire was being run at that time. Hawkins technically outranked Seabert, but she remained IC in charge of firefighting operations. This was a proper procedure; Cal Fire contracts with county and other local agencies to provide fire protection service, and Hawkins was the agency's top executive for Riverside County. When Hawkins walked in to the ICP, he saw Seabert working in one place, the sheriff's representative sixty or so feet away, and Forest Service personnel huddled at a distance. "That's not unified command," Hawkins said. "I should have pulled them together, unified command or not, and had them coordinate among themselves." Hawkins blames himself to this day for not doing so.

Acknowledging the seriousness of the fire even before the burnover, a high-ranking unit, Cal Fire Incident Command Team 8, based in southern California, was alerted during the night to take over the fire. By 7:00 AM most of the team members had checked in for a telephone conference call. Dale Hutchinson, Cal Fire's assistant regional chief for southern California, was briefing the team by phone when the first reports of the burnover reached him. Hutchinson suddenly broke off. "I have to step away; something has happened," he said. Some of the team's forty-five members started for the fire by 9:00 AM, but they had long drives ahead, and there were other delays. "There was difficulty finding enough qualified people to fill assignments," said Phill Veneris, Team 8's night operations chief. A shortage of branch directors and division supervisors meant that weary initial attack personnel had to be held over to fill those jobs. Equipment and crews had been ordered early but were slow to arrive. And so Team 8's official takeover did not occur until the regular 7:00 AM briefing the next morning, October 27, the second day of the fire, which meant long shifts for the ICs, Seabert, Wakoski, and many others.

♦ ♦ ♦

IN THE SQUAD room of the county's Central Homicide Unit at the Palm Desert station south of Palm Springs, a half dozen detectives clustered around a TV watching the first sketchy news reports about the Esperanza Fire: possible fatalities, hints of arson, out-of-control flames, Santa Ana winds, and mass evacuations. Among the dramatic footage was a video showing a Cal Fire pickup and a civilian vehicle appearing out of a curtain of fire and smoke on Highway 243. "They barely made it!" reported the photographer who took the footage, Tyrone Johnson, a stringer for Fox News. "You can see them coming through the flames." Johnson's footage would become an icon of the fire, shown over and over as a touchstone for local and national television news reports. Johnson reported that the driver of the Cal Fire pickup had been injured and taken to a hospital by helicopter, apparently confusing the driver with one of the injured at the Octagon House. The driver of the pickup was not hurt: he was Branch Director Toups, whose identity was never established in the newscasts.

As the detectives watched the flashing screen, Sergeant Brandon Ford, the homicide unit leader, came out of his office. "I think we're going to have to send someone over there," Ford said.

"Do we investigate arson now?" a detective said.

"This may be a homicide," Ford said.

"If it is, you're going to have to send more than two of us."

Sergeant Ford went back to his office but emerged again in minutes.

"Everybody get ready," he said, "we're going to roll."

When the homicide squad arrived in Cabazon, they realized that the command post, which had been moved by now from the Cal Fire station to a larger community building nearby, was no place to run a major arson-murder investigation. On top of dealing with emotional trauma and the rapidly expanding fire operation, the fire supervisors had to run a complex rescue and body recovery operation, which would require everything from family liaison to body removal to memorial services. "We needed to snuff out the fire as quick as we could," said Mike Wakoski, the Forest Service IC. "People say, 'Let it burn; it's good for the land.' People who don't live in southern California don't understand; you can't let a fire burn in southern Cal. The quicker you put it out, the less chance you have of killing somebody."

An immediate decision was made to pull Forest Service personnel off the fire lines so they could "gather their thoughts and prayers," an agency spokesman said. Some of them, however, insisted on finishing their shifts. The burnover was separated from the firefighting operation into an "incident within an incident" and assigned its own management team. The burnover support team arranged or helped to arrange family liaison, five funerals, and a memorial service held just ten days later in Devore; it was attended by as many as ten thousand people. "It was a little rocky at first," said one member of the support team, which eventually numbered more than seventy. "One mother had moved, and we sent people to the wrong address. But it was a success because of what we had learned on previous fires."

Meanwhile, Gilbert briefed the arriving homicide detectives on the fatalities and the background of the Banning Pass arson series. When the lawmen asked to drive up to the Octagon House so they could view the crime scene, they were told that smoke and flames had closed Highway 243. They could, however, visit the site of another possible arson fire, the Seminole Road Fire, which Gearhart's Engine 51 had fought. They drove there only to discover that the point of origin had been trampled over and there was nothing for them to see.

Bristling with frustration, Detective Scott Michaels asked Gilbert, "What else can we do? What else have you got?" Did the arson squad have any likely suspects under investigation? Were they following leads that would give the homicide detectives a place to start?

Many suspects had been investigated since May, Gilbert said, but none had checked out. In addition, surveillance cameras had been placed on utility poles around the Banning Pass in spots where arson fires might be expected to occur. Nine such pole cameras had been set out, recording and storing images of passing vehicles, but none near the source of the Esperanza Fire.

One of the pole cameras, though, had recorded images of vehicles driving past the site of another arson fire, the Mias Canyon Fire, which had burned four days earlier, on October 22, on the opposite side of the Banning Pass from the Esperanza Fire. By coincidence, the Mias Canyon Fire had been attacked and extinguished by the same Forest Service engine crews who were fighting the Esperanza Fire. The weather that day had been mild, with light winds, and the fire had been held to 40 acres. Two of the engine captains, Gearhart and Loutzenhiser, had remarked to each other at the time how much more troublesome the fire would have been if a Santa Ana wind had been blowing.

The pole camera had taken photos of ten or more vehicles going past the site around the time of the fire, Gilbert said. There hadn't been time yet to make a thorough investigation based on the images. The downloading chore was usually done at night to keep the camera locations secret, and that meant an inevitable delay. The cameras were aimed to take images of license plates, not fires, but those images were timed and could be matched to the time of an arson start. Several vehicles had aroused suspicion, but the most suspicious was a battered Ford Taurus. Five images showed the Taurus entering a side road at 3:02 PM in the area where the fire occurred, and five more images showed it coming out again about eight minutes later. The fire had been reported barely a quarter of an hour after that, at 3:26 PM, just enough time for a smoke column to develop. The images of the Taurus were blurry, the face of the driver was obscured, and it appeared a second person was seated next to the driver, which later proved to be untrue: it was a baby seat. The license number, though, could be clearly made out: California plate 3CWG869. There hadn't been time yet to check out the plate.

Gilbert gave Michaels a long, hand-printed list of all the license numbers photographed around the relevant time. "We had nothing but the license plates to go on at that point," Michaels said. He took the numbers back to an analyst at the Central Homicide Unit, and she ran them through a state Department of Motor Vehicles database. The news wasn't all that could be hoped, but it was a start. The Taurus was registered to an auto salvage shop in Banning and not to an individual. The auto shop was only a dozen miles away, so Michaels and his partner, Gary LeClair, headed over. By the time they arrived the place was closed for the day, and a cruise around the neighborhood failed to turn up the Taurus; further investigation would have to wait for the next day.

◆ ◆ ◆

MARIA LOUTZENHISER AWAKENED about 8:00 AM at the family home in Idyllwild, but something held her in bed. "I didn't want to get up. It was like I was in a trance," she said. A ringing cell phone finally made her get up, and when she answered the phone, the caller said there was trouble.

"Tell me!" she demanded.

But the caller couldn't—or wouldn't—be more specific.

"We didn't know anything," Maria said. "It was not a premonition, but it felt like we were in contact, like he was trying to get hold of me. It was like I was with him the whole time."

Freddie Espinoza's wife, Janey, had heard about the burnover when she had come into work at the Forest Service office at 8:00 AM, and she called Maria and asked if she wanted her to come over. Maria, who was distraught and alone with her children, was glad of the offer and said yes. Then several calls came to the house reporting that Mark and another firefighter had been injured and were on their way to the hospital. *Oh, God, thank you!* Maria thought. *Mark's alive!*

She and Janey had to arrange for someone to take care of the youngest children and get the older ones ready for school. Neither of the women was in fit condition to drive; at this point they thought the other engines, including Engine 56 and Janey's husband, Freddie, might be involved. "Our hearts were being wrung out as we speculated who might be alive or dead," Janey Espinoza said. "I didn't want to think about having my close friend that I grew up with—my husband—included in this nightmare." Another friend, Jan Boss, owner of the Red Kettle, came over and offered to do the driving. Maria dressed in the car as they headed down the mountain.

"It's the kind of stuff that doesn't happen in Idyllwild," Maria said. "Not to me. Not to Mark." With Highway 243 closed by flames, they had to go the long way around to the south. Doctors met them when they arrived at the burn center and told Maria they were working on Mark, and if she went into the room now, there was a risk of infection. She would have to wait.

"I want to see him. There's something he needs to know," Maria said.

The doctors again refused, but Maria persisted. As the confrontation grew heated, a group of doctors filed into the room. Maria knew what that meant.

"Ma'am, we did everything we could. We tried our best," one of the doctors said. "Is there anything we can do for you?"

"Yes," she said. "You could have let me go see him when I had the chance." She and Mark had been having some issues; there were things she'd wanted to say to him, things that needed to be said.

She could have told him she loved him and forgave him. In fact, she still could.

"Okay," said the doctor. "You want to see him now?"

"Yes," she said.

In the treatment room, Mark was lying under a sheet that covered his body except for his face. Maria thought she saw his eyes twinkle with recognition.

"He's alive!" Maria said.

"No, ma'am," said the doctor. "He's not. He's dead."

Maria hugged Mark and felt his body warm in her arms.

"That was my gift from God," she said later. "I told him what I wanted to say, and I calmed down."

♦ ♦ ♦

FANNED BY THE Santa Ana wind and gaining strength from the hot sunshine, the Esperanza Fire raged unchecked, driving seven hundred residents from their homes along Twin Pines Road and at Poppet Flats and trapping about four hundred others at the Silent Valley Club, an RV park about ten miles south of Banning off Highway 243. Large RVs and narrow roads meant a mass evacuation from the park would be a dangerous shambles. The area around the Silent Valley Club had been cleared of vegetation as a firebreak, except for one section several hundred yards long that was awaiting completion. After handing over his IC duties, Andrew Bennett had driven to the RV park, seen the gap in the firebreak, and ordered up a bulldozer to finish the job. With that task under way, firefighters adopted a "shelter-in-place" strategy: the RVs and the four hundred people there would ride out the fire at the park. Fire engines and hand crews were deployed throughout the park grounds to protect people and property. Helicopters and air tankers flew overhead, dropping water and retardant. Other firefighters lit a ring of fire around the park for added protection, a variation on the burnout used by the Forest Service engine crews at the double-wide. "The fire department is taking great care of us," club manager Jo Ann Trosper told a television reporter. The fire had made a run at the park, she said, but had passed around the sides, deflected by the deliberate burning, and the Silent Valley Club was left untouched.

Charles Miner, 42, who lived with his parents and sister in a modular home on Woodcliff Drive, one of the dirt roads leading off Twin Pines Road, was not so lucky. As flames approached the home, Miner told other family members to get out. He stayed behind to try to save a new $50,000 backhoe. "There were fireballs shooting over our heads," Miner said in a television interview. "I drove it out of there. I drove right through the flames, right through the flames. There was flames everywhere. I couldn't see nothing. I didn't think I'd make it. And I just drove as far as I could. I drove miles down through the flames. I made it. That's all that matters."

Behind him, the family home burned to the ground.

Miner, who suffered burns on his face and right hand, was the only civilian requiring hospitalization as a result of injuries from the Esperanza Fire. Southern California's massive "fire siege" three years earlier, in October 2003, had caused many improvements in dealing with evacuations that well may have saved lives on the Esperanza Fire. The fires of 2003 proved to be the most devastating wildland fire disaster in southern California history but one that taught a simple lesson that probably has saved many lives since then. In addition to the deaths of twenty-three civilians and one firefighter, flames from the fourteen fires that made up the siege blackened 750,043 acres and destroyed 3,710 homes. Many of the civilian deaths occurred when people who had waited too long to evacuate were caught in their vehicles on smoke-covered roads; they got lost, drove off the road, or crashed into each other. The lesson was straightforward: early evacuations save lives. In the aftermath, Cal Fire and agencies at other levels of government, along with civilians themselves, made a major effort to improve public evacuation procedures, including identifying and clearing evacuation corridors and setting up notification systems. The evacuation on the Esperanza Fire began in the dark, when air tankers and helicopters were restricted from flying, and thus there were no aircraft noises to awaken residents. Nonetheless, the evacuation started early, thanks in large part to the volunteer telephone notification system set up by residents and the house-by-house check by firefighters and others on Twin Pines Ridge. As incident commander, Seabert ordered the mandatory evacuation at 4:00 am and Riverside County sheriff's deputies carried it out. Overall, the evacuation was a major success: Miner, the only civilian injured, was bandaged and released from the hospital, and there were no civilian fatalities.

There were plenty of close brushes with fire, though, and one of the closest involved Toups and his pickup. After he left Engine 57 and the others at the double-wide, Toups drove back to Twin Pines Road, which by now was covered with smoke and threatened by flames. "I could go about zero miles an hour," Toups said. Many of the homes along the north side of the road were aflame, though those on the south side, away from the ridge face, fared better. Cal Fire engine crews were ready with hose lays around many homes. Toups figured that a couple of bulldozers on the south side of the ridge, where the fire was not so intense, could cut a line that would help keep flames from jumping Highway 243.

He radioed the operations chief, Mike Ritchey, told him his plan for bulldozers, and started driving back along Twin Pines Road to meet Ritchey. "There were hundreds of ignitions, multiple fire embers; there were reports of people not wanting to evacuate," Toups said. He saw one engine crew defending a large home at the end of a beautiful alley of oak trees; the second-story windows of the home suddenly blew out, and flames drove the firefighters back down the alley.

Toups joined Ritchey, and they decided to drive in separate vehicles south along Highway 243 to check conditions for the bulldozer line. They had driven about a half mile when a woman hailed them, screaming that her husband had run down the road after livestock and had disappeared in the thicket of oak trees and brush alongside the road. *If that's true, he's dead*, Toups thought. Flames had already reached the brush.

Ritchey started ahead down Highway 243 toward the flames, the direction the woman said her husband had gone, while Toups tried to get the woman calmed down, into her car, and headed off to the south, away from the flames. By the time Toups was able to follow Ritchey, smoke blanketed Highway 243.

"There was orange all around me; oak trees were burning. All I could see was the yellow line in the middle of the road and I followed that," Toups said. He forced himself to drive slowly, to avoid an accident and to stay on the road. As a consequence, his pickup emerged in controlled fashion rather than popping out of a wall of flame when he finally made it to safety. This was the iconic event filmed by the Fox News stringer Tyrone Johnson.

The missing husband was later found uninjured.

The many hundreds who made it out ahead of the fire gathered at evacuation centers, including a community hall in Banning, the Fellowship of the Pass Church in Beaumont, and Hemet High School. All waited anxiously to hear whether their homes were still standing. One evacuee at the Banning center had watched television footage of a neighbor's house going up in flames but had no word about his place. "That's all I got left," he told a television reporter. "I'm just on Social Security and that was it, so I'm sitting here waiting. I just grabbed the papers, a couple of shirts, and left."

A child fearfully recounted how family members had gathered things from their house while she waited in a truck with the family pets. "I just waited in the truck and talked to the animals," she said. A mother visiting her two daughters remembered being awakened in darkness for a nightmarish journey to safety. "I figured we were going to get burned up, so I was ready to go," said the mother, who suffered from lung cancer and needed oxygen. Her daughters loaded her into the car. "We walked out the front door and the flames were, I would guess, a city block from the house," one of the daughters said. "I could hear the roar of the fire; it sounded like a train. We jumped in the car and vamoosed."

The owner of the double-wide, Neil Garner, gave several interviews. He said the last he'd heard, his neighbor's house—the Octagon House—had been destroyed. "But my place was untouched. Just luck of the draw and placement of the house, the way the land runs up there, the hills and the gullies," Garner said. "I'd like to get up the hill and see what's going on."

It would be days, however, before Highway 243 would be reopened and homeowners allowed back on Twin Pines Ridge.

By mid-afternoon of that first day, the Esperanza Fire had become a concern not only for locals but also for politicians and agencies at every level of government—local, county, state, and federal—and eventually the White House. At an afternoon press conference held outdoors near the ICP, political figures joined representatives of Cal Fire, the Forest Service, and the Riverside County sheriff's office to report on the situation.

Representative Mary Bono Mack, a Republican whose district includes Idyllwild, said she had been in Idyllwild only a few days before talking with residents and officials about how to address the dangers of wildland fire. "Like all of us in southern California, every time the Santa Ana winds pick up, we wonder who's going to be next," Bono said as the Santa Ana wind blew her hair across her face. The live broadcast of the conference included the Toups escape footage playing on the screen in a separate panel.

Cal Fire's Chief Hawkins gave an early estimate of losses. By noon, he said, the fire had burned about 10,000 acres, though heavy smoke made an accurate estimate impossible. About one thousand firefighters already were working on the fire, and three times that number might be needed. "You feel the enemy. The enemy blows in our face right now; it's a Santa Ana wind," Hawkins said. "The Santa Ana wind drives the fire. It not only has a pushing effect, it feeds more oxygen to the fire, but it also dries out already critically dry vegetation." Hawkins left no doubt that an arsonist was to blame for the fire. "I'm going to tell you right up front, this is an arson fire," he said. "This is a deliberately set arson fire. A deliberately set arson fire that leads to the death of anyone constitutes murder."

A month earlier, in September, an article by Hawkins ran in *Wildland Firefighter* magazine, describing a training exercise held in Idyllwild for just such an event as the Esperanza Fire. In 2005 the Riverside County Mountain Area Safety Taskforce had conducted a drill centered in Idyllwild that simulated conditions in a major fire in the wildland–urban interface. The drill involved elected officials, governmental agencies, public utilities, and private organizations, as well as the fire community. Idyllwild was chosen because it was such a good example of the problem. "The field exercise took six months to develop and about four to execute," Hawkins wrote. More than fifty sheriff's deputies participated, gaining experience in handling evacuations. One of the findings concerned the need for multijurisdictional or unified command in situations like this, a problem repeatedly cited in investigations of the Esperanza Fire.

Several announcements were made about funding issues. FEMA, the Federal Emergency Management Agency, had agreed to fund 75 percent of firefighting costs. The Riverside County Board of Supervisors had set up a post office box to accept donations for the families of the fallen firefighters. Governor Arnold Schwarzenegger had pledged $100,000 to a reward fund for information leading to the arrest and conviction of whoever was responsible for the fire; that fund eventually would grow to $550,000. And Marion Ashley of the Riverside Board of Supervisors announced that the sheriff had set up an arson hotline. He urged anyone with information to call the number. "It might be some friend or family member who knows something about it," Ashley said. "Get him in jail and keep him there for a long long time. Turn that scum in, please."

12.

On Friday, October 27, the arson investigation went into full swing, and the Esperanza Fire burned virtually unchecked. The blaze had grown overnight to 24,000 acres, more than thirty-seven square miles; firefighters had built line around only 5 percent of the perimeter. The flames threatened Lamb Canyon and Highway 79, a major artery that roughly parallels Highway 243 to the west at a distance ranging from a half dozen to a dozen miles. Though the Santa Ana continued to blow, there was one piece of good news: weather forecasters predicted diminishing winds for the next day, Saturday.

"Breaking news at 8:55: Just moments ago, the U.S. Forest Service identified the firefighters who were overrun by flames: four of them killed; one injured," a CBS affiliate station announced. Cerda was reported in "grave condition," with burns over 95 percent of his body. The CBS announcer rattled off more excited headlines: "Mile after mile on fire. Hundreds forced from their homes in new evacuations. The Esperanza Fire is out of control. The battle to contain the deadliest fire in the past five years grows." The Fox News affiliate exclaimed, "More than just a monster blaze—it's murder!"

Detective Scott Michaels started his drive early from home to the Banning Pass, knowing the smoke would slow the morning traffic. "It was like a war zone out there," Michaels said. He was eager to check more license numbers from the pole camera photos taken at the Mias Canyon Fire, especially the one from the battered Ford Taurus. Michaels picked up his partner, Gary LeClair, and they headed for the Banning auto salvage shop that was registered as owner of the Taurus. They met the shop owner, Charlie Price, at 10:05 AM, according to Michaels' log.

Price remembered buying the Taurus about a year earlier from "a white kid with blond hair." The youngster had been in a hurry and had offered the vehicle cheap, for $50. Price had sold it later the same day for $100 to an employee named Ray, but he couldn't remember Ray's last name. "I felt sorry for him," Price said. "For the first month, he worked out pretty good." Later, Price said, he had begun to suspect Ray of stealing items from the shop and had fired him. He had heard that Ray had found a job at another auto shop, this one in Beaumont.

Michaels and LeClair headed for the place, Highland Springs Automotive. When they arrived there at about 10:50 AM, they were startled—and excited—to see parked across the street a Ford Taurus matching the one in the pole camera photo. As they approached the car on foot, they saw someone asleep in the backseat. Figuring this could be their man, the detectives rousted the sleeper, who emerged from the car disheveled and alarmed.

While LeClair talked to the sleeper, Michaels looked inside the car. "Something was off about it," Michaels said, a description he would use repeatedly during the investigation, as though an extra sense was signaling him that something was wrong. Cigarette butts littered the car floor; the Cal Fire arson investigators had said that cigarettes had been used in the arson devices recovered from the Banning Pass series. The vehicle's right front tire was flat and the back window broken; it was a car with a careless owner, and that fit too.

The sleeper identified himself as Daniel Contreras and said a friend named Ray Oyler owned the Taurus. He didn't know where

Oyler was, but he felt sure that his friend Ray wouldn't mind if he
slept in his car; it was that kind of relationship. "Contreras was odd
and disjointed, but he was also upfront and confident," Michaels said.

The questioning drew the attention of workers at the auto shop
across the street. "We were in civilian clothes, but it was obvious we
were cops," Michaels said. After a few minutes, one of the workers
beckoned to Michaels, who went over. The man handed Michaels a
telephone with a worried Raymond Oyler on the other end of the
line. Oyler's coworkers had called to alert him to the police interest
in his car. When Oyler asked what was going on, Michaels again
had the feeling that something was off.

Contreras was the natural suspect, a homeless drifter who had been
sleeping rough in a car linked to an arson fire. Contreras, however,
was able to explain himself in an apparently candid manner. Oyler,
to the contrary, sounded frightened and dumbfounded that a police
officer would want to question him. "Oyler wasn't communicating
right; he seemed to be hiding something," the detective said. Oyler
agreed to meet with the detectives, however, and gave Michaels his
home address, a few blocks away. Michaels and LeClair decided to
let Contreras go, though he was still a suspect. They took photos of
him and directed him to a local shelter.

It was about noon when the detectives arrived at the address Oyler
had given them. It was a gated blue-collar complex in Beaumont
called the Noble Creek Apartments. The grounds were clean, the
lawns well trimmed, the modest low-rise buildings in apparent
good repair. Across the street from the complex was an open field
where, Michaels would learn later, one of the Banning Pass arson
fires had been started more than a month earlier. Oyler lived in
apartment 28, a second-story unit at the rear of the complex. He
shared the apartment with his girlfriend, Crystal Breazile (whose
name is pronounced like the country Brazil), and their infant
daughter, Diamond Belle.

When Michaels and LeClair climbed the stairs to Oyler's apartment, they noticed that a large ashtray on the outside landing was filled with Marlboro cigarette butts, the same brand used in the Banning Pass arson devices. When Oyler opened the door to Michaels' knock, the detective went on high alert. Oyler had "full sleeve" tattoos on both arms: red and black flames interspersed with death's head skulls. Oyler later proudly described his arm "art" to a jailer as a "skull, a snake, and some flames, and skulls, a bunch of those skulls . . . eyeballs." The tattoos were a telltale, but there was more. Over Oyler's shoulder, Michaels could see a poster in the apartment that showed a faceless devil made of flames stretching out a bony, skeletal hand, a poster for a hard-core hip-hop group called Insane Clown Posse.

This is the guy! Michaels thought.

Oyler answered the detectives' questions without raising his eyes to theirs or allowing them inside the apartment. He gave off a coldness of spirit, Michaels thought, as though he inhabited a separate, remote world. "Oyler wasn't crazy or stupid or retarded," Michaels said. "He was *off*. Everything in there was off; it had a coldness and darkness to it." The apartment reminded him of the house of horrors in the film *The Silence of the Lambs*, the one the murderer used as a torture chamber.

Michaels couldn't shake the feeling, first prompted by his look into Oyler's Taurus, that some unseen force was nudging him along and pointing him in Oyler's direction. It sounded weird, but it felt right. As the two detectives asked questions about the Taurus and Oyler's whereabouts, his responses were vague and evasive; he couldn't tell a story the same way twice. He was acting like a child who had been caught doing something wrong, Michaels thought, a dangerous grown-up child. As the interview progressed, Michaels' intuition told him that he was in the presence of a killer, as he had often been before.

During previous investigations, Michaels had observed criminals transform before his eyes from confident and arrogant personalities to craven, empty shells. It didn't happen every time: some kept up a front throughout. But others had been able to sustain an inner, distorted reality in which they felt all-powerful, until the day detectives appeared on their doorsteps and the questions began. Perhaps for years they had gotten away with murder, arson, or other serious crimes, their sense of power and control swollen by success. Perhaps family and friends had been aware of what was going on, however dimly, and had shrunk from interfering, adding to that sense of invincibility. No one had ever seriously challenged their inner reality, the place where they truly lived, until that fateful day when they heard the knock on the door.

"It's almost like they're dying," Michaels said. "It's almost like you have ahold of a piece of their life, whatever it is that fuels them, a soul, a life force. It's like you're holding something that's not meant to be touched. A good cop clues in on that; the better the cop, the better he is at reading that reaction. There's a certain faint level of panic and chaos. A light in them starts to extinguish."

Initially, Michaels was the only investigator who believed strongly that there was a connection between Oyler and the Esperanza Fire. He had no hard evidence to back up his hunch, at least not at first. He had intuition, like every good cop, but more important was the feeling he had of being guided or driven by a powerful force, one he did not fully understand but nonetheless welcomed. As he stood on the landing of Oyler's apartment, he felt guided by an invisible hand, as though the men who had died in the fire were standing behind him, urging him to play a role in something bigger than himself. "There were greater forces than me at work," Michaels said. "I felt a stronger presence than me. I could feel those fallen firefighters right there with me, telling me what questions to ask, telling me to keep going. But I stayed objective."

♦ ♦ ♦

AS MICHAELS QUESTIONED Oyler at the apartment in Beaumont on the second day of the Esperanza Fire, he could not get a straight story out of him. Oyler's account of his movements at the time of the Mias Canyon Fire was garbled. While he acknowledged that the Ford Taurus was his, he made conflicting statements about who had been in possession of it at relevant times, blaming his bad memory on heavy marijuana use. "He changed his story regarding the drivers, those who had possession of the car, and the times the vehicle was driven," Michaels said. "He appeared very upset and nervous but did not directly ask why I was there to talk to him." Surely, an innocent man would ask why police detectives were on his doorstep.

Michaels told Oyler he wasn't buying the excuse about selective memory loss from smoking pot. "I did not believe it was possible to remember some things and forget others," Michaels said. Oyler responded by piling on details, but they didn't add up either. At that point, Michaels asked Oyler if he was willing to go to the sheriff's substation at Cabazon, give a formal statement, and take a lie detector test. He didn't have to go; he wasn't under arrest. But if he wanted to be eliminated as a suspect, he needed to do a better job of explaining himself, the detective said. Oyler agreed to go.

Michaels left the apartment to call his superior, Sergeant Ford, and report on his progress. The exchange did not go smoothly. "Nobody but me was convinced it was Oyler," Michaels said. "There was so much at stake that I think people froze or slowed down out of fear of screwing up." A fading light in the eyes of a suspect and a sense of being guided by an unseen hand are not the kinds of things that convince hardheaded, overburdened police supervisors to commit scarce resources. Sergeant Ford was in the middle of what was becoming a massive investigation, pulling in scores of state, county, and federal agents, each jealous of their prerogatives, to check a gusher of leads. The tip hotline set up the previous day already was jammed with leads, some of them very promising and most of them requiring follow-up. Committing manpower to investigate a different, earlier fire with no evidence of a link to the Esperanza Fire was a long stretch. Despite his misgivings, Ford told Michaels that he was the case agent for Oyler and to go ahead and bring him into the substation for an interview.

Michaels was back at Oyler's apartment by 12:32 PM, according to his incident log. Oyler asked him to wait a minute while he found his shoes and cigarettes.

"What kind of cigarettes do you smoke?" Michaels asked, casually.

"Kools," Oyler said, after a pause.

Ashtrays in the apartment indeed had a few butts from Kools, Michaels observed, but many more from Marlboros, the cigarette of choice of the Banning Pass arsonist. Michaels eventually sorted out all the cigarette butts found in the ashtray on the apartment landing, where apparently Oyler did most of his smoking at home. Michaels counted dozens of Marlboro butts and one Kool.

The moment the two men stepped out the door of the apartment, they could see the smoke cloud from the Esperanza Fire stretched across the sky like a storm front.

"Man, that's something else right there," Oyler said. "That fire right there, that's terrible, all the animals and people losing their homes and stuff."

On the drive to the station, Oyler kept his head down and did not look again at the fire. He had followed the fire story on television, he told Michaels, but never once during the drive did Oyler mention the dead firefighters, the suspicion that the fire was set by an arsonist, or the accusations of murder.

♦ ♦ ♦

THE RIVERSIDE COUNTY sheriff's substation in Cabazon, a small but modern building, served as the cramped headquarters for the Esperanza Fire arson-murder investigation. Michaels seated Oyler in a spartan interview room with a table, chairs, and a recording camera hidden in a clock. As Michaels began the interview at 1:50 PM, he had an attentive audience. Mayman, the DA's arson specialist, and Gilbert from the state arson squad settled down in a nearby room to watch on closed-circuit television.

Michaels began by thanking Oyler for agreeing to talk. Michaels told Oyler that he wasn't going to get in trouble for his admission about smoking pot; they had more important things to discuss. He then pressed Oyler to account for his whereabouts at the times of the Mias and Esperanza fires. Oyler's responses were confused and defensive. On the night of the Esperanza Fire, Oyler said, he had quarreled with his girlfriend, Crystal, and had left their apartment in frustration. He and Crystal had fought, as usual, about raising the baby, Diamond Belle. "I got four kids by four different women. They live all over the place," Oyler said. He became weepy as he acknowledged that he had never helped raise any of his children.

After leaving the apartment that night, Oyler said, he had driven to the Morongo Casino in Cabazon and had arrived there about 1 AM—just minutes before the discovery of the Esperanza Fire. He had parked on the top, fifth floor of the casino parking lot because, he said, "it seems like when I park on top I win." He didn't win this time: he stayed at the casino long enough to lose $30 and then went back to his car.

"Where'd you go after you left the casino?" Michaels asked.

"I leave the casino and the fuckin' hill's on fire," Oyler said. "I see these big old humongous flames. I was like, *damn*." After a stop or two at gas stations to buy cigarettes, Oyler returned to his apartment.

Oyler had committed a major blunder by trying to use a casino as an alibi. Probably no commercial enterprise has more security cameras than a gambling establishment. Investigators spent hundreds of hours examining the casino's surveillance videos taken that night, including from the parking garage, but not a single frame showed Oyler.

When Michaels asked about the Mias Canyon Fire, Oyler acknowledged that the Taurus in the surveillance images was his. He claimed, though, that someone else had been driving it. Friends like Contreras, whom he knew as Danny Cat, were always borrowing the car without his permission, he said. They even slept in it, which was true. After much back and forth, Michaels turned up the pressure.

"Okay, we need to talk here," Michaels said. "Why did you think you were here? If you had to put two and two together, why did you think you were here?"

"I don't know," Oyler said. "Something to do with my car. I don't know."

"The reason you're here is because I need to talk to you about these fires," Michaels said. "I need to talk to you about where your car was and where you were, okay, when these fires occurred."

"I don't know about no fire. I really don't," Oyler said. "I did not light no fire and I—I don't—I don't have nothing to do with no fires. I don't light no fires or anything."

Oyler yanked a knit cap off and put it back on, wept, and buried his face in his hands. He appeared to be physically sick from nervousness. He was breaking down, and Michaels figured he was on the point of confession. He needed only a little nudge, and Michaels gave him a big one.

"There's evidence left behind," Michaels told Oyler. "Often when people pull off in areas, they leave tire impressions."

"Right," Oyler said.

"What I'm telling you is that your car was in the area where the fire began," Michaels said. The Taurus's tire marks had been found near the ignition point of the Esperanza Fire, Michaels implied. Maybe Oyler had been driving by and had tossed a cigarette butt out the car window, not thinking of the consequences, Michaels said. Maybe Oyler had pulled over to the side of the road to relieve himself, which would account for the tire marks, and had dropped a cigarette butt on the ground. "Things can happen by accident," Michaels said encouragingly.

Michaels was lying, or to use the legal term, he was attempting a ruse. "When they work right, it's awesome," Michaels said later. "When you guess wrong, it stops the interview." In fact, the Taurus's tire marks had not been found at the Esperanza Fire. What Michaels did not know at the time was that the Taurus had broken down and was not drivable that night. It was parked in the lot of a shopping mall, where it was photographed by a surveillance camera with a time stamp within minutes of the first report of the Esperanza Fire. Oyler knew for certain that his car could not have left tire marks near the site of the Esperanza Fire.

He visibly straightened in his chair.

"Explain to me how your tire impressions got at these locations," Michaels said.

"I have no . . . I don't know. I can't tell you that man," Oyler replied. "I can tell looking in your eyeball you don't believe me. I don't know how my car or my fuckin' tire tracks got by there or anything. I don't know."

"You think some magic or a ghost put your car where you're saying it wasn't?" Michaels asked.

Oyler repeatedly denied that he had any responsibility for either fire. "I would not do that. That's cruel. People get hurt, man. You're treating me like I'm lying to you. Something's wrong, man. You're going after the wrong person. I'm telling you."

The confessional moment had passed, and Michaels decided to cut his losses.

"I'm totally mad right now," Oyler said.

"It's understandable. I would be too," Michaels said.

"Yeah, I want to go talk to my mom."

"Okay, I can arrange that."

Michaels told Oyler it would go a long way to eliminating him as a suspect if he voluntarily gave a DNA sample and took a polygraph test. Oyler agreed to the DNA test but not the polygraph. Michaels produced a DNA test kit and brushed a cotton swab similar to a Q-tip inside Oyler's cheek. He took the kit, his tape recorder, the cotton swab, and his notebook, and as he tried to push open the door of the interview room, he dropped the swab on the floor, contaminating it. The DNA kit, perhaps in anticipation of high stress in a test situation, contained two swabs. Michaels got a good swipe with the second one, though he had no way of knowing at the time exactly how good it was.

Oyler was thoroughly spooked by now and asked for a lawyer, which put an end to the questioning.

"I feel like I'm being violated," Oyler said. "I'm being accused of something I'm not doing and I need to go talk to my mom."

Michaels told him he was free to leave the station any time.

"Okay, I'm leaving," Oyler said.

"Okay, I'll show you the way out," Michaels said.

Mayman and Gilbert watched on closed-circuit television from the room nearby as Oyler got to his feet. They already had been convinced that whoever had been in the driver's seat of the Taurus when it was photographed at the site of the Mias Canyon Fire was also the Esperanza arsonist. As Oyler departed, Mayman had the same thought Michaels had had when he first encountered Oyler: *That's our guy.*

◆ ◆ ◆

ON THE SECOND day of the Esperanza Fire, as daylight faded toward dusk, the fire had grown from 24,000 to 40,000 acres, or more than sixty-two square miles. Firefighters had made a stand along the fire's leading edge, at Highway 79, which proved to be an effective firebreak and allowed engines and hand crews to patrol and quickly attack flames. Some crews assaulted the fire so aggressively, supervisors said later, that it smacked of retribution. Firefighters, now numbering over two thousand, made a special effort to save high-voltage lines along highways 243 and 79 to spare the region a major blackout. During the day, they had built and held about six miles of fire line out of a total fire perimeter of fifteen miles. That took the morning's 5 percent containment to 40 percent by nightfall. Flames advanced toward mountain towns including Idyllwild, and fire crews cut lines between the fire and the towns to protect them. The towns were considered safe unless the wind changed direction. Five firefighters sustained minor injuries during the first two days of the fire, but there were no additional serious injuries to firefighters or civilians on any subsequent day. "It's always in the backs of our minds that there were lives taken in this fire," said Chris Woods of the Los Padres Hotshots. "But our tactics didn't change. It's a sad thing, but it's our job."

Nearly all seven hundred evacuees from Twin Pines Ridge and Poppet Flats remained at shelters or other accommodations in the area, as did another one hundred evacuees who were forced from homes in the foothills. Late in the day, a few homeowners were allowed to return with escorts to make brief checks on their homes. The toll of homes known to be lost rose by one, bringing the total to five, plus five other structures. The numbers would increase as more homes were checked. The four hundred residents and temporary campers sheltering in place at the Silent Valley Club stayed put, protected by numerous engines and hand crews. "Apparently we're safe," one said. "We're still here."

The winds had died down during the day, to everyone's relief; the red flag warning expired as predicted at 9:00 PM. But Cal Fire's Chief Hawkins cautioned that the Santa Ana could still cause trouble. "The most dangerous period of a Santa Ana is a reversing Santa Ana," Hawkins told a television interviewer. "When the wind changes from offshore to onshore, there is usually a one-hour lull. During that period the fire can change direction and burn back uphill. That's of great concern to us because of the risk to firefighters and the risk to property."

The firefighting effort was helped on the second day by a full-force air show. The number of familiar aircraft deployed was impressive enough: ten air tankers and twenty helicopters. In addition, Cal Fire brought a new weapon to the fray, a DC-10 used as an air tanker. Developed by a private company, 10 Tanker Air Carrier, the DC-10 was in its first season for Cal Fire. The DC-10 took off from its base at Victorville and made six drops on the fire, as media in hovering helicopters filmed the visual dramatics.

The volume of retardant the DC-10 put on the ground is impressive; a DC-10 can drop a maximum of 11,600 gallons of retardant in under ten seconds, four times the load of other heavy air tankers or helitankers. The DC-10 did not come cheap, though. The rate for contracting the DC-10 was $26,500 per hour, with at least three hours a day guaranteed for pay by the agency. Cal Fire subsequently put the DC-10 on contract, at $7 million a year, but then cancelled the contract in 2011 because of the state's budget problems.

As the fire operation reached its maximum effort, Cerda was fighting for his life at Arrowhead Regional Medical Center's burn clinic in Colton, where Cerda underwent surgery early in the day to remove burned tissue. Governor Schwarzenegger visited the hospital and met privately with Cerda's family. Dr. David T. Wong, the chief of the trauma center, spoke later at a press conference. He said Cerda's oxygen intake and renal function both showed slight improvement, perhaps enough to allow another needed surgery. Cerda's lungs had been damaged too. Patients had survived with similar burns, said Wong, though Cerda's case was one of the worst he had ever seen.

"What is the prognosis?" a reporter asked.

"Poor," Wong replied without hesitation.

13.

A S THE WEEKEND BEGAN, THE Santa Ana wind died down and the Esperanza Fire passed its peak. The arson investigation, to the contrary, broadened and intensified as a swarm of federal, state, and local investigators joined the hunt for a killer. The Riverside County sheriff's office alone put more than forty detectives on the case. "We are searching for the arsonists. We will find them and we will punish them," promised Governor Schwarzenegger. He spent several days touring the area, inspecting fire damage, and meeting privately with families who had lost homes and loved ones. Several leads showed promise. Residents of a Cabazon trailer park reported seeing "two young strangers" acting suspiciously as the fire burned behind them on a hillside. "When they saw that we noticed them, they turned away from us and started walking away real fast," said a neighbor, Edy Bowers. "They didn't say anything, and if they'd been locals they would have."

With leads like that to pursue, Michaels had a lonely day ahead of him following his instinct that Oyler was the Esperanza arsonist. "I didn't have any facts; I had a hunch," Michaels said. "And what if I was wrong and tied up all these resources?" Maybe he could find a solid clue by searching Oyler's Taurus. He drove back to Oyler's apartment on Saturday morning, this time carrying a consent form that would allow him to search the car. Oyler answered the door and in response to Michaels' request said he would like to cooperate. After calling his lawyer, he signed the consent form.

It took until Saturday afternoon to tow the Taurus to the sheriff's substation in Cabazon. Michaels had no idea what he was looking for, but as he searched the Taurus, he found plenty of things that could be used as fire starters—so many, in fact, that Michaels later described the Taurus as "an arsonist's laboratory." The most suspicious items were two five-gallon gasoline cans. An auto mechanic might have a use for gas cans, but so would an arsonist. The car was littered with wads of newspaper and trash that would make good fire starters. There was a lighter. There were a woman's black wig and piles of clothing, mostly sweatshirts and pants "which were potential disguises," or so Michaels wrote in his report. He found a wrist "rocket type" slingshot with burn marks on it. An arsonist could have used the slingshot to propel an incendiary device from a car, Michaels figured, without getting out or even stopping. There were surgical gloves, wire, and cigarette butts in profusion and empty packs of Marlboros. The stuff was suggestive of arson but far short of proof.

The most intriguing item of all, though, was a notebook with a sentence scratched in it that read, "So I, the fucken world came to the end then ware would I stand." Michaels took the sentence to mean, "If the world came to an end, where would I be?" Whoever wrote it, presumably Oyler, was clearly both desperate and dangerously self-centered. Michaels was certain that such suggestive material would overcome resistance on the investigation team to pursuing Oyler as a primary suspect, and in this he was proved wrong.

"I was dumbfounded by the lack of interest," Michaels said. "The evidence in the car was significant." He presented his case in a heated argument with a supervisor in which they "came as close to blows over the phone as you can come, and later in person." Michaels, ordered to join the detectives working on leads with specific links to the Esperanza Fire, had little choice but to comply if he wanted to keep his job. He picked up a few lead sheets for checking, but his heart wasn't in it. He managed to slip in time to brief Mayman and the DA's homicide expert, Michael Hestrin, who had been called out the night before, about his suspicions concerning Oyler and the stuff he had found in the Taurus. At last he found a receptive audience.

Hestrin had been driving home after work the previous evening, Friday, when District Attorney–Elect Rod Pacheco had called him on his cell phone and told him to come back to the DA's office in Riverside for a "face-to-face" talk. When Hestrin arrived, Mayman already was there. He had driven to Riverside after observing Oyler's interview with Michaels in the Cabazon sheriff's substation. Mayman laid out the developing case. There was the link connecting Oyler's Taurus to the Mias Canyon Fire and thus to the Banning Pass arson series. Mayman also described Oyler's guilty behavior during the interview with Michaels, especially his waffling over and eventual refusal to take a polygraph test. Mayman had been involved in the prosecution of five previous cases of serial arson, and when he assured Pacheco and Hestrin that in his judgment Oyler may very well have set the Esperanza Fire, they took action.

Pacheco directed Mayman and Hestrin to go to Cabazon, find a motel, and be prepared for a long stay. He didn't have to tell them the case was likely to be the biggest one of their careers. Firefighter deaths strike home no matter where they occur, but in combustible southern California, they rank in a special category, doubly so when arson is involved. It was also a testing moment for Pacheco, who had been elected district attorney in June but would not take office until January. "He didn't have to explain," Hestrin said. "It was a critical moment for him and for our office." Pacheco promised to provide all the resources they needed.

The sheriff's substation in Cabazon had become a madhouse by the time Hestrin arrived there on Saturday morning. Corridors were jam-packed. Every detective in the county seemed to be working the case. "They had whiteboards on every wall and suspects on every whiteboard," Hestrin said. The FBI had sent in a team of profilers— young, well dressed, and computer savvy—who interviewed detectives as they returned from the field. "The profilers were bright and well-meaning," Hestrin said, "and a few of the detectives became a little starstruck." The FBI team had dismissed Oyler as a suspect because he didn't fit the agency's standard profile for a serial arsonist: a white blue-collar male, aged 27 or younger, unable to hold a job or maintain a relationship with a woman, and with a history of abuse by parents or others. Serial arsonists most often are social outcasts with criminal records as firebugs. Serial arsonists are also serial murderers in the making; nearly all, if not all, serial murderers begin as arsonists and, like every addict, require increasing amounts of stimulation as time goes on. Psychologists who have interviewed serial criminals report experiencing an "involuntary skin-crawling sensation." The most notorious example of the grim evolution from fire to murder is David "Son of Sam" Berkowitz, who terrorized New York City with a spree of murdering young women in 1976–1977. Berkowitz kept a meticulous record of 1,488 arson attacks he'd carried out before he became a killer. After he pleaded guilty to six counts of murder and eight counts of attempted murder, Berkowitz was sentenced to 365 years in prison with no possibility of parole.

Oyler was 36 years old, well beyond the profile age limit. He had a job and a girlfriend. He regularly visited his mother and father, Florence and Donovan, who lived nearby in Banning, and he maintained some ties to his sisters, Joanna and Jennifer, and his brother, Jeffrey. His father, Donovan, was a truck driver who spent much time away from home; no evidence was ever found of parental abuse.

Oyler had a lengthy criminal record for drug, theft, and other relatively minor offenses but none for arson or arson-related crimes. In April 1995, Oyler was arrested for taking a vehicle without the owner's consent in San Bernardino County. He failed to appear for sentencing and moved away, to Missouri, where he worked as a house painter and mechanic. He was arrested several times in Missouri from 1997 to 1999 on charges involving stolen cars, hit-and-run, and domestic violence. He had a relationship with a woman there named Christy, who complained to police in 1999 that Oyler was using and perhaps cooking up crystal meth, or methamphetamine, in their home. She accused him of entering the home in violation of a court order and taking a pit bull puppy and possibly a shotgun. Oyler returned to California, where he was given probation on the 1995 auto theft conviction. Two years later he was convicted of drug possession and was sentenced in 2001 to a year and four months in state prison. In January 2006 he was cited for having three dogs off leashes; he kept pit bulls. In June he was ordered to begin paying $683 in fines from traffic violations, and in August a failure-to-pay warrant was issued.

Despite being told to put his Oyler inquiry on a back burner, Michaels found an excuse over the weekend to interview him again. When Oyler failed to pick up the Taurus after it had been searched, Michaels and another detective, Ed Rose, went to Oyler's parents' home at 720 Eighth Street in Banning to meet with Oyler. Inside the house, Michaels took note of the family tableau: the father, Donovan, stood to one side and said next to nothing. His wife, Florence, and daughter Joanna seemed to dominate the scene, and Oyler appeared to meekly allow the women the dominant role. Responding to the detectives' questions, Oyler said the wig and a pair of shoes found in the Taurus did not belong to him, but he acknowledged that the other items were his. He said he needed the gas cans because he was always running out of gas; the slingshot was a nephew's toy.

If he was innocent, as he protested, the detectives said, why not come in for a lie detector test and help prove it? A technician would ask a standard set of questions; there would be no tricks. Detective Rose began asking Oyler sample questions to show him how easy the lie test would be. Oyler began answering back, as though he were actually taking the test, and the detectives recorded the exchange.

"Is your name Ray Oyler?" Rose asked.

"Yes," Oyler said.

"Do you live in the state of California?"

"Yeah."

"He will ask you your date of birth, whatever it is. Do you understand what I'm saying?"

"Yeah."

"Does your mother-in-law or whoever live at this address, 720 Eighth Street?"

"Yes."

"In regards to the Esperanza Fire, did you start it?"

"Yes."

Oyler answered the last question in what sounded to Michaels like an honest tone. When the questions ended, Oyler told the detectives he would think about taking the test for real, but he wasn't ready to do it now. As the detectives got back in their car, Michaels was near to bursting.

"Brother, he just confessed!" Michaels said to his partner. "You asked him did he set the fire and what did he answer?"

"Yes!" Rose said, repeating Oyler's answer with a grin.

But when Michaels repeated the answer to the prosecutors, Hestrin and Mayman, they reacted skeptically. A defense lawyer would argue that Oyler thought he was participating in a hypothetical test and thus his answers were hypothetical. Even if Oyler had said the same things during an actual polygraph, California law requires that both defense and prosecution consent to the use of polygraph material in court. Hestrin decided against making any use of Oyler's "confession," much to Michaels' dismay. "I'm dying over this," Michaels said later.

The prosecutors, though, were more than willing to help Michaels carry on investigating Oyler. The "confession" may not have been good enough for court, but it was one more link between Oyler and the Esperanza Fire. With the prosecutors' support, Michaels obtained a search warrant for Oyler's apartment. By now, the "confession" and search of the Taurus had sparked growing interest in Oyler within the sheriff's department, and as a result Michaels also obtained approval to keep Oyler under electronic surveillance. The Banning Pass is notorious with police as a difficult place to carry out surveillance, because so many in the population are familiar with police tactics. Aware of the problem, Sergeant Ford and the overall case agent, Detective Ben Ramirez, approved a loose surveillance of Oyler, which meant putting electronic trackers on the Taurus and another car Oyler was in the process of buying.

What the sheriff's officers did not know at the time, however, was that the DA's office, motivated in part by the previous lack of interest in Oyler by the investigation team, had independently ordered surveillance of Oyler by their own investigators, unfortunately using an unmarked car that was easily recognizable as a police vehicle. Neither the sheriff nor the DA's investigators knew what the other was doing, and as a result potentially important evidence very likely was lost. The DA's investigators tailing Oyler watched as he left his apartment carrying a filled white garbage bag. Oyler put the bag in his car and drove off. They tried to follow him in the unmarked car, but he apparently had spotted them and lost them in traffic. The garbage bag was never recovered; Oyler's girlfriend, Crystal Breazile, would later say that Oyler kept a plastic baggie full of newspaper clippings about arson in a hall closet. These were never recovered either. When the sheriff's investigators learned of the double surveillance and the lost garbage bag, a major row broke out with the DA's office.

Now having to act quickly and with a search warrant in hand, Michaels collected a team of detectives and went to Oyler's apartment. When there was no answer to their knock, they broke down the door. As they were entering the apartment, Oyler drove up and parked. Seeing his apartment swarming with police, he took off running. Michaels ran after him, across lawns, driveways, and parking areas, and caught up with Oyler in front of a neighbor's apartment. Oyler's frantic knocks were going unanswered: he was trapped. He waited in front of the door, with his head down and a sulky expression on his face, for Michaels to catch up. Michaels slowed to a walk and put his hands in his pockets, and when he got a few feet away he bent over so he could look Oyler in the eye.

"Raymond, I know it's you," Michaels said. "I know it's you, Raymond."

Then Michaels walked away and left Oyler frozen at the neighbor's door.

◆ ◆ ◆

BY SUNDAY MORNING, the fourth day of the Esperanza Fire, a team of California's most experienced fire investigators had begun scouring the fire's point of origin for a clue to the arsonist's identity. Cal Fire battalion chief James Engel, who had long experience in the Banning Pass, had been summoned from his current duty station in northern California to lead the team. Engel got the nod because he had investigated more than one thousand fires and had spent most of his twenty-one years with Cal Fire stationed in the Banning Pass. He also taught Cal Fire's class on serial arson; two members of his Esperanza investigation team were recent graduates.

When Engel met with other investigators, no arson device had yet been found at the Esperanza Fire. The working theory was that the fire was a "hot start," lit by hand with a match or ignition device that probably was taken away from the scene. Engel realized that the investigation was likely to be the most important one of his career and determined to take whatever time necessary to make a thorough search. When he and his investigation team went to the site for the first time, late on Friday, they found an engine company standing by but no police. Engel requested a police guard, and one was assigned. By Friday night, more than twenty-four hours after the fire, the site was secure.

One of the first things Engel's team did, in order to have no preconceived boundaries for their search, was take down the flagging tape that had been stretched along Esperanza Avenue to preserve the scene. By the time they began their search of the site the next day, Saturday, they had a good idea of where the fire had begun. An aerial image showed that the fire had fanned out in a classic tomahawk or V pattern, starting from a sharp point just a dozen feet from Esperanza Avenue. Luckily for generations of fire investigators, fires seldom burn back on themselves and destroy the evidence of their origin.

The team identified roughly 2 acres of ground as the outer limit of the point of origin. The plan was to check the ground with the naked eye for signs such as the angle of char on trees to determine the fire's path of spread and then to set out a grid on the likeliest ground for the ignition point, using metal posts and string to divide the ground into foot-square blocks or quadrants. The investigators then would get down on their hands and knees with magnifying glasses and study the blocks, sifting dirt much like archaeologists uncovering an ancient site. By the end of the day on Saturday, they had made an initial examination of the entire 2 acres, except for a small burned strip next to Esperanza Avenue. When they resumed work on Sunday, they started with the narrow strip. Engel was standing along the roadway taking a break with another veteran investigator, Cal Fire captain Gary Eidsmoe, when something caught Eidsmoe's eye.

"What do you think of that?" Eidsmoe asked, pointing to a patch of twigs embedded in light grass a dozen feet from the road. There was a pattern to the twigs, as though arranged by a designing hand. When Eidsmoe and Engel knelt and examined the patch more closely, they could make out a bundle of scorched matches, a cigarette butt, and a rubber band: the signature device of the Banning Pass arsonist. "Eidsmoe just had an eye for detail," Engel said later. "I had walked by that spot numerous times."

The media were out in force along the roadway, and the wind was blowing hard. Engel covered the device with a helmet to hide it and keep it intact. No one touched it until it had been photographed in place; only then was it carefully extracted from its setting and wrapped in cotton. Upon closer observation, the Marlboro brand name could be seen on the cigarette butt. There were no fewer than four and perhaps as many as six partially burned wooden matches. The rubber band was a bluish-green, the same color as rubber bands in other Banning Pass arson devices. The only thing missing, Engel said later, was the cigarette's ash. The device would act on a simple time delay, allowing minutes for an arsonist to get away from the scene; for good reason is arson known as the crime of the coward. Later tests with similar materials showed that the delay with this particular device would have been four to eight minutes. Charlie Dehart, the Cal Fire investigator who had investigated the arson series starting with the first fires in May, was chosen to drive the collected device to the state Department of Justice crime lab in Riverside for analysis.

The search was far from over. Engel's team staked out a grid and got busy with magnifying glasses and little shovels. "When you make a find like that, it's encouraging," Engel said, "but you still have to go through the process." The search would continue for another two and a half days, until Tuesday, but the cigarette–match device was the only find. "It started the fire," Engel said.

◆ ◆ ◆

OVER THE WEEKEND, the families and friends of the Engine 57 firefighters spoke at press conferences and vigils about what the living presence of their loved ones had meant to them and to the community. Aunts, uncles, cousins, and friends of Pablo Cerda maintained vigil with his father, Pablo Sr., and his sister, Claudia, at Arrowhead Medical Center, where Cerda's life hung in the balance. The family, facing difficult choices, talked among themselves in Spanish.

Cerda liked being around other people and never wanted to be alone, friends said. He went from the soccer team in high school to playing sports and video games with the Engine 57 crew at the station house, particularly with McLean and McKay. A devoted Dallas Cowboys fan, he especially liked playing Madden football on PlayStation 2. Cerda had been trying for a job closer to home, with the Santa Ana Fire Department, so he could spend more time with his widowed father. "He didn't drink; he didn't smoke. He was just a good guy," said Martin Ruiz, 28, a friend and fellow firefighter who joined the vigil at the hospital. "He was a little kid trapped in a big body."

Short, peppery Jess McLean was remembered as an outdoorsman and "man of nature" but also as someone who had discovered a vocation for teaching through his job as a firefighter. John Clays, McLean's brother-in-law and also a firefighter, spoke for the McLean family at a press gathering. Standing behind Clays in red crew T-shirts was the Vista Grande Hotshot crew, on which McLean had served. Other uniformed Forest Service personnel stood by, their badges crossed with black mourning bands. "He touched so many people," Clays said in an emotional address. "He wanted to be a firefighter for a long time. But working for the Forest Service allowed him to realize his other passion, which was teaching. He was able to teach past and present firefighters through the Forest Service, not only in the classroom but in everyday life, with strong leadership skills."

A prayer vigil for Najera was held at the 9/11 memorial site at Fire Station 88 in Sherman Oaks. He was remembered as the youngest member of the Engine 57 crew. His mother, who had married again and become Gloria Ayala, said that at 20 years of age, Daniel was "too young, too green" to be fighting the blaze. "As the ashes come down I keep thinking, that's part of my baby, coming down on me," she said through tears.

Najera's grandfather Patrick, who had helped raise him and referred to him as "my son," held up a copy of the *Press-Enterprise*, which carried the headline "They Had No Chance." "I'm going to be looking at this for the rest of my life, because I lost something very precious," Najera said. "He was a baby that anyone would want in their lives. This baby became a man; he died as a man. He died as a hero."

In Idyllwild, the town went into mourning. At the Forest Service headquarters, the American and Forest Service flags flew at half-mast. Flowers and candles appeared at a makeshift memorial at Engine 57's Alandale station house, where a bronze plaque with the names and faces of the Engine 57 crew would later be erected as a permanent memorial. In the center of town, donation jars were put out at Jo'An's Restaurant & Bar to aid the Loutzenhiser children. "We're a close community; they came in here for dinner a lot," said Jessica John, a restaurant employee. "My sons are in school with her twin sons in third grade. Our hearts go out to them, and we just want to be as helpful to them as best as we can." Maria

Loutzenhiser invited cameras into her home, and with Mark's friend and fellow captain Chris Fogle seated next to her on a sofa, made a brief, composed statement. "I especially want to thank all Mark's firefighter friends who were there with him at the time. I know that he was under great care. I know they all love him."

McKay's mother, Bonnie, spoke at a press conference she requested in order to make a point: the Forest Service was not to blame for what had happened to her son, she said. Jason was well trained, loved his job, and was an experienced firefighter. It was the arsonist who was to blame, along with his family, who probably were aware of what was going on and had failed to stop it. "You already know that you have a problem," McKay said, addressing the arsonist. "I truly believe that you didn't think things were going to turn out the way they did. But they did. Don't let the remorse eat you alive. Come forward."

By the close of the weekend, the Santa Ana wind had collapsed, the temperature was dropping, there was fog at night, and firefighters had gained the upper hand on the flames. The fire had burned 40,200 acres, almost sixty-three square miles, but the prognosis by fire managers was that the flames would be fully contained in one more day. As firefighters and residents made their way into the burn area, the tally of lost homes rose to thirty-four, with another twenty outbuildings burned. Though the fire was not yet controlled, no more homes or structures—or lives—would be lost.

14.

On Monday, October 30, the fifth day of the Esperanza Fire, sheriff's police cars pulled up at a pinkish stucco house at the foot of Cabazon Peak, a half a mile to the east of the Esperanza Fire's ignition point, where James Engel's investigation team was still busy with its grid search. It was a neighborhood of modest dwellings, mobile homes, snarling dogs, rusted gates, and dirt driveways. Two young men with shaved heads and tattooed arms got out of the patrol cars and were immediately pursued by a crowd of media. The men hurried into the stucco house, at 51621 Ida Avenue in Cabazon, without speaking.

The deputies had picked up William "Billy" Hutson, 28, who had served prison time for arson, and his brother Jason, 26, as "persons of interest," but that didn't stop them from regarding the brothers as primary suspects. Not only did the Hutsons live just blocks from the fire's point of origin, but Billy Hutson was a good fit for the FBI's serial arsonist profile: he was about the right age, from the right blue-collar social class, and had served a six-year prison term for arson. He had set a neighbor's mobile home on fire in Texas in 1998. (He claimed it was an accident.) A Hutson girlfriend who was in the house when officers took the brothers into custody was briefly detained. She was released when it was determined that she had no connection to the case;

nonetheless, footage of her in handcuffs made teaser material for television stations.

Billy Hutson acknowledged to *Press-Enterprise* reporters that police had grilled him about the Esperanza Fire and that he had failed a polygraph test. He claimed a bad case of nerves had caused him to flunk the test and denied any connection to the fire. After checking their statements, investigators determined that the Hutson brothers had not set the fire, and they were released and driven home.

The case was moving at such bewildering speed that certainties could not keep up with facts. One minute the lead investigators were united in the conviction that the Hutsons were the arsonists, and everyone, including Scott Michaels, was enlisted to help prove it. The next minute, when the mass effort cleared the Hutsons, the investigation team was left groping for a new prime suspect. The team returned to the routine of checking out people with records for arson, knocking on doors in search of witnesses, and following up leads that continued to pour in on the telephone tip line; out of about 265 leads, ten to fifteen were considered substantial. "This is the kind of fire investigators are not going to let go of," said Douglas Allen, the retired chief arson investigator for Cal Fire. He appeared on television urging the public to be patient. He said he once had an arson case that took sixteen years to solve and that arson investigators were used to lengthy pursuits. "They are driving themselves to find out who did this."

While investigators searched for a new focus, firefighters had their best day so far. A switch in the wind from offshore to onshore drove what was left of the dying fire back on itself. Containment lines were expanded by hand crews, bulldozers, and aircraft. Temperatures fell into the seventies and humidity levels rose into double digits, helping tamp down flames. At 6:00 AM, the fire was said to be 85 percent contained, and full containment was predicted for that evening, at 6:00 PM. As the day progressed, evacuation orders were lifted and residents of the Twin Pines and Poppet Flats neighborhoods were able at last to return to their homes, often to scenes of devastation.

Lili Arroyo, the 76-year-old woman whose life almost surely had been saved when she gave in to pleas to evacuate her mobile home on Twin Pines Ridge, returned to her home to discover it had become a charred heap of wreckage. As Arroyo picked through the ashy remains, she told reporters: "It's so hard to see the fire coming. I didn't think it was going to burn. I told the firemen, 'Don't let my trailer burn.' But of course you can see it did." Digging through the debris, she found one intact object, a small statue of Saint Jude, patron saint of desperate and lost causes. "It's a miracle!" said Arroyo. The find encouraged her, she said, to think of rebuilding on the site where she had lived for the past twelve years.

The Esperanza Fire, as predicted, was declared 100 percent contained at 6:00 PM, and an initial five hundred weary firefighters were released and sent home.

◆ ◆ ◆

ON THE FOLLOWING day, Tuesday, October 31, Detective Michaels tried to find an inconspicuous place to sit at a morning meeting of the investigative team, in a conference room at the sheriff's substation in Cabazon. The room was too small for the crowd of DA's men, sheriff's police, and federal agents, all in a quarrelsome mood. "The situation was becoming strained," Hestrin acknowledged later. "Everyone was short on sleep; tempers were frayed. Cops were tired of listening to lawyers argue endlessly about everything. The lawyers were tired of computer kids challenging their well-honed instincts. Nobody was screaming . . . at least not yet."

Michaels tried to disappear into his chair. "They were shutting me down," he said. The search of Oyler's apartment had turned up nothing incriminating, and with that, Michaels' investigation had come to a dead end. Despite his bravado in telling Oyler, "Raymond, I know it's you," Michaels had no hard evidence to back up the accusation, only that extra sense telling him Oyler was the one. Michaels figured Oyler had put newspaper clippings and other mementoes or trophies of arson fires in the garbage bag, the one he had dumped after losing the DA's men assigned to tail him. The lost bag was one of the things the DA's men and the sheriff's police were quarreling about in the conference room right now.

When Michaels' cell phone rang, he whispered into it that he was in a conference.

"Hey, I need to talk to you!" the caller replied.

Michaels slipped outside the room and put the phone to his ear. The caller was Lynn Melgoza, who handled arson cases for the state Department of Justice crime lab. Melgoza was speaking so excitedly that Michaels couldn't understand a word.

"Slow down, get calm, and repeat that again," Michaels said.

Melgoza had news.

"We've got a positive DNA match for your suspect Raymond Oyler!" she said.

Michaels took a breath.

The Esperanza Fire had become the top priority for the crime lab from the moment Melgoza had learned there was DNA available from a suspect, namely the DNA swab Michaels had taken during his first interrogation of Oyler. Crime lab personnel had worked virtually nonstop through the weekend to test dozens of previously recovered arson devices from the Banning Pass series and to check any DNA found against the Oyler sample. They had made two matches. Traces of DNA were discovered on devices used to start fires in flat grassland in Banning on June 9 and 10. Both matched

Oyler's DNA. The two devices were made up of wooden matches placed on Marlboro cigarettes, six matches at the first fire, seven at the second, making up what prosecutors later described as "layover devices." Both devices had been found about ten feet from a roadway, similar to the placement of many of the Banning Pass arson devices. Oyler apparently had gotten out of a vehicle, taken a few puffs on a cigarette, placed the cigarette on the ground, and laid the matches over it. As with all the devices, the matches would ignite when the cigarette burned down to them. DNA had been found on the filter tips, which did not burn as readily as tobacco and paper. Later, the crime lab would analyze the matches from the devices, which would prove to be identical, chemically and structurally, to each other and to matches found at the home of Laura Breazile, the mother of Oyler's girlfriend, Crystal. At the time of Melgoza's call, the arson device from the Esperanza Fire site had not yet been analyzed. But her call meant that Oyler now was linked to three fires in the Banning Pass series: the two June fires for which there were DNA matches and the Mias Canyon Fire, where his Taurus had been sighted.

Michaels told Melgoza he was going to put her call on hold and when he came back on the line she should repeat exactly what she had told him. Michaels went back into the conference room where the angry, frustrated investigation team was trying to plot a way forward.

"It was the biggest moment of my investigative career," Michaels said. "I went back in the conference room and told people to shut the fuck up. I put my phone on the desk and turned on the speaker. I told her to say it again, and she said, 'We have a positive match to Raymond Oyler—it's confirmed.' And I got to watch the reaction on everybody's face."

That moment proved to be the turning point for the investigation. "The DNA changed everything," Hestrin said later. "The disagreements disappeared. Everybody respected that DNA hit. Now everybody knew, *Oyler is our guy.*" Key witnesses had yet to be found. More lab tests had to be run, more forensic analyses made. Specific charges had to be drawn up, an arrest made, experts summoned for testimony, motions filed, rulings made, jurors selected, and witnesses prepared for testimony. That one cell phone call, however, turned what had been a determined but frustrated investigative effort onto a path that led, in a few short years, to the capital murder trial of Raymond Oyler.

Once the decision was made to arrest Oyler, however, a fresh dispute broke out over who should have the honor of handcuffing him, a very touchy matter in police circles. Michaels badly wanted to be the one to snap the cuffs. "It was me who did it," Michaels said later, plaintively. "To take that arrest away from me was difficult. But it wasn't me that solved it. It was those firefighters. They were there, as if they were putting the words into my mouth."

Michaels had identified Oyler as a prime suspect from their first meeting. He had obtained the crucial DNA sample that linked Oyler to the Banning Pass arson series. Oyler's genetic blueprint was not in any law enforcement data bank; California law has required mandatory DNA collection from anyone arrested on felony charges only since 2009, three years after the Esperanza Fire. If Oyler had not voluntarily given Michaels a sample of his DNA, the DNA found on the June 9 and 10 devices might never have been traced to him. The link between Oyler and the Esperanza Fire might never have been made, or it could have taken much longer. And Michaels had pursued Oyler in the face of opposition, potentially jeopardizing his career.

Many other investigators, though, had had a hand in building the case against Oyler, as Michaels willingly acknowledged later on. Despite severe doubts, Sergeant Ford and Detective Ramirez gave Michaels enough leeway to continue his investigation, and full support once they were convinced of Oyler's involvement. The foundation for the court case, however, was the painstaking collection of arson devices and other evidence by the Cal Fire arson squad and others beginning back in May. The arson squad investigators had recognized from the first day that they were dealing with a serial arsonist. They had alerted Cal Fire and Forest Service fire crews to preserve points of origin for fires in and around the Banning Pass. The fire crews had responded, and the investigators had recovered one fragile device after another and carefully stored them for future reference. The prosecution was able to introduce twenty-five photos of arson devices during Oyler's trial. Essential, too, was the effort of state Department of Justice crime lab technicians and supervisors, who worked feverishly and produced the DNA matches within days, not the weeks and months it usually takes.

It was decided that Gilbert, representing the Cal Fire arson squad, would put the cuffs on Oyler. "It was a political issue; I had a huge argument over it," Michaels said. "We had a tracker on his car. We still wanted a confession. Why pick him up? To take that arrest away from me was difficult, because I had solved it. In my heart, I knew the deceased firefighters had guided me. It's important that those families know their firefighters participated in it."

The matter, however, had been decided. Michaels and Gilbert drove together toward the Banning-Beaumont area, guided by the electronic tracker that was still on Oyler's vehicle. They found Oyler, and Gilbert put the cuffs on him at approximately 1:30 PM Tuesday, the sixth day of the Esperanza Fire. During the drive back to the sheriff's substation, Oyler appeared upset and nervous but said nothing. "At the end of the day there's something gone in him," Michaels said of Oyler. "You can't look Raymond Oyler in the eye and make a human connection." Michaels, assigned to conduct Oyler's arrest interview, left him in a chair in the interview room and went to report to his superiors. When he returned a few minutes later, Oyler's whole body was shaking so badly that he was slipping off the chair.

"He made it all the way to the floor and started flopping around like a fish," Michaels said. "I thought he was faking, but it was my obligation to protect life, so I called for an ambulance."

A female police officer came into the room and tried to get Oyler to sit up.

"You'll be much more comfortable that way," the officer said. "Work with me here, okay? Just sit on your butt. Take slow, deep breaths."

After a few moments, Oyler was able to speak and said his chest felt tight and his head hurt. An ambulance arrived with a paramedic.

"Hey, Ray, my name's Chuck," the paramedic said. "It sounds like you had a little bit of a hyperventilatory issue, breathing a little fast. How are you feeling right now?"

"Weak," Oyler replied.

Oyler was taken to a hospital emergency room, where it was determined he had no serious medical problems. He was returned to the substation, where Michaels read him his rights and tried one final time to get Oyler to talk. How did his DNA come to be on the cigarette butts? Why was his Taurus at the Mias Canyon Fire site? And trying the phony ruse again, Michaels asked him how his tire marks wound up at the site of the Esperanza Fire?

Oyler said his lawyer had told him not to answer questions, and after he repeated this statement several times, Michaels gave up and left the room to begin the lengthy booking process. A surveillance device, though, continued to operate as Oyler's girlfriend, Crystal, came into the room.

"I need to get bailed out," Oyler told Breazile, sounding desperate. "Tell mom to find out what bail is and then to get me bailed out."

"We don't have that kind of money," Breazile replied.

"Call Jason," Oyler pleaded. "Tell Jason I need to get bailed out of jail." Oyler named other friends and acquaintances who might help, urging Breazile over and over to find "some way, somehow . . . get the bail."

To the listening law enforcement officers, it sounded as though Oyler was planning a hasty exit from California.

♦ ♦ ♦

WHILE OYLER WAS being booked at the substation, Pablo Cerda's family gathered at Arrowhead Regional Medical Center to make the most difficult decision of their lives. They could authorize another surgery for him, to remove more burned tissue and to treat his severe inhalation injuries, or they could let him go. Dr. Dev GnanaDev, medical director of the hospital, described Cerda as "a great fighter" who had not been expected to live more than a few hours when he had arrived at the hospital six days before. GnanaDev said doctors had done all they could for Cerda and that the prognosis for him was "very very poor." As firefighters and others held vigil outside the hospital, Cerda's father and sister made the decision, at about 3:00 PM, an hour and a half after Oyler's arrest, to allow doctors to withdraw life support. Sustaining measures were gradually withdrawn, and Cerda died at 5:08 PM.

♦ ♦ ♦

OYLER'S DESPERATE PLEADINGS with Breazile to bail him out put the prosecution team in a difficult position. Oyler's remarks clearly indicated he was a flight risk if he made bail. On the other hand, charging him with murder, which meant he could be held without bail, would alert his family and supporters that he was in very serious trouble and probably would limit their cooperation with police, a fear that turned out to be well founded. "We were concerned about talking to people before they had a chance to rally around Ray," Hestrin said. "If Crystal had realized early on the amount of trouble Ray was in, she might not have been so forthcoming." Indeed, when Michaels and another detective, Robert Dean Spivacke, interviewed Crystal the next day, Wednesday, November 1, they gathered information that proved vital during the trial—and that Crystal later tried to disavow.

The prosecutors decided to charge Oyler initially with just the two June fires and hope that he couldn't make bail. The DA's office tried to obtain sealed warrants on murder charges as well, to make certain he stayed in jail, but a judge ruled there were insufficient legal grounds to keep the warrants secret. The prosecutors decided at that point to hold off on the more serious charges. When the prosecutors heard a rumor that friends of Oyler had raised his $25,000 bail and were on their way to post it, however, they switched plans.

Oyler was charged with murder on Thursday, November 2, a week and a day after the start of the Esperanza Fire. Riverside County undersheriff Neil Lingle made the announcement at an outdoor press conference surrounded by a crowd of state, county, and federal politicians and other officials. Oyler was charged with five counts of first-degree murder, eleven counts of arson of forest land, and ten counts of use of incendiary devices in those arsons. (More charges were added later, bringing the total number to forty-five.) Lingle thanked the Riverside County Central Homicide Unit, Cal Fire's arson investigators, and many others for the swift arrest. "We have worked tirelessly to find those responsible for the crimes of arson and murder," he said. "I am proud to share with you today that we have done our job. Our hearts go out to all the families who have suffered a loss of a loved one on the Esperanza Fire and to all our brothers and sisters in the fire service."

The time had arrived for a final tally of the fire, though it would be years before some cost figures became clear. The Esperanza

Fire burned for five days before it was fully contained. The 40,200 acres it burned is a large area, but in southern California fires of over 100,000 acres are not infrequent. The thirty-four homes and twenty other structures it destroyed is also a large number, but nowhere near a record for California. The following year, 2007, a series of fires in southern California would burn 500,000 acres and destroy more than 1,500 homes. The financial cost of the Esperanza Fire was understated at the time as about $9.9 million, which is substantial enough. The real figure, though, is almost twice that amount.

On the day the fire started, FEMA approved fire management assistance grants for the Esperanza Fire. The grant program is used to defray 75 percent of the costs for state and local government agencies for fires that are or threaten to become major disasters, to try to limit damage by quickly opening the federal coffer. Of the costs approved by FEMA for the Esperanza Fire, the largest was $10,239,006 for Cal Fire for firefighting actions. Other costs show how widespread the firefighting effort was: $9,325 for Cal Fire for administrative expenses; $534,439 for Riverside County; $186,923 for the Governor's Office of Emergency Services; $61,944 for the California Highway Patrol; $9,325 for the state Department of Transportation; $12,821 for the city of Banning; and $7,275 for the city of Beaumont. The total of approved costs was $11,061,058, of which FEMA paid $8,312,949, or approximately 75 percent.

The Forest Service costs were not eligible for reimbursement by FEMA because one federal agency cannot pay another: the money comes from the same source. Forest Service costs, obtained through a Freedom of Information request, totaled an additional $5,154,741. Added to the state and local figures, the price tag for the Esperanza Fire was no less than $16,215,799. The financial cost of the fire was not extreme by comparison with other California fires: in the first decade of the new century, six fires in California cost more than $75 million each to suppress.

The highest and incalculable cost was the lives of the five men of Engine 57. For the first time, flames had wiped out an entire wildland fire engine crew, the greatest loss of life for wildland firefighters on a single fire since the South Canyon Fire of 1994 in Colorado and its loss of fourteen lives.

15.

THE ROBERT PRESLEY HALL OF Justice, where the trial of Raymond Oyler took place, is a 1991-vintage building sited to its disadvantage next to the Ionic-columned Riverside County Courthouse, one of the most beautiful structures in southern California. The historic courthouse is a reminder of the days when "citrus was king," Riverside County was the one of the richest places in the world, and county fathers could afford the best. The state's legendary citrus industry began in 1873 when Eliza Tibbets, an East Coast matron who had moved to southern California after the Civil War, planted three Brazilian navel orange trees sent to her by a friend and botanist, William Saunders, the director of the U.S. Department of Agriculture. A cow destroyed one tree but the other two thrived. The thick skins of the naval oranges made them easy to transport, endless groves were planted, and the growers became very rich. It was a different kind of California gold rush and it lasted a lot longer, earning the region the nickname Inland Empire.

When time came to build a courthouse, the county hired a noted Los Angeles architect, Franklin Pierce Burnham, who used as a model the beaux arts facade of the 1900 Paris Exposition's Grand Palace of the Fine Arts. Begun in 1903 and completed the next year, the building, with its Ionic columns, classical sculptures, and graceful proportions, has made a backdrop for numerous movies and television shows, especially those set in the 1920s. Today Riverside County ranks in the bottom half of counties in the state in per-capita income, but it's still a leader—only now in population growth. Plenty of land plus proximity to Los Angeles made it the fastest growing county in California in the first decade of the twenty-first century: the population soared by 41.7 percent to 2.19 million, which greatly extended the reach of housing into previously wild and open areas, not without consequence. The rising population outstripped the county's legal facilities, and by the time of the Oyler trial in 2009, the historic courthouse had been hemmed in by a high-rise parking garage, a detention center, and the cube-shaped, utilitarian Robert Presley Hall of Justice, which was built to handle civil matters. The historic county courthouse handled criminal trials until a series of escapes emphasized the building's lack of modern-day security. Adult criminal trials were then moved to the Hall of Justice.

♦ ♦ ♦

WHEN THE PROSECUTION and defense finally rested forty-seven days after jury selection had begun in the Raymond Oyler trial, Judge W. Charles Morgan issued his instructions and the jurors solemnly filed from the courtroom. As Deputy David Holland locked the door of the deliberation room behind them, most felt a palpable sense of release. The room was small and sparsely furnished. Two tables pushed together occupied most of the space. Blank whiteboards hung on a wall, and a picture window opened on a bland view. For most of the six-week trial the jurors had been forbidden to talk with family and friends or even each other about the disturbing narrative they'd listened to each day; now, at last, they were free to speak their minds.

"We didn't know each other; we'd never had time to sit down and learn much about each other," said Janis McManigal, an events coordinator who had occupied a seat in the jury box closest to the courtroom's public seats. From there, during the trial, she had overheard whispered comments from victims' family members and their supporters. "It got harder and harder as the story moved along," McManigal said. "These are families, the firemen. By virtue of where I sat I could hear them, 'Oh please God, oh please God.'" She had watched Andrew Bennett, the first incident commander for the Esperanza Fire, as his shoulders slumped and his head dropped down. "I knew he was crying," she said. "It wasn't staged. It was real. I could hear the quiet crying. I started looking down at the carpet."

The first order of business for the jury was the selection of a foreman, and it did not go well. At least two jurors wanted the job: Don Estep, a retired real estate man with a handsome shock of white hair, and Judi Voss, a teacher transplanted from the Midwest to California. But it was Estep who declared, "I'll be it!" Everyone became quiet. No one wanted to ruffle feathers.

"The foreman picked himself," Voss said later. She had wanted the foreman job but also wondered why she was on the jury in the first place. "I couldn't imagine how I got picked. I look too conservative. But if I had been the foreman things would have run differently."

Estep didn't see it that way. "We just went in there and I said, I'll take the job if nobody else really wants it," Estep said. "After a couple of days I realized being foreman wasn't the fun job."

Estep began the proceedings by calling for a show of hands, to see how matters stood. Nine hands went up for guilty, three for not guilty. Estep cast one of the not-guilty votes, he said later, to make sure the process continued to the discussion stage. But the split vote disclosed a division that would endure for many days.

By happenstance, the seating arrangement in the jury room exactly fitted the way the vote kept splitting. Two women jurors, the holdouts, who will be identified here as Stephanie and Amanda (not their real names), were seated together at one corner of the table. Stephanie and Amanda could not accept the prosecution's theory that all the fires were connected or that Raymond Oyler or any other single person was responsible for them. There were too many fires. They couldn't see a consistent pattern. They kept raising the suspicion that a second arsonist might have been at work, which was a justifiable concern: defense attorneys had hinted at the presence of a second arsonist operating in the Banning Pass, and the judge had instructed the jurors to disregard the reference. But as every courtroom lawyer knows, such an admonition does not erase from the minds of jurors the memory of what was said. "We caught the innuendo," McManigal said later.

Seated together at the opposite corner were three other women jurors, all of whom strongly favored conviction: McManigal, Voss, and Ethel Nwandu, a social worker and graduate school student. "The three of us felt we needed to do right by these firefighters; we felt a responsibility to the families," Voss said. "We didn't discuss it among ourselves. It just happened." The three women, self-described as the "power corner," used photographs, documents, arguments, and eventually a transcript of crucial testimony to try to win over the two holdouts.

Those at the "power corner" thought that an excess of sympathy for Oyler was clouding Stephanie's judgment. During the trial, Stephanie's gaze had softened when she looked at Oyler and hardened when Hestrin spoke for the prosecution. Stephanie was from the "other side of the tracks," one juror said. "She had had a hard life, she was an underdog, and she saw Raymond Oyler as an underdog too." Amanda seemed to other jurors like a deer caught in headlights. "Those two women were not getting it, they couldn't see the pattern, they almost put blinders on," said McManigal.

The atmosphere in the jury room became heated, though descriptions of the intensity vary a good deal. "Everyone was congenial; it was a nice bunch of people, though I had to cool it down once or twice," said the jury foreman, Estep. "It wasn't that we didn't agree. We talked it over to make sure we weren't making a mistake. It was so hard for us to say this man is guilty of five murders."

Others remember the exchanges quite differently. "There was a lot of venom in that room," said McManigal, who stopped taking breaks with the others because she didn't want to be around Stephanie and Amanda. At one point, Nwandu snapped at Estep for making jokes and trying to lighten the atmosphere. "I got up and challenged him," she said. "I told him to shut up. I said, 'I didn't come here to sing, to make jokes. It is my duty to take responsibility. We are talking about a human life here, about five lives!' And he apologized."

The jury proceeded in chronological fashion, starting with the first fires in the Banning Pass series on May 16. Estep, the foreman, said that when there was too much jumping from one fire to another, he intervened to pull the discussion back on track. The courtroom testimony about the fires had been tedious, but it wove together a case that depended on connections made of delicate threads. Prosecutors deliberately chose women for the jury, they said, because they could sew facts together.

Day after day, a different Cal Fire engine captain in a trim blue uniform with brass bugles on the collar took the stand and described how he and his crew had arrived at the site of a fire and what pains they had taken to avoid disturbing the point of ignition. Directly after the series had begun, the word had gone out to fire stations in the Banning Pass area to take special care because a serial arsonist was at work. "We knew we had an active arsonist, but those law enforcement guys are close mouthed about details—and they're supposed to be," one engine captain testified. Once a captain had described a fire, Dehart, Gilbert, or another Cal Fire arson investigator would testify about what they had found at that site, from a full-fledged ignition device to a couple of charred matches.

As the jury went over the fires, they found many points of dispute. Had there even been a Banning Pass arson series? Were there enough similarities in how the fires started to show links and an evolution? Could the dozens of fires from May 16 onward truly have been the work of a single man as charged? Oyler had not testified, but did the alibis offered on his behalf hold up? And perhaps most mysterious of all, what kind of man was Raymond Oyler? What kind of man would delight in setting fires knowing they might kill?

For McManigal, it was easy to conclude that the fires were connected. For one thing, she was familiar with the Banning Pass and understood that the fires had been set within easy driving distance of Oyler's residence and workplace. Voss, too, had no trouble seeing patterns. But she had never encountered anyone like Oyler and his courtroom supporters before. "They were sleeping back there in the back row of the courtroom," Voss said with visible disgust. "There's somebody on trial for their life and you're sleeping?"

Photographs, maps, and other exhibits went up on the whiteboards, peppered over with yellow post-its to identify specific spots and make points. The walls came to resemble the inner sanctum of an obsessive madman, or so it seemed to prosecutors who looked in later.

The defense case had focused on the lack of hard evidence linking Oyler to the Esperanza Fire. Oyler's lawyer, Mark McDonald, had had little choice except to admit that Oyler was responsible for the two fires in June where his DNA matched the DNA found on the cigarettes used in the ignition devices. But he tried to turn the admission to Oyler's advantage. McDonald told the jury to go ahead and find Oyler guilty of all ten fires that occurred in June, every one of which employed the layover ignition device, and the Mias Canyon Fire where his Taurus had been seen as well. Bear in mind, McDonald cautioned, that the June fires prove absolutely nothing about Esperanza: the state crime lab had found no DNA on the crucial Esperanza ignition device. Further, the wooden matches used to set the Esperanza Fire were chemically different from the Diamond matches recovered at Laura Breazile's home, the ones found to be similar to those from the June 9 and 10 fires. And the Esperanza device, rather than being an example of an evolution in construction methods, which was the foundation of the prosecution's case, looked a lot like the earliest devices, namely a large bundle of matches held around a cigarette with rubber bands.

Hestrin later acknowledged that the DNA matches, damning as they were, had handed the defense its best argument. "The DNA told us Oyler was our guy," said the chief prosecutor. "But it also gave the defense a strategy: okay, Oyler did these two fires. But he didn't do Esperanza, where no DNA had been found."

McDonald, who had represented Oyler in some of his previous brushes with the law, claimed immediately after Oyler's arrest that his client was flat-out innocent of all charges. McDonald said Oyler was a victim of a "rush to judgment" and a "lynch mob" atmosphere and that he had become virtually "catatonic" with fear and distress. "The finger is pointing at him, but he adamantly denies involvement," McDonald said. In a brief jailhouse interview with the *Press-Enterprise*, Oyler appeared deeply shaken. "I have never done anything with any fires," Oyler said. "Fires hurt people."

Oyler had a good alibi for the one o'clock hour when the Esperanza Fire was set, McDonald said. His sister Joanna, who was with him for part of the fateful night, said Oyler was at home at that hour taking care of the infant Diamond Belle. Oyler's girlfriend and the child's mother, Crystal Breazile, was out shopping at a big box store after finishing a late shift as a waitress at a fast-food restaurant. Crystal would never have left Diamond Belle alone, or even in the care of Joanna Oyler, whom she did not trust, McDonald claimed. And Crystal's departure for a shopping trip had left Oyler without a car to make the fourteen-mile round-trip from apartment to fire scene and back. For her shopping trip, Crystal had taken a car the couple was purchasing, because the infamous Ford Taurus had broken down some time before. It had been left in a shopping mall parking lot many miles from the fire scene. A security camera at that mall took an image of the Taurus at 1:08 AM, only minutes before the Esperanza Fire was reported. So how did Oyler make the round-trip?

McDonald said the prosecution theory that the ignition devices were all the work of the same arsonist was fanciful; cigarettes, wooden matches, and rubber bands have been used for decades to start arson fires. McDonald said no fewer than seven different kinds of incendiary devices had been used in the Banning Pass series, which indicated the presence of two, possibly three, arsonists. McDonald called to the stand an arson expert, David Smith, who testified that the Banning Pass series was "the work of multiple, unrelated arsonists." Once an arsonist discovered a device that worked, Smith said, he never changed the pattern. Smith said he knew of dozens of arson cases where wooden matches were used, including some in California. Smith's credibility suffered a blow, however, when the prosecution drew from him the admission that he had never investigated a serial arson case in his life. Called to the stand to rebut Smith was Douglas Allen, the retired Cal Fire arson investigator, who began by saying he had participated in more than one hundred arson investigations. Serial arsonists typically learn from experience, Allen said, and they do change their ways to avoid detection and to light bigger and more destructive fires. The Banning Pass series showed every sign of an evolutionary pattern, he said, and certainly could have been the work of one person.

That in essence was the case for the defense, with one notable exception: the specter of another suspect, a second arsonist at work in the Banning Pass. Oyler had set some of the fires for certain, but in the jury room, the holdouts, Amanda and Stephanie, repeatedly asked the same troubling question, "How could one person have started *all* these fires?" They had more reason to ask than they knew.

Only a few weeks before the Oyler trial began, a Forest Service "confidential" investigation report about arson in the Banning Pass had come to light. The report, compiled in 2008, named a Forest Service firefighter, Michael McNeil, as a possible suspect in some of the 2006 fires in the Banning Pass. The report, apparently written to support an ultimately successful effort to dismiss McNeil from the Forest Service, said that nineteen fires in 2006 "may possibly be associated with McNeil." Of that number, five were on Oyler's charge sheet; the report made no mention of the Esperanza Fire. At the time of Oyler's trial, McNeil was in jail on arson and criminal threat charges in an unrelated case in which he allegedly made violent threats to discredit his wife.

News of the "confidential" report, publicly disclosed on the eve of the Oyler trial in a story by Richard K. De Atley, a well-respected courthouse reporter for the *Press-Enterprise,* brought a surge of hope to the defense—and consternation to the prosecution. In effect, the report said that even two years after Oyler was charged with murdering five Forest Service firefighters, the agency suspected one of its own of setting fires in the Banning Pass series. If that suspicion could be backed up by evidence, it would hand the defense a powerful weapon to argue for reasonable doubt that Oyler was the lone arsonist in the series and guilty of setting the Esperanza Fire.

The Forest Service report, in a section on southern California's 2006 fire season, noted that wildland arson fires that year had "rocketed to levels rarely observed." More than eighty fires had been identified as arson. About 90 percent of those fires, the report said, occurred on or very near McNeil's assigned prevention patrol area, the San Jacinto District, where many of the Banning Pass fires occurred. The eleven-page document, written by Special Agent Diane Welton, was based mostly on information supplied by Special Agent Ron Huxman, who had years of acquaintance with McNeil that Huxman characterized as "only a very distant working relationship."

Huxman had good reason to distance himself from McNeil, whose long and troubled history as a firefighter was well documented in the Forest Service report. It seemed every time McNeil joined a fire department, the number of fire starts jumped exponentially, but then dropped off as soon as he left. McNeil would show up at fires minutes after they were reported and had an uncanny ability to locate points of origin. Fellow employees more than once had refused to work with him, citing disturbed and offensive behavior. "All indicators of a firefighter-arsonist were present," the Forest Service report stated.

One reported incident was typical: McNeil moved from California to Utah in 1995 and joined the Apple Valley Township fire department as a volunteer. Fire Chief Louie Ford became suspicious after McNeil reported a number of wildland fires, which were starting up with unusual regularity. McNeil often was first on the scene and quickly discovered ignition devices. "The device McNeil found which threw Chief Ford over the edge was a rolled-up piece of paper, a bunch of matches, and a cigarette," the Forest Service report said, describing a device with an eerie similarity to ones used in the Banning Pass series. After Chief Ford confronted McNeil and he left the area, the report said, the rash of fires came to a halt.

McNeil bounced from job to job, with the Forest Service and U.S. Fish and Wildlife Service, and then was hired again by the Forest Service in June 2005. He was assigned as a "fire prevention technician" at the Banning Pass station on the San Jacinto Ranger District, just in time for the Banning Pass arson series. "I didn't like McNeil from the first day," said B.J. Scott, the Vista Grande Hotshot whose family home along Twin Pines Road had been threatened by the Esperanza Fire. "We don't have blue lights like cops, but he used to make traffic stops in town, stuff like that. We'd go looking for a fire, engines going up roads all over the place and finding nothing, and he'd lead us right to the spot. That kind of thing just doesn't happen. You don't find fires like that."

The Forest Service report details McNeil's many misadventures, but it has a glaring omission. It fails to note that McNeil had been eliminated as a suspect in the Banning Pass series long before the report was written. McNeil was an obvious and early suspect. At one point in mid-June, as fires popped up with increasing regularity, agents placed a tracking device on McNeil's fire vehicle, as they did on many others. The device stayed there for over a month, from June 16 to July 25, during which time at least nine arson fires occurred, nearly all in and around Banning. The tracker exonerated McNeil as a suspect in those fires. If that wasn't enough, his vehicle had been searched, and a container he used as a spittoon yielded DNA, which was analyzed and found to be different from the DNA recovered from the devices found at the two June arson fires.

The failure of the Forest Service report to note that McNeil had been discounted as a suspect was not lost on the prosecutors. "I was beside myself; that was the low point of the trial," said Hestrin. "That was the worst report I've ever seen. There was nothing there to link him to the fires, just the 'could be a suspect' statement. That doesn't cut it. There is no evidence McNeil was responsible for any of the fires in that series—subsequent behavior, proximity, nothing. But there is hard evidence to show he was not connected to the fires. They put out that report without even calling or contacting us. If they had called I would have said, 'You're going to include the hard evidence, right? The evidence showing he was *not* linked to the fire?' This guy McNeil is not our arsonist."

In a hearing before Judge Morgan, without the jury present, the prosecution and defense attorneys argued whether or not the Forest Service report should be allowed as evidence in Oyler's trial. The chief witness was Huxman, who said he had first encountered McNeil in 2004, when Huxman was a special investigator for the Forest Service on the San Bernardino National Forest. McNeil had repeatedly telephoned him to offer his services as a fire investigator. "He kept calling me about getting hired," said Huxman, who found it strange that McNeil also offered to bring along a dog supposedly trained to sniff out arson. McNeil's behavior had aroused suspicions as early as 2005, Huxman said, though nothing was done about it. The next year, as the Banning Pass series began, Huxman began checking into McNeil's past.

"Soon after McNeil was hired, suspicious fires increased where there had been no fires before?" McDonald asked Huxman.

"Yes, that did occur," Huxman replied.

The case against McNeil as a second Banning Pass arsonist began to break down, however, as Hestrin cross-examined Huxman, who acknowledged that of the nineteen fires associated with McNeil in the Forest Service report, twelve were later found not even to be arson fires or were of "undetermined causes." The five fires in the Banning Pass series that the report "possibly associated" with McNeil were the three small fires that began the series on May 16, a 7-acre fire on June 14, and a 3-acre fire on October 22.

"Is there any evidence that Michael McNeil was involved in any of the fires in the Banning Pass area?" Hestrin asked.

Huxman, who appeared relieved to be able to disavow any link between McNeil and the Esperanza Fire, replied, "There is no evidence direct or circumstantial. Our suspicions were relieved with Mr. McNeil." Huxman said he drew up the investigation report because McNeil, who had been transferred to a different national forest by 2008, had become a "thorn in the side of the Forest Service." In June of 2008, just days before the July 1 date of the report, the Forest Service filed a "Notice of Proposed Removal" for McNeil and subsequently fired him. Long after the Oyler trial, in 2011, McNeil was sentenced to nineteen years in California state prison after he pleaded no contest to six counts of making criminal threats and three counts of attempted criminal threats against elected officials and others during a divorce battle with his wife. His one-time lawyer, Lassen County public defender David Marcus, said the threats were delusional but alarming. "He threatened to blow us all up with dirty bombs," Marcus said. "I don't know that he really had that capability. But you couldn't ignore them either."

At the conclusion of the hearing about whether to tell the Oyler jury about McNeil, Judge Morgan observed that no link had been established between McNeil and any of the fires in the Banning Pass series. "The Forest Service didn't like this guy," the judge said. "He was a bad seed everywhere he has been. But even saying this, they haven't linked him to any fire. There has to be some nexus to one of the crimes, direct or circumstantial. And there has been no showing of that." The judge ruled that the Forest Service report could not be entered as evidence in Oyler's trial.

The matter did not end there. As the jurors returned from lunch on the day of closing arguments, several found a copy of a *Los Angeles Times* article about the Forest Service report on McNeil tucked under the windshield wiper blades of their vehicles, which were parked in a lot reserved for jurors. Three of the jurors reported the incident to the court. An infuriated Judge Morgan ordered the courtroom closed and summoned the jurors, one by one, to determine whether or not they could continue with the case. The prospect of a mistrial loomed.

The jurors had to walk from an elevator past a throng of spectators and media to enter the courtroom. They marched by wordlessly, their facial expressions pregnant with secret knowledge. Excited rumors swept the gathered press corps, and one rumor turned out to be true: there had been jury tampering. The closed courtroom session lasted for nearly an hour. The judge determined that the jury had not been tainted, and the trial resumed without public explanation. From that time forward, however, sheriff's deputies escorted the jurors to and from the jury room. Meanwhile, the confiscated newspaper articles were sent to the state forensic lab for analysis.

Less than a month later, the lab reported that a fingerprint on one of the copies matched that of Christopher Vaughn Hillman, 47, who was married to Oyler's sister Jennifer. Hillman had been a regular attendee at Oyler's trial, giving the media hard looks. Hillman turned himself in to police and claimed he had been out of town when the clippings were put under the wiper blades. During his trial in July 2010, Hillman's attorney suggested that Hillman had touched the fliers when he discovered them at home and had angrily tried to grab and destroy them. A jury found Hillman guilty of seven counts of jury tampering. Deputy District Attorney Tim Cross argued for jail time, but Hillman was sentenced to three hundred hours of community service and three years' probation and was fined $4,200. "I think it's unfathomable that someone can attempt to influence a jury in a capital murder case—one of the most important cases in the history of this county—and a judge gives no jail time," Cross told the *Press-Enterprise*.

The jury tampering case was a sideshow to the main event, the

Oyler trial, and while the newspaper clipping had no apparent effect on the Oyler jurors, they had plenty of other matters to consider and dispute. For a time it looked as though they had reached an impasse and would never agree.

16.

THE JURY LABORED IN ISOLATION, day after day recording split votes of ten to two for conviction. Stephanie and Amanda would not budge; the women at the "power corner" continued to throw out arguments for conviction. The DNA matches for the two June fires were solid facts, but there was other evidence linking Oyler to the arson series, including sightings of Oyler, or someone who looked just like him, at several of the arson fire sites. The truck driver James Carney Jr., who had identified Oyler as the figure lurking at the Shell station on the night of the Esperanza Fire, was not the only eyewitness.

On June 11, a driver had parked along Highway 243 at Mount Edna Road, near the site of the 1998 fire in which air tanker pilot Gary Nagel had been killed, to give his dog a run. The driver, John C. Lawrence, had noticed a Ford coming down Highway 243 and said it was either a Taurus or a Sable. The vehicle had been amateurishly spray-painted, Lawrence testified, in a color that could be described as brown, blue, or black. He said he was certain, though, that he saw red-and-black flame tattoos on the male driver's left arm, from elbow to wrist, as the Ford passed by. Minutes later, Lawrence saw a puff of smoke and then flames from the direction the Ford had come.

"Look around the court," said the prosecutor, Hestrin. "Do you see that man?"

"He's that gentleman sitting right over there," Lawrence said without hesitation, indicating Oyler. Throughout the trial, Oyler had been dressed in shirts and suit jackets that covered his tattoos.

Another witness, Ronald McKay, had testified that he saw the Ford Taurus, described this time as brown. He saw it on June 14, three days after Lawrence's sighting, as he walked to his brother-in-law's house in Banning. McKay waved at the driver, who had short hair and a mustache. As he drove off, smoke from a wildfire appeared where the Taurus had been. McKay identified the Ford Taurus from photos but could not positively identify Oyler as the driver.

In a bizarre twist, Oyler's second cousin Jill Frame testified that just days before the Esperanza Fire, Oyler had talked about "setting the mountain on fire" as a diversion so he could free his pet pit bulls from an animal shelter where they had been impounded. It was a strange and confusing story. For one thing, the dogs had been released by the time of the fire. But the phrase "setting the mountain on fire" was a memorable one. During cross-examination, however, defense counsel McDonald accused Frame of turning in her cousin solely for the reward money. She in fact had told her mother that was what she was going to do. When McDonald confronted Frame with her own words, she said it had been a joke. McDonald's charge stung, however, and years later Frame would take a revenge of sorts.

The fuel truck driver, Carney, proved to be the only eyewitness who could link Oyler directly to the Esperanza Fire, and he made the point in dramatic fashion. Carney's initial testimony for the prosecution was straightforward. Carney told how he had watched a hunched figure of a man scuttle back and forth among gasoline pumps at the Shell station where Carney was making a delivery. The man had sounded so authoritative in describing the fire behavior they were watching on Cabazon Peak that Carney thought he must be a firefighter. "The fire's acting just how I thought it ought to, just the way I thought it would," the man had said, according to Carney. He described how he had identified Oyler as the man at the station from police mug shots, and then he identified him again in court. McDonald, however, attacked Carney's credibility as an observer. Carney had been attending to the gasoline delivery and it was dark outside. The man he saw was hunched and muffled in a jacket. Carney had been very hesitant in identifying Oyler when first interviewed by police, McDonald said. "Considering how tentative you were in the tape-recorded interview with detectives, how have you become so certain now?" the defense lawyer asked.

Carney stiffened. Being a credible observer was obviously a matter of pride to him. He said he hadn't been "tentative" at all when he picked out Oyler from mug shots. He merely had warned detectives that he wanted to be absolutely certain before committing himself. That wasn't good enough for McDonald, who kept hammering away until at last Carney had had enough. He straightened in the witness chair, looked out at the audience in the courtroom, and surprised everyone, including prosecutors who had put him on the stand, by announcing that he could be so certain in making the identification because he had been a photo analyst for the air force for five years during the Vietnam War. McDonald appeared to deflate. Carney, dressed in a black open shirt and black trousers that gave him a Johnny Cash look, knew he had made an impression. He proudly tilted his head and took a slow walk past the jury box on his way out of court, looking right past McDonald.

Eyewitness accounts are dramatic, compelling, and notoriously unreliable, and the eyewitness sightings in the Oyler trial did not convince the jury's holdouts, Stephanie and Amanda, to change their votes. They had less trouble over the issue of whether Oyler had a car available that night: the prosecution had established that an acquaintance's car was available to Oyler. Finally, facing deadlock, the jurors began separating the twenty-three fires on the charge sheet into groups depending on the weight of evidence for each. Into one group they placed the eleven fires that the defense admitted Oyler had set: the ten June fires in which layover devices were used, including the two that yielded Oyler's DNA, and the Mias Canyon Fire. Stephanie and Amanda agreed to vote guilty on those counts. In another group they placed the three fires that had no physical evidence of a link to Oyler—no ignition device, no witnesses, no surveillance photos. Stephanie and Amanda said they would never vote to convict on those fires, two on May 29 and one on May 31. The crucial murder and arson charges connected to the Esperanza Fire made up a separate group.

The dispute finally came down to a single point. Stephanie and Amanda said that Oyler had never admitted setting a single fire, not to his girlfriend Crystal Breazile, not to anyone. They remembered her testifying that he had threatened to set fires but not that he had actually set one. Breazile had been an unwilling witness, and her testimony had been disjointed and confusing. She had done her best to exonerate Oyler, insisting that he would have been at home with their child, Diamond Belle, at the time the Esperanza Fire was set. At one point, prosecutors had confronted her with an interview she gave police directly after Oyler's arrest, before he was charged with murder and the gravity of the case against him became apparent. Breazile had ducked and dodged and claimed memory loss, making for very disjointed testimony. Several of the jurors had taken notes, however, that indicated Oyler had told Breazile that he had set fires, maybe more than one. Stephanie and Amanda had taken no notes. If Oyler had admitted to setting fires, the two holdouts conceded, they would consider changing their minds and voting for conviction. There was only one way to settle the matter, and the jury sent for the transcript of Breazile's testimony.

♦ ♦ ♦

ON WEDNESDAY, NOVEMBER 1, the day after Oyler's arrest, Detective Michaels went to interview Breazile at the apartment of her mother, Laura, in Cherry Valley, just north of Beaumont, where Crystal was staying. At the time, Oyler had been charged only with two counts of arson for the June 9 and 10 fires. Michaels had chosen another Riverside County detective, Robert Dean Spivacke, to join him for the interview, because he had worked with him before and admired his interview technique. The two detectives, it turned out, had just this one chance to win the trust of mother and daughter before murder charges were filed and made public, which happened the next day, and the family went on the defensive. "We know how the game is played," Spivacke said later. "Family members circle the wagons irrespective of guilt. Their attitude is, anything to protect him."

The detectives had a hard time getting past the Breaziles' front door. "When we got there Crystal was a bit defensive," Spivacke said. "We took our time; we wanted her cooperative." After several minutes of chatting, the women let the detectives into the apartment. The atmosphere was polite but tense. Crystal sat on a sofa and her mother sat protectively close, on the arm of the sofa; Crystal kept nervously groping for a missing button on her sweater.

Spivacke told the women that it was time to focus on what was going to happen to them rather than to Oyler. Crystal needed to think of herself and her baby, Diamond Belle. The detectives needed to hear the truth and they needed to hear it now, while the investigation was at an early stage. They were out to solve a crime, not to railroad someone. They would work just as hard to prove innocence as guilt. DNA evidence, however, tied Oyler to fires set on June 9 and 10. Oyler was an arsonist for sure. This was the moment for them to talk.

After a half hour, Laura Breazile asked the detectives if they would like a drink of water. Spivacke had to stop himself from winking at Michaels. "That's when I knew she had accepted us; the mother was mellow," Spivacke said.

It was a tricky moment. When Laura went for the water, Michaels saw a chance to separate mother and daughter, if only for a minute or two. He figured Crystal probably had been lying to her mother and would have a hard time changing her story with her mother hovering nearby. But if Crystal had a few private minutes with Spivacke, she might find the courage to tell the truth. So when Laura came back with the water, Michaels began a separate conversation with her.

"It felt like clockwork," Michaels said. "The gears were aligned."

Spivacke, also sensing the opportunity, watched Crystal for nonverbal signs of an attitude change. Sure enough, her body relaxed. She put her face in her hands and turned confessional. "This wasn't fluff; I could tell by the words she was using that we were on the right road," Spivacke said. "It's hard to cry and lie at the same time."

Oyler had bragged about having set fires, Crystal admitted, and she had threatened to leave him if he didn't stop—the timing for the ultimatum, it was later determined, would account for the summer hiatus in the Banning Pass arson series. During a quarrel in their apartment, she said, Oyler had pointed to the TV they were watching and claimed he had started the fire that was being reported right then. Another time Oyler had claimed he used cigarettes and matches to start fires in a way to implicate relatives he thought were keeping him from one of his children. Still another time, Crystal had found a baggie full of newspaper clippings about arson fires hidden in a cupboard in their apartment. And Oyler was always listening to fire calls on a scanner.

"I pinned her down by coaxing and convincing, saying things like, 'I want to make sure I'm good on this, that I'm clear on this,'" Spivacke said. "She would give a little and then become hesitant.

It's a process. I gave constant positive reinforcement, saying things like, 'You're doing good; you're doing the right thing.'"

After several hours the detectives thanked the women and walked outside to their car. Until that moment, they had maintained a calm, serious demeanor. "No nonverbal body celebration," Spivacke said. Once outside, they could hardly restrain themselves. "I was happy because I knew Crystal had burned him to the ground," Spivacke said. "I knew we were golden. There was no ambiguity. I knew it was going to be important. I knew it would play a part."

Afterward, though, Michaels had a sense of sadness about the encounter. "I can still to this day picture every detail of that room down to the missing button in Crystal's sweater," Michaels said. "Spivacke and I knew there were no second chances. When she was tired of him, I talked; when she was tired of me, he talked, until the truth was her only option. It was sad in a way, because I knew she would never be the same person again after we left."

When the transcript of Crystal Breazile's testimony arrived in the jury room, it was no easy task to figure out exactly what she had said. Breazile had refused to be interviewed by the prosecution before court proceedings began, but at the preliminary hearing she acknowledged that she had decided to leave Oyler at one point because he admitted he was setting fires. Hestrin leaned over to Mayman after that answer and said, "Did she just say what I think she said?" The job of the prosecutors then was to get the same admission out of her at the formal trial, but it had been a struggle. Her interview with the two detectives, which had been publicly reported, had made her a pariah in the Oyler family. At the murder trial, she tried her best to deny what she had said to Michaels and Spivacke. A typical exchange:

"Just look at that page to yourself, please; let me know when you're finished," Hestrin said, handing a transcript of the interview with detectives to Breazile.

"Even reading it, I really can't remember saying that," Breazile said.

"Can you just—did you get a chance to read it?"

"I read it."

"Okay."

"But I don't remember saying that."

Under heavy prodding, Breazile acknowledged that Oyler had told her he had set fires, but claimed it had happened in early 2006, before the Banning Pass series began.

"You said that Mr. Oyler told you he set the fire that was on TV," Hestrin said.

"Yes," Breazile replied.

"And you said this fire was where?"

"Moreno Valley."

"Did you and Mr. Oyler continue to have an argument about it?"

"It was a long argument."

"But was the argument you had about him specifically setting fires?"

"Him saying that he did, yes."

"And at some point you gave him an ultimatum. What was the ultimatum that you gave him?"

"That if he was doing this, I was going to leave."

"You told the detectives in your previous interview that you had your bags packed."

"Yes."

"And that was because you believed he was starting fires at that moment, right?"

"It was my concern, yes."

After further discussion, Hestrin asked, "When he talked to you about starting fires, did he ever talk to you about his tactics or plans that he used to start fires? In other words, how he did it?"

"With a cigarette and a match."

"Do you remember telling detectives that he had told you some things about how he did it?"

"With a cigarette and a match."

That was enough even for Stephanie and Amanda.

"Oh, damn, he really did it to himself, didn't he?" Stephanie said.

She and Amanda were prepared to vote guilty on the murder charges, but there was one more hurdle to clear: the three fires in May. Stephanie and Amanda had vowed never to vote guilty on those three. The jury had reached deadlock. They sent a note to Judge Morgan explaining the breakdown, which caused another round of rumors about a mistrial. Only a judge, however, can declare a mistrial. "Step back and it may become clearer," Judge Morgan advised. "You have to consider everything substantial. We're here to help. Send us notes. Send us requests. Is that clear?"

The jurors decided to put the three disputed fires aside and vote on the other charges. The list was long, and they did not finish until late in the day. Drained by the effort, they went home for the night. When they returned to the jury room the next day, they spent the morning doing paperwork left over from the previous day's marathon session. It was not until 11:45 AM that Sheriff's Deputy Holland told two observers who were on watch outside the courtroom—Richard De Atley of the *Press-Enterprise* and me—that the jury had reached a verdict. It would be announced in precisely two hours, Holland said, which was barely time for all the firefighter families, some of whom lived many miles away, to get back to the courtroom. The families had set up an alert network for just such a contingency, but the deliberations had gone on so long that no family representative was stationed at the courthouse. The families had a right to be there, so I stepped out of the observer role for a moment and called a family representative, who spread the news. Two hours later, as the jury filed into a tension-laden courtroom, the last of the families slipped into their seats.

The Oyler clan was well represented, scattered in the backbenches. Several, though, came into court crying. "They seemed to know," said Vivian Najera. "His sister had a face full of tears."

The jurors struggled to keep their faces blank, but their expressions were full of repressed knowledge, a solemn sense of responsibility, and awareness of being the center of attention. After quick glances around, they took their seats and stared at nothing. "Walking into that courtroom was the hardest thing I ever did," McManigal said. The jury handed over a fat stack of verdict forms to Judge Morgan. After reading through them for a few minutes, he raised his head with a stern look, sending a shock wave through the spectator seats and the jury box. Had something vital gone wrong at this, the ultimate moment? To everyone's relief, the judge ordered the jury to retire and fix a minor clerical error in signing and dating forms.

At 1:54 PM on Friday, March 6, after six days of jury deliberations and less than two and a half years after the Esperanza Fire, the judge handed the forms to the court clerk, Gina Gurrola, who read out the verdicts in a strong, clear voice, starting with the murder charges. "Guilty," she said, and a wave of emotion swept the courtroom. There were gasps but no general outcry. On the firefighter side of the room, some held hands and pressed against each other. Some wept silent tears of release. Seated in rows behind the families were more than a dozen uniformed firefighters, their eyes shining with powerful emotion. One of them put his head on a friend's shoulder and left it there. Oyler's supporters put their arms around each other, hugged, and tried to stifle sobs.

Gurrola asked the jurors after each finding if that was their verdict, and they replied in unison, "Yes." It took thirty-five minutes to deal with the charge list. The jury found Oyler guilty of five counts of first-degree murder, twenty counts of arson, and seventeen counts of use of an incendiary device. They declared themselves deadlocked on the three disputed fires, the ones Stephanie and Amanda said they would never vote on for conviction, and Judge Morgan declared a mistrial on those charges, in effect dismissing them.

The courtroom began to empty. Sheriff's deputies shackled Oyler hand and foot and started to lead him out a side door. Dressed in a gray suit, blue shirt, and striped tie, Oyler had shown no emotion as the verdicts were read. When family members cried out to him, "I love you, Raymond!" he cast a final stricken glance over his shoulder. Then he was led away and the courtroom door closed behind him.

17.

FATAL FIRES DIE DOWN BUT they never die out. A fatal fire burns for generations, scarring forever the lives of those who knew the risks but lived in the hope that a much-loved face would always turn up again at the kitchen door, tired and dirty but smiling and alive. There are "gifts of the fire" to be sure: an outpouring of compassion, a reaffirmation of the brotherhood of fire, lessons learned. But the penalty phase of the trial of Raymond Oyler, which followed the guilty verdicts, was not about gifts. Rather it was about what remains when the embers have cooled, the memorial services are over, the old bedrooms of sons or daughters have been preserved in the amber of remembrance—with all things kept as they were then—and the reality of irretrievable loss has settled in.

The guilty verdicts required a follow-on proceeding before the same jury to decide whether Oyler should be imprisoned for life without parole or face the death penalty. Each juror had been asked before being selected whether he or she could impose the ultimate penalty, if circumstances warranted, and all had said they could. Under California law, there are seventeen special circumstances justifying the death penalty. A few of these special circumstances are directly connected to arson. Two of these are murder done while committing an act of arson, and the murder of a firefighter engaged in professional duties when the murderer knew or should have known the victim was a firefighter. The prosecutors instead chose the simplest of the special circumstances: conviction for more than one murder in the same incident.

The mood of a death penalty hearing is very different from that of a trial to determine guilt or innocence. A trial is supposed to deal primarily with facts. It's like a puzzle in search of a solution—a solution that may or may not be convincing. The theme of a death penalty hearing, by contrast, is about loss: the loss for family and loved ones of the fallen, and the potential loss of life for the defendant. The first person to break down during the death penalty hearing was Oyler. His behavior, which had been relatively composed during the guilt phase, turned bizarre at an administrative hearing held even before the jury was called in.

As the hearing began at 9:00 AM, he greeted his two defense counsels with a "Good afternoon." He wore a shirt and tie but for the first time no jacket—his shirtsleeves were down and covered his flame-and-death's-head tattoos. He made little shrugs of his shoulders, mumbled, jerked his head one way or another, and stared at a courtroom clock. He told his lawyers he could see little men marching across the defense table. When the behavior continued into the next day, the judge ordered an examination by a court-appointed physician, Dr. Robert Suiter; no claim was ever made that Oyler was mentally incompetent to stand trial. Dr. Suiter determined that while Oyler was not mentally deficient, he was at the time returning to his jail cell so late in the day, on account of court proceedings, that he was missing his medications. He had prescriptions for seven different medications to treat high blood pressure, depression, stomach upset, and tremors. "This is a bad time in his life. He's in a place he doesn't want to be; it's a very anxious time," Judge Morgan said. He ruled that the proceedings continue—and that Oyler would receive his medications.

On Tuesday, March 10, with the jury back in the courtroom for the death penalty hearing, Hestrin cautioned that the testimony and exhibits would be both graphic and emotional. Oyler was not only guilty of setting fires, Hestrin said, he was also capable of cruelty, and the jury would be given evidence to show his cruelty. Family members and loved ones would testify about what the loss of the men of Engine 57 meant to them. "You have to determine the loss to families and the community," Hestrin said. "They were real men, living, breathing, with dreams and hopes."

The rules about evidence would be different too. Judge Morgan ruled that Hestrin could describe for the jury two extra Banning Pass arson fires, where too little evidence had been recovered to justify bringing charges. The first of these two fires was reported at 7:30 AM on the morning of the Esperanza Fire, within minutes of the time the area ignition swept the crew of Engine 57. Oyler had clocked in at the auto shop twenty-two minutes later, at 7:52 AM, which gave him time to set that fire before work.

A TV at the auto shop was on all that day, and the fatalities were the talk of the workplace, a coworker would testify. There were no more arson fires during the day, while Oyler was at work. A surveillance camera at a gasoline station spotted him in a giddy mood after work, at 4:51 PM. The camera caught Oyler in the gas station kiosk grinning and patting a blonde woman on her bottom. The second arson fire was started seven minutes later.

And with that, the Banning Pass arson series of fires came to an end.

Judge Morgan ruled that the jury could see autopsy photos that he had excluded as inflammatory during the guilt phase of the trial. The judge warned that the photos were "horrible," the most disturbing he had seen in more than two decades on the bench. (Family members were cautioned the day before the photos were shown that they might not want to attend. "You are all welcome to come to court," a family liaison officer wrote in an e-mail.

"However, these picts are not something I am recommending any of you view!")

In his opening remarks, Hestrin warned the jury that he would take them on a journey of the imagination and spirit back to the mountain where the men of Engine 57 had met their fate. He would ask them to consider the meaning of the bits of clothing and gear left there, the footprints and the body locations, and to join insofar as possible the crew of Engine 57 during their final moments. "We're going to have to go back up to that mountain and consider their last moments and decisions and their struggle for life," Hestrin said. Before this, Hestrin said, he had talked about five men. Now, *they would have faces.*

The Forest Service captains who had been with Engine 57 on Twin Pines Ridge were the first to take the stand and tell their tale. The engine captains wore their hair a little longer, their green-and-tan uniforms a little looser than Cal Fire's more regimented ranks; "woodsy owls," some called them. Fogle was the first to testify. He said he had worked with Loutzenhiser for sixteen years and had been best friends with him for much of that time. As Fogle told his story, the prosecution showed the jury still images and video clips taken by Fogle's crew from the Tile House, the same time the area ignition had engulfed the Octagon House. The ignition had happened so quickly, Fogle said, "there isn't a measurable rate of speed." He told the jury how he had tried to reach Loutzenhiser by radio, calling, "Captain 57, Captain 52," how he had walked up the driveway and found Cerda and Loutzenhiser, and how after spending a few moments with his best friend he had gone in search of those still missing. He related how he and fellow captains had used canteens to douse flames still burning on one of the bodies.

After Fogle finished his testimony, Gearhart took the stand and described how he and the others at the double-wide location had "burned out around our area to ensure our survival." As he described the ordeal of the aftermath, when he had declared the crew of Engine 57 dead and then reversed himself, several members of fire families became so emotional that they had to leave the courtroom; they composed themselves and returned within minutes.

Dinkel and Espinoza took the stand in turn. They related how they had helped put Cerda onto a backboard to be airlifted from the site. "Everything's okay, they're coming up to help," Espinoza had told Pablo.

Hestrin asked Espinoza what lessons the fire had taught him. Espinoza had to pause for thought. "I don't trust the judgment of a lot of fire supervisors until I get a chance to check it myself," Espinoza said.

The jury sat mesmerized. There was no longer a question of guilt or innocence to decide, and most of the jurors appeared to follow the testimony with utter credulity. They tried to check their reactions and appear neutral, but their bodies leaned in their chairs toward the witness box and their eyes burned with sympathy. The dissenters, Stephanie and Amanda, seemed troubled, however, as though they were wrestling with powerful emotions they could not control and would rather not feel.

Maria Loutzenhiser was the first family member to testify. After taking her seat in the witness box and glancing nervously around the courtroom, she looked straight at the jurors. Her narrative jumped around a bit, but the jury had no trouble following her meaning. Mark Loutzenhiser was "the calm, patient one, not crazy like me," she said. She had driven him nuts sometimes because she would call him three times a day, just to hear his voice and feel the calm of his presence. They had done everything together: fought fire, played volleyball, raised children. Loving friends had rallied for her after Mark's death; Janey Espinoza had virtually moved in with her for most of a year. Friends, neighbors, and a community group had rebuilt the Loutzenhiser house in Idyllwild from the foundation up. Maria had an abiding faith in God, much encouraged by others. But Mark had been the foundation of her life, her anchor, and she was left now with a great emptiness.

When she had raced down the mountain to see Mark at the hospital, she said, she had been grateful that he looked presentable: his face appeared to be sunburned and a blanket covered his body. He hadn't spoken, and the doctors kept insisting he was dead. They were wrong, she told the jurors; she could see it in his eyes. He had lived until she was finished saying things to him, things that had to be said. It was tough raising the children, three boys including the twins, plus the two girls, without having Mark around. "Just because I can run a chain saw, it's not the same thing," she said. "It's been real hard. Friends help out a lot, but it's not the same. I loved him. It makes me real angry. I miss his laugh, his smile. I miss a lot of stuff."

When Maria was finished, Hestrin asked the judge for a break and left the courtroom. A few minutes later, Hestrin stood in the corridor outside with tears in his eyes.

For each member of the Engine 57 crew, the prosecution showed the jury a slide show assembled from family photos. The scenes of childhood, growing up, and adulthood brought an occasional light moment: a photo of the Loutzenhiser daughter Savannah wearing goofy, oversize sunglasses brought a giggle from Savannah and smiles from others.

The rest of the families each took a turn in the witness box. Jason McKay had been the man in his family from the time he was 12 years old, when his father ran off, and had lived with his mother, three sisters, and grandmother until he was 25. With all those women around, his mother, Bonnie, joked to the jury, "He had to be ornery to survive." He was the one the McKay women counted on to lift their spirits. "He had a rough start, but he was a beautiful young man," she said. She related with sadness the story of her last communication with Jason, a series of instant messages on the computer. She had been upset that he hadn't checked in with her since August; he had missed his grandmother Penny's birthday on September 16. Jason finally sent an electronic message and asked Bonnie how she was doing. Angry at his long silence, Bonnie said she abruptly typed back a reply: "Fine, busy. In fact I'm busy right now."

"I guess I have to let you go then," Jason responded.

"Yes, yes you do," she wrote back, and those last words left behind an echoing silence.

The photos of Pablo Cerda in family settings, as a soccer player and as a graduate of the fire academy, portray a young man who found a footing in society through sports, hard work, and strong family ties. "We were together all the time; he was very supportive of me," his father, Pablo Sr., told the jury through an interpreter. When Pablo Sr. and his daughter, Claudia, arrived at Arrowhead Medical Center, where Pablo was being treated, they were told he was in a coma and would not survive. Father and sister were the ones who made the decision six days later to end the medical life support. Pablo Sr. said that ever since then he had not been able to work or concentrate on much of anything. "As long as I have, I'm never going to be able to get rid of this," Pablo Sr. said. "It's on my mind all the time."

Daniel Najera had a rough start in life and a rocky adolescence—crazy hair, heavy alcohol use. After being passed from his birth mother, Gloria Ayala, to the care of his grandparents and aunt, Vivian Najera, he was passed back again as a teenager to Gloria. He was basically a fun-loving and happy-go-lucky personality, and once he turned his behavior around, he was seldom without a skateboard and a smile. When he joined the fire service, he seemed to have found himself.

"Danny is no longer down the hallway, no longer a conversation away," Ayala said. "I still speak to him often, and I trust in his silence that he's listening. I regret never having the opportunity to see my son experience what it's like to be a husband, a father, or an example to his younger sister and brother, Monica and Michael. My only hope with this pain is that no other mother would have to go through the experience I'm feeling."

Jess McLean had had to contend with the loss of a father, as had McKay and Najera, and the experience had been sobering. McLean, a troublesome youngster, small in size but a fierce competitor, became the one who held things together for others. As soon as he was old enough, his older brother, Joshua, told the jury, Jess was down at the Cabazon fire station trying to join the department. In the courtroom, a photo of McLean as a hotshot went up on a screen. He was taking a break in an idyllic mountain meadow, leaning back, sporting wraparound sunglasses, with a blue bandana wrapped around his head under his hard hat. The composed look on his face told the tale: he was a poster boy for wildland firefighters.

Joshua then said what many others had felt. The words came slowly and evenly, as though they had been in his mind for a long time.

"He didn't go up that mountain to die," Joshua told the jury. "The way he died pisses me off. If my brother would have died in a fire that was started by lightning, it would have been easier to deal with. My brother got murdered, and that's something I don't know how to deal with. He should not be dead. I have a rage that I can't even explain to you. He knew the risk of his job. It will never be right."

The defense began its presentation with a photomontage of its own, showing Oyler as a child and youth. The oldest of Oyler's four daughters, 21-year-old Heather, said he had been a good influence in her life, even though she had lived away from him and visited only occasionally in the summer. Her mother, who had drug problems, had abandoned her when she was 2, Heather said, and her maternal grandparents took her in. "He was always there to help me; he taught me to roller-skate for the first time," she said. "That's my heart, that's my daddy right there. I would do anything for him." Heather undercut her impact, however, by appearing on the stand and later in front of television cameras wearing hoop earrings with dangling Playboy Bunny charms. But she was right about a bond with her father: Oyler had Heather's name tattooed in large, italicized letters on one arm, directly above a set of flames.

The defense recalled Breazile to speak on Oyler's behalf, but she managed to dig the hole deeper. Oyler may have made mistakes, Breazile told the jury, but he wasn't the kind of man who would intentionally kill anyone. "I know he didn't do at least two of those fires," she said, including Esperanza. As she spoke, Hestrin and Mayman held a whispered conference at the prosecution table. They had a key piece of evidence they hoped to use to impeach Breazile's credibility, a taped jailhouse telephone conversation in which she and Oyler had gloated over the prospect of suing Riverside County for wrongful prosecution. In the conversation, Oyler chortled that he wakened every morning with the thought, "Cha-ching! I'm going to make more money every day that I'm in jail," and he promised her jewels and other baubles. The prosecutors needed the testimony of a jail guard to establish that jailhouse calls routinely were recorded, but matters had been moving so swiftly that they'd forgotten to set it up. Mayman left the courtroom as quickly as decorum would allow and then ran flat out to the jail across the street, hoping to find a guard there who was familiar with telephone procedure.

As Breazile concluded her defense of Oyler, Mayman still hadn't appeared, and in fact he didn't make it back in time. Hestrin visibly braced himself and began his cross-examination.

"Ms. Breazile, you're here to tell the truth with all your heart," he said, his voice ringing with authority.

"That's correct," she replied, primly.

Hestrin solicited an admission that she and Oyler had talked by telephone while he was in jail, which was natural enough, and that she knew their conversations were recorded. If at this point she had challenged the prosecutor and said something like, "What are you talking about? I didn't know they were recorded?" the burden of proof would have fallen on Hestrin and the exchange could well have ended there. But she did not and he sprung the trap.

"And do you remember talking and laughing about how much money the two of you were going to make after this trial?" he asked.

Breazile, appearing flustered, gave a rambling answer that ended by confirming the conversation. "That's what people do," she said, "they retaliate and they get money for being blamed for something that they didn't do."

Hestrin asked next if she would be surprised to hear that she and Raymond, talking about the money they were going to make by suing the county, had used the expression "cha-ching!" to imitate the sound of a cash register? Breazile, by now fully alarmed, stammered that she couldn't remember such a conversation. Even after Hestrin handed her the transcript of the exchange, she said she couldn't remember it, which only made matters worse. Hestrin read on in the transcript, asking Breazile if she remembered other damming excerpts. "One million, two million, hah hah hah!" Oyler had said. "You can have rings on each of your fingers. . . . This is going to be the best thing that ever happened to our family!" One thing they had not mentioned on the phone, Hestrin said pointedly, was the loss of five lives on the Esperanza Fire. For the jury, the exchange and especially the term "cha-ching!" would ring in memory. "It was disturbing; it came up in the jury room," Voss said. "Poor Crystal. She'd do anything to get him out."

The defense next tried to put the fire on trial, to show the jury that it had been not Oyler but flames and bad decisions that had killed the firefighters. The strategy risked alienating the jury by laying blame on the firefighters, and McDonald proceeded in a very gingerly manner, careful always to refer to the fallen men as "the brave firefighters," just as Hestrin had. McDonald called as a witness Cal Fire battalion chief Jeff Brand, his agency's chief investigator for the *Esperanza Fire Accident Investigation Factual Report*. Brand was anything but a willing defense witness. In response to McDonald's questions, he gave brief, polite answers and strongly defended the presence of the firefighters at the Octagon House. Under similar circumstances, he said, he probably would have acted as they had. Should anyone have been sent to a place like the Octagon House, marked by a red warning dot on a fire map, unoccupied, and very difficult to defend? McDonald asked.

"Yes," Brand said. "Honestly, about every house out there could have been a red dot under those conditions. We still are going to send resources out to defend homes. There are a lot of homes that we saved that day."

An unintended consequence for the defense was that Brand disclosed some previously unknown details about the final moments of the men at the Octagon House and as a result helped the prosecution paint a picture for the jury of the agony of Engine 57. The climactic scene of a fatal wildland fire by definition occurs under a shroud of smoke and flame. Some of what happened is forever lost to living memory. Those moments, though, are the last testament of individuals who have paid the ultimate price to defend lives, property, and wildlands. Reclaiming from the ashes the bits and pieces left behind serves as a reminder to those who live with fire, whether they fight fire or count on those who do, of how high that price can be.

As the sun rose over the Banning Pass just after 7:00 AM that October morning, the Santa Ana wind arrived with the force of a gale. It spread along the floor of the Pass at speeds exceeding sixty miles an hour, powerful enough to uproot trees and topple light poles. Attack helicopters had taken to the skies at first light and now hovered above the Pass, ready to begin a day of water drops. One pilot flying his ship above the unnamed creek drainage took a photo of a heavy ribbon of smoke lying low in the drainage. Churning flames like sinews of raw muscle broke through the smoke in several spots. Cal Fire investigators later estimated that there were at least three spot fires, each one a substantial 40 to 50 acres in size, in the drainage at the time.

The wind raced along the floor of the Pass and reached an abandoned gravel mine or quarry directly east of the mouth of the unnamed creek drainage. The tailings pile there, which extended out from the mine, acted the way a boulder does in a stream, causing the wind to eddy downstream from it, just as flowing water forms an eddy below a rock. An offshoot of the swirling air turned and shot up the unnamed creek drainage, gaining velocity as the narrow passage compressed it. The torrent of fresh, compressed air was glutted with oxygen, and when it struck the spot fires in the drainage, they came to life with blinding speed. Driven by the wind, the spot fires reached outstretched fingers of flame to the next spot fire ahead, which was already exploding, and the fingers from the spot fires intertwined and became one and swept on and upward until the whole length of the unnamed creek drainage was a single, raging river of heat and flame.

From his post at the Tile House, Fogle saw the golden nugget of flame at the narrow spot in the drainage throb and then burst. He estimated the time as between 7:10 and 7:15 AM. First a bolt of superheated air that was shot through with swirling heat waves exploded out of the drainage and in seconds swept over the Octagon House. Then a column of smoke, light gray with streaks of white and interspersed with ribbons of scarlet flame, spewed out of the drainage behind the heat wave. As this happened, a shuddering blast of wind drove heat, smoke, and flame with so much force that the entire inferno was held tight to the ground. In technical terms, this was an area ignition, but the description everyone repeated afterward was, "It was as though someone had laid down a blowtorch in the drainage." The area ignition was so swift, Fogle said, that there was "no measurable rate of speed." Cal Fire investigators, pressed in court to put a number on the rate of fire spread, said it was "beyond extreme," maybe thirty miles an hour. The official fire report states that winds at the Octagon House reached between fifty and seventy miles an hour, velocities achieved by tropical storms. At a few miles more an hour, seventy-four miles an hour to be exact, a tropical storm is designated a hurricane.

In a snap of time, the air around the crew of Engine 57 came alive with heat waves of searing intensity. The mad war of the elements seemed to come from nowhere and to be everywhere in an instant, deadly and unexpected. No one from Engine 57 had time to unlimber a fire shelter. McLean and McKay were standing near the engine in front of the garage when the blast of superheated air hit them. McLean's body was found next to the engine near a rear wheel. Fire investigators said there was no evidence McLean had moved more than a step or two after being struck. As engineer, it would have been natural for him to be at the rear of the engine manning the controls. Perhaps he started toward the cab for protection; the cab door was open a few inches. The day after the fire, Norm Walker, McLean's division supervisor, returned to the scene and timed himself walking the steps from the rear of the engine to where McLean's body was found: it took only three to four seconds. McLean might have had that much time but not more.

McKay was found a short distance from the engine, between a parked Volkswagen and a tractor in front of the garage. A hose lay ran from the engine past him around the side of the garage; a nozzle was found nearby. Walker traced a path for McKay, too, following what was left of the hose. Again, it took only three to four seconds to get from the engine to where McKay had died, roughly the same amount of time as for McLean. McKay may have been standing where his body was found or just beyond, perhaps holding a nozzle. Or he may have been near McLean and stumbled a few steps seeking shelter. The wave of superheated air would have seared the men's nasal passages and throats, and the muscles in their throats would have constricted with the insult, blocking the flow of air. Suffocation would have followed, but death by suffocation is not instant death. McLean and McKay may have seen the coming shroud of smoke and flame, or that first heat blast may have mercifully stunned them unconscious, or nearly, and any movement that followed was merely stumbling. Walker, who had witnessed an area ignition early in his career, believes it is possible that the heat blast struck down both men where they stood. The power of an area ignition is overwhelming, Walker said. The one he witnessed, while on a hotshot crew during his first year fighting fire, had burned so intensely that the crew had held their hard hats like shields to protect themselves—even though the flames were a quarter of a mile away.

Cal Fire investigators told the jury that McLean's and McKay's bodies were found in the prone position, indicating they had followed standard escape training and dived to the ground, covering their heads with their hands. That may be wishful thinking: the condition of the bodies, as shown by the Eddie Harper photos, makes it nearly impossible to infer deliberate action. As Dr. Joseph Cohen, chief forensic pathologist for the Riverside County Coroner's Bureau, told the court, the two men's bodies were "about as bad as you can get short of cremation."

Harper's photo of Engine 57 taken directly after the fire establishes for certain that preparations for a burnout operation had barely begun. In the photo, the two drip torches carried on Engine 57 are on the ground next to the engine and are not ready for operation. The torches are heavy metal cylinders with screw-on caps and handles. The cap on one of Engine 57's drip torches hasn't been unscrewed, but a wand from inside a torch is lying on the ground several feet away. It's not clear how the drip torches wound up where they did; they are carried in a compartment on the engine, and an exploded oxygen bottle, which can be seen in the photo, may have knocked them out. The simpler and more likely explanation is that one or more firefighters had pulled the drip torches from the engine to get them ready for the burnout and unscrewed the cap and taken out the wand from the second drip torch, which is not wholly visible in the photo.

From that evidence, it's reasonable to conclude that the crew was not counting much on the burnout for protection. Most of the preparation work was done at the swimming pool. Loutzenhiser had the two least-experienced crewmen, Najera and Cerda, there with him—Cerda "the mule" and Najera "just thrilled to be there," as Hestrin described them. It would have been natural for the captain to keep the rookies close to him and to leave the veterans McLean and McKay back with the engine. The pool contained between two thousand and three thousand gallons of water, many times more than the five hundred gallons carried by the Forest Service engines. A portable pump had been carried to the swimming pool, and an intake hose with a strainer run into it. Fire investigators found the pump, described as "the size of a watermelon," with the throttle in the on position and a nearly full tank of gas. A one-hundred-foot hose line led from the pump to the rear of the Octagon House, where a gated wye divided the hose into two smaller hoses that ran around the sides of the house. The melted rubber from the smaller hose lines left snakeskin-like marks on the concrete walkway, visible even at the five-year anniversary mark.

Najera probably was at the hose line on the side of the house farthest from the driveway when the area ignition occurred.

According to fire investigators, the design of the house both partially deflected the fire and also helped its advance. The house did offer some protection, and firefighters are taught to take shelter when necessary behind houses. But the octagonal shape acted like an airplane wing, according to the investigators, and allowed the fire to slip around the house, slightly accelerating along the way. A lingering question is why Loutzenhiser and the two others did not jump into the pool. Perhaps they were too far away, perhaps the fire swirling around the Octagon House flanked and cut them off, perhaps they didn't trust the pool. Some questions can't be answered.

When the fire struck, overwhelming evidence indicates that Najera ran for his life. The crew had been at the Octagon House for nearly two hours, and the site was covered with boot prints. But fire investigators said a trail of prints showing long strides and heavy indentations at the toe, indicative of a runner, went around the front of the house, across the driveway, and down a bank. It was also rumored among firefighters but never confirmed that one boot print had been found on top of a propane tank on the slope below the house, indicating that someone, possibly Najera, had leapt atop the tank in a downhill race to escape the fire. A metal buckle and other bits of gear were found along the trail of footprints. "The clothing and gear matched the footprints, which were continuous," a Cal Fire investigator testified. At the end of the footprints was a disturbed patch of dirt, as though someone had fallen or dropped and rolled to extinguish flames. Najera's body came to rest at the end of the trail, lodged against a scorched tree stump at the edge of a steep bank.

"Would Daniel have been on fire the whole time?" Hestrin asked.

"Yes."

"How long?"

"Well over thirty seconds."

Cerda and Loutzenhiser were better protected, probably close together on the opposite side of the house from Najera. Taking a contrary view, Fogle believes the fire caught all three men together on the driveway, where they had just finished a quick scouting walk in preparation for the burnout, and that they scattered from there. Fogle's scenario is possible, but it also seems likely that at least one or two of the men, if not all three, were up near the swimming pool, where preparations were more advanced. They may even have had seconds of warning of what was to come: Loutzenhiser's broken radio call to Espinoza asking for help may have happened at or near the commencement of the area ignition. The desperate cry of a young male voice on the radio picked up on a video camera recording by one of Fogle's crew, beginning "Engine 57" and trailing into incomprehensibility, occurred at or close to this time.

However it came about, Cerda and Loutzenhiser were badly burned but alive, thanks to the protection of the house and the knoll. The scorching heat that entered their mouths and noses caused damage but not enough to destroy the nasal passageways and shut down the breath reflex. They stumbled in separate orbits along the driveway, leaving behind patches of clothing and bits of gear. Cerda was farthest down the driveway, on his back, his face frozen by heat into an expressionless mask. A score of yards up the driveway, Loutzenhiser was staggered by the heat blast. The straps holding his radio melted and the radio fell to the ground. The front of his shirt disintegrated and a pack of cigarettes fell out of a shirt pocket. He came to rest on his back, which was not as badly burned as his front, indicating that he had faced the heat blast. However he got to the ground, he was quickly rendered immobile. The thundering fire drowned out all sound except its roar. Fire of such ferocious intensity cannot be sustained for long, and as the roar died down, Loutzenhiser's still-working radio on the ground nearby brought him voices from what seemed another world.

"Lotz, how you doing over there?" Gearhart asked.

"Captain 57, Captain 52," Fogle called over and over.

Minutes passed and then Gearhart came on the air again, said everyone was dead, paused, and then corrected himself. Loutzenhiser lay within earshot of the radio for half an hour, unable to reach the radio to answer it or to shut it off. "His last moments on this earth were a living hell," Hestrin told the jury. "He knew he was going to die." The loss of the firefighters, Hestrin said, was the direct responsibility of Oyler and justified the death penalty. "This is not recklessness," he said. "This is murder."

♦ ♦ ♦

McDONALD'S CO-COUNSEL THOMAS Eckhardt, made the closing remarks for the defense. He acknowledged Oyler's guilt and said his crime was "unforgivable." Oyler had not intended to kill anyone, Eckhardt claimed, and the deaths had occurred as a result of recklessness, not evil intent. Oyler was going to die in prison no matter what, and there was nothing to be gained by his execution. "Please, when you consider what you are going to do with Mr. Oyler, try on in your mind what it must be like to spend the rest of your life in prison," Eckhardt said. "It's a severe punishment." If the jurors voted for execution, Eckhardt concluded, in a remark several jurors later said they found deeply offensive, they would have "blood on their hands."

The jury retired to deliberate. As the discussion got under way, McManigal sat at the table with an envelope in her lap, the kind of envelope used for photographs. Several jurors became fearful that she was going to make them look again at the ghastly autopsy photos. When the discussion started to bog down, McManigal took out the photos one by one and placed them on the table. They were

the family photos—McLean in the meadow; Cerda graduating
from fire academy; the Loutzenhiser family together; McKay and
his girlfriend, Staci Burger, being affectionate. "Folks, this is what
it's all about," McManigal said. "It's not about Oyler. It's about
what happened to these people. These are the photos that will take
us to the place we need to be."

The jury deliberated for less than seven hours and then voted.

Oyler returned to court in shackles to hear the verdict, surrounded
by a half dozen sheriff's deputies. He wore a suit and tie, but he
was unshaven and looked meek and downcast. The court clerk,
Gurrola, read the jury's one-word decision: "Death." At sentencing
in June, three months away, Judge Morgan would follow the jury's
recommendation.

Families and spectators streamed outside the Hall of Justice
to a wide pavilion, where reporters and a lineup of television
cameras awaited them. Fire families and their supporters spoke
from a podium banked by a photo display of the victims. Maria
Loutzenhiser expressed relief that Oyler was in jail where he could
do no more harm. Bonnie McKay called on family members who
become aware that a loved one is starting fires to report the guilty
people, to save lives and to spare themselves the agony that Oyler's
family was suffering. Gloria Ayala said of Oyler, "I harbor no anger,
only hope. Hope that you will understand the depth of pain you
have caused so many families, including your own."

Four of the jurors—Estep the foreman, Voss, McManigal, and
Nwandu—came out to the pavilion and began hugging family
members. McDonald later complained that it was inappropriate
for the jury to display bias like this, but the jurors said the trial
was over and they wanted to show their feelings. "This has been a
life-altering event; that's why we came out here," Voss said. Estep
said the jury had an easier time deciding on the death penalty than

on the guilty verdicts, but there had been tears nonetheless. "You're putting someone to death; you get all worked up," he said. Seeing the family photos spread out on the jury table, Estep said, had sealed the decision.

18.

THE SUN ROSE AS A fiery red ball in the mouth of the Banning Pass on an unseasonably cold morning in early fall, at what normally is the height of the fire season. Drizzle fell from broken cloud cover. At about 7:00 AM, close to the minute and five years to the day after the area ignition exploded, the American and Forest Service flags rose for the first time at the Octagon House memorial to Engine 57: a stone as high as a man set on a concrete and brick platform at the entrance to the driveway. Conducting the flag raising were Chris Fogle, who had been promoted in the interim from captain to battalion chief; Norm Walker, who had retired from the Forest Service and become fire chief in Idyllwild; and Dan Felix, who had been promoted from battalion chief to division chief. Longtime friends and fellow workers, they raised the flags respectfully but without fanfare. The memorial was now ready for the families, who would arrive in a few hours, after the sun had warmed the site. At the five-year mark, many of the surviving family members and firefighters felt they had passed an emotional landmark. The slow, ongoing process of absorbing loss had worn down the feelings of rage and despair. Tears still came, but they no longer fell without ceasing; survivors could smile when they got together; life moved on. "It was a year of adjustment," said Vivian Najera, Daniel Najera's aunt.

The wind, which always seems to blow at this place, unfurled the flags and shook them out in the gray dawn. The memorial, constructed by Greg Koeller and volunteers, was ready just in time for this anniversary day. Koeller had dug out the huge stone from a nearby embankment, hoisted it somehow onto the platform, and constructed a heavy-duty wrought-iron fence around it. There was a bench inside the fence where visitors could sit in contemplation. A plaque installed on the stone the day before read, "In loving memory of Engine 57, who in the midst of chaos and strife, acted with selfless courage to protect life and property. We will always remember your sacrifice and valor." The plaque named the five men, but in the rush to make the anniversary deadline, Daniel Najera's name was misspelled Najara. Even people who care deeply about their work can make mistakes, which must be one of the more enduring lessons of the Esperanza Fire.

As the clock ticked toward 7:10 AM, the approximate minute at which the area ignition commenced, a few hardy firefighters at the site hunched against the chill in hooded sweatshirts. They stood their posts like shrouded sentinels. One burly firefighter with a red, Irish face and wearing shorts, a sweatshirt, and no hat walked alone to visit the simple crosses made of rebar that mark the spots where the men of Engine 57 were found. He knelt on bare knees, crossed himself, and bowed his head.

Fogle, Felix, and Walker left the monument and walked slowly up the driveway, a trail of many memories.

"Winter's come early," someone said.

"Yes, but it'll be summer by afternoon," Felix said with a smile. Southern California was still southern California.

The rising sun poured a bright glow into the Pass and turned the rain clouds, drifting off to the northeast, from gray to rosy pink. The shell of the Octagon House stood like an abandoned sentry post on the top of the knoll, its empty windows staring vacantly at the unnamed creek drainage below and on to the breathtaking emptiness of the Banning Pass. As 7:10 approached, it seemed as though time should do something dramatic to acknowledge the moment—maybe extend itself like one of the dripping watches painted by Salvador Dalí, or curve or skip a beat altogether. The minutes kept to a measured pace, and the future arrived without pause. Those who had come for this moment slowly made their way to trucks and utility vehicles parked near the memorial and drove off, back up the face of the ridge to Twin Pines Road.

The families arrived at mid-morning, after the rain clouds had moved off. It was warmer, but the wind continued to gust. The Cerdas and McKays didn't make it this year; Jess McLean's widow, Karen, and her new husband, Conrad Meyen, had promised to attend and they did. Maria Loutzenhiser, wearing a baseball jacket with Engine 57 and Mark Loutzenhiser's name emblazoned on the back, played the role of captain's wife: she smiled and shared welcoming hugs with the two other mothers, Cecilia McLean and Gloria Ayala. The mothers carried bouquets of flowers and went from one cross to another, placing flowers at each one.

The Najera family—Ayala and her two children, Monica and Michael, along with her sister Vivian and her son Rikk—were for the first time able to walk easily to Daniel's marker. The crew of Engine 51 had the day before cut a trail with a gentle incline from the roadway across the steep slope to the marker. The family members walked up the trail and huddled together at the marker. Later, Rikk, for whom Daniel had been more like a brother than a cousin, went back alone for a few minutes. It can take decades, but sometimes those who were young or even unborn at the time of fatal fires, and who led altered lives as a result, find their way back to the rocky hillsides where lives ended and legends began, and sometimes with healing results.

It was time for group pictures. Maria Loutzenhiser encouraged the family members to stand around the memorial stone and smile. They did, even if they had to force a smile. As noon approached, someone turned a fire radio to high volume. Maria encouraged everyone to stand in a circle in front of the memorial, hold hands, and bow heads. At noon precisely, the area dispatcher announced over the radio a moment of silence for Engine 57, as had happened every year for the past five years. The dispatcher read out the names of the fallen crew. And then for a minute the only sound was the wind.

◆ ◆ ◆

DURING THE INTERVENING five years, the Octagon House became a pilgrimage destination for families, survivors of the fire, and others. They walked the ground singly or in small groups, some with measuring tapes and cameras seeking practical answers, and some only with memories. It was four years after the fire before Detective Scott Michaels stood for the first time at the site where the men of Engine 57 had met their fate and was able to test against reality what had been until then a dreamlike experience.

It was a clear day in early fall. I had tried to contact Michaels earlier and discovered that he, like other investigators on the case, was not free to talk because of ongoing legal action against Oyler. Time had passed, the trial was over, and Michaels had discovered that I was writing a book about the Esperanza Fire. A mutual friend gave him my e-mail address, and he sent me the following message. "If you ever want to know what really happened inside that investigation I would be happy to share it with you." What author could resist? A few months later, we stood together at the Octagon House.

In wildland firefighting as in war, there is no substitute for knowing the ground. Terrain drives action. What struck Michaels as he stood at the fatality site for the first time, a perspective denied him at the time of the fire on account of heat and smoke, was the commanding view. Because it was a clear day, you could see down into the Banning Pass to the town of Beaumont—and by a stretch of imagination to Oyler's apartment complex. What struck Michaels most forcefully was the discovery that what had been for him just a dreamscape actually existed in the waking world, for the Octagon House looked almost exactly the way he had imagined it: a house perched high atop a promontory, surrounded by blackened chaparral and overlooking the entire locale of the arson-murder investigation.

Leaving our car at the foot of the driveway, we walked up toward the house and immediately ran into the owner, Greg Koeller, who was doing some work around the place. It was a chilly, windy day, but Koeller, his face red from the weather, was dressed in light bib overalls and boots. Koeller had built the house to get away from people, he said. After the fire, he could have isolated himself from the powerful emotions and memories that people such as Michaels and I bring to it. Instead, he welcomed anyone pursuing a serious interest in the fire, especially survivors and kin of the fallen. Eventually he had to put a chain across his driveway to deter casual visitors. But a yellow fire shirt remained a passport to his property.

I took a photo of Koeller and Michaels together, smiling and standing in the middle of what was left of the Octagon House. Koeller had scrubbed the place as clean as a mausoleum, but hadn't been able to face rebuilding and living in it again; it was one thing to work there, he said, but quite another to think of treating it like home. The concrete walkway around the house still bore the black marks of melted rubber, like a shed snakeskin, where the crew of Engine 57 had pulled hose lays from the portable pump they'd set up in the swimming pool.

After a while, Michaels stuck his hands in his jeans pockets, hunched his shoulders, and walked off on his own. The detective stopped at the edge of the site, his back to us, and made a brooding, solitary silhouette against the almost limitless backdrop of the Banning Pass. From where he stood, he could see the whole story of the Esperanza Fire: the ignition point, the gaping mouth of the Banning Pass where the Santa Ana wind had entered, the rugged unnamed creek drainage below, and miles and miles away to the town of Beaumont and the haunts of Raymond Oyler.

Michaels came back to us with a pensive look on his face. It was time to go, and we said our good-byes to Koeller. As we were driving up the ridge face, I asked Michaels what he had made of the visit. Looking into the Pass, he said, had made him realize the physical connection, the clear sight line, between the Octagon House and Oyler's apartment. The physical link, he said, helped explain the feeling, which he still carried with him, of being in contact with the men of Engine 57, of a spirit so strong and compelling that he could almost touch it.

◆ ◆ ◆

REMEMBRANCES DIRECTLY AFTER the fire had been on a very different scale. A huge memorial occasion had been organized a bare ten days after the fatal event; everything about the Esperanza Fire seemed to move at exceptional speed, from the area ignition to the capture of Oyler to this giant gathering at Devore. A crowd estimated at eight to ten thousand assembled at the Hyundai Pavilion, an open-air amphitheater within sight of the San Bernardino National Forest that is often used as a staging ground for firefighting. Firefighters came from up and down California, across the West, and as far away as New York City. Uniformed Forest Service firefighters lined the entrance roadway and saluted as limousines entered carrying the families, followed by the Forest Service engines of the San Jacinto District. Above a crowded stage hung an enormous banner with the names of the five men of Engine 57 and the words "Always Remember." Dozens of fire engines parked along the rim of the amphitheater. Family members, looking shattered, took seats in front rows, their children huddled like embryos in mothers' laps. There were tears and skirling bagpipes, hymns and songs, a flyover by a fleet of air tankers and attack helicopters, and speeches—Governor Schwarzenegger, Senator Dianne Feinstein, and others paid their respects. There was an overpowering sense that an extended family, the fire family, had suffered grievous loss. "We are wildland firefighters," said Tom Harbour, Forest Service director of fire and aviation. "We do our work where cities and wildland meet. In doing that work, we become brothers and sisters."

People opened their wallets as well as their hearts. The Central County United Way accepted more than $1.3 million in donations from across the nation and abroad. The Wildland Firefighter Foundation, which aids firefighter families, distributed $248,842 in contributions. Through the federal Public Safety Officers' Benefits Programs, each family received a payment of $295,194, a figure adjusted for inflation each year in early October, in this case right before the fire happened. Congress and the California legislature both passed special legislation that granted United Way and the Wildland Firefighter Foundation a one-time exemption from rules about nonprofit organizations that allowed them to give the money they had collected directly to the families, without tax consequences for the organizations or the donors. The sum for each family from these three sources was no less than $604,962.

Mike Dietrich, the fire chief of the San Bernardino National Forest, told the audience that one significant way to give meaning to the lives of the men of Engine 57 was to work to prevent and vigorously prosecute the crime of arson. "The scourge of arson is nothing less than domestic terrorism," Dietrich said. "I'm here to tell you that if this fire had started a few hours earlier, or if the wind had blown a little harder, much of the community could not have been evacuated in time, threatening the lives of our law enforcement officers and the citizens who live in those areas, who may not have been able to escape. We have no control over natural disasters like earthquakes and flood, but we must address this heinous crime."

Walker offered the audience a fond remembrance of Loutzenhiser and McLean that brought a ripple of subdued laughter. He recounted how the pair had renovated the Alandale fire station, consulting him as division chief only when absolutely necessary. "Lotzy and Gus became very good at calling me and partially explaining what they had in mind," Walker said. "If I agreed, it was a short conversation. If I didn't, they'd say, 'Hey, chief, you want your car washed?' In the end I would lose, the plans they had would prevail, and I would drive away with a clean car."

Five years later, it was Walker who offered a toast to Engine 57 at a fifth anniversary gathering held in the mountains near Idyllwild the weekend before the actual day. Originally intended as a small, informal get-together, the event expanded by popular demand into a dinner that drew more than two hundred people.

"Here's to Engine 57. May we never forget!" Walker said, and he raised a foamy cup of beer to a sea of smiling faces.

A highlight of the evening was the presentation of commemorative awards to thirty-one fire personnel who had fought the fire and taken part in the rescue operation.

The honorees were Captain Richard Gearhart and the Engine 51 crew: Shawn Evans, John Fakehany, Eddie Harper, Darrell Arrellano, and Mike Christian; Captain Chris Fogle and the Engine 52 crew: Josh Richardson, Paul Jacobs, and Aaron Reyes; Captain Anna Dinkel and the Engine 54 crew: Josh Spoon, Jarod Baker, Adan Castro, and Ian Governale; Captain Freddie Espinoza and the Engine 56 crew: David Goldstein, Doug Donahoo, Ryan Henninger, and Chris Matthews; the March Brush 10 crew: Rod Rambayon and Gary Bicondova; Forest Service patrol officer Chris Hardy; H535 pilot Chris Templeton; H535's helitack crew: Daniel Sepulveda, Daniel Diaz, Randy Ruiz, and Ryan Gonzalez; H301 pilot Dave Patrick; and H305 pilot George Karcher.

Each received a "challenge coin" symbolizing high honor, a tradition started in the military. The coin bore on one side the insignia of the National Fallen Firefighters Memorial in Emmitsburg, Maryland, and on the other an image of Tahquitz Peak, the site of a lookout tower, at 8,828 feet the highest in the San Bernardino National Forest. The firefighters also received certificates of recognition and letters noting their "courage and determination" signed by Representative Mary Bono Mack.

When Gearhart received his coin, he remarked, "I said I'd either be getting a medal or getting fired—I got the medal!" He had to leave the gathering early, to check back on a 10-acre fire that had started earlier in the day along Mount Edna Road off Highway 243, now the Esperanza Firefighters Memorial Highway. The fire was near the spot where Gary Nagel's air tanker had crashed during the 1998 Mount Edna Fire, an event Gearhart had witnessed. By the time Gearhart arrived back at the fire, which was suspected as arson, it was under control and he wasn't needed after all. The fire had been easy to contain because the Esperanza Fire had burned over the site five years earlier.

At the five-year mark, too, the feeling persisted that the fire community had not been well served by the state and federal Esperanza Fire investigations. The point of official investigations is to gather a trustworthy account, identify negligence if it exists, and highlight lessons to be learned to prevent a future repetition of the event. That was especially the task of the investigation team that produced the *Esperanza Fire Accident Investigation Factual Report*, a joint effort of the Forest Service and Cal Fire. Though staffed by an eighteen-member team and fourteen technical specialists, the joint report suffered from an apparent excess of haste and sloppy editing. The most serious charge against the report, however, was that Cal Fire deliberately skewed its findings to lessen the agency's responsibility for the Forest Service deaths. The charge lingered for years after it had become well established that the joint report had been wrong to assert that the Forest Service shared equal or unified command with Cal Fire at the time of the fatalities. The question of who was in command at that time raised the broad issue of blame and the specific issue of criminal liability. If the Esperanza Fire had resulted in criminal charges against the incident commander, as had happened after the 2001 Thirtymile Fire, and if the fire *had been* in unified command as claimed in the joint report, then a Forest Service supervisor would have been in jeopardy, along with the Cal Fire IC.

"The report was a whitewash to protect Cal Fire," Mike Dietrich told me several years after the fire. Dietrich was one of three supervisors at the command post that morning who might have served as Forest Service IC, the others being Walker and Felix. Dietrich said he told the joint report's investigators that the Forest Service had not joined unified command until later in the morning, after the fatalities, but his remarks were ignored. "Cal Fire wanted to share the responsibility for decision making with the Forest Service, or they wanted to disburse the blame. They knew about unified command; they knew about it upfront. It was brought out several times by a few of the team members, subject matter experts, prior to the report going forward, just on the unified command issue."

The joint report's assertion about unified command had a factual basis: the radio transmission to that effect at 3:10 AM, hours before the fatalities occurred. George Solverson, the Forest Service's chief investigator, said the team relied on that radio transmission for its finding. It was not difficult to discover, however, that the transmission was in error and that unified command between Cal Fire and the Forest Service was not instituted until 9:00 AM, when Mike Wakoski took the IC post for the Forest Service. The failure of the joint report to spell out the details created the impression, justified or not, of bad faith. The point should be made again that no serious analyst of the fire has ever claimed that the addition of a Forest Service IC before the fatal hour would have changed the outcome for Engine 57, and none have blamed Cal Fire's IC, Brenda Seabert, for what went wrong. In fact, Solverson said Seabert turned in an admirable and underrated performance, repeatedly asking why someone higher up did not take over the fire and warning on the radio about 5:00 AM that the fire was going to sweep the ridge.

Errors of fact in the joint report are simply too numerous for a document claiming to be a definitive "factual" account. A hand-drawn map showing travel paths of the victims transposed the positions of Loutzenhiser's and Cerda's bodies. The report states that all the firefighters at the double-wide "sought refuge in their engines for protection from smoke and billowing embers," when in fact only three of seventeen did. The executive summary states that the fire was "several hundred acres in size" at the time of the burnover and then in the body of the report correctly states that it was about 2,200 acres just before the area ignition occurred. Toups is misidentified once as a branch chief rather than identified by his proper title, branch director. Hall's Grade is misidentified as Hallis Grade not once but several times.

More consequential questions abound, and they undermine the report's usefulness as a lesson guide. The report does not deal forthrightly with Toups's account of his meeting with Loutzenhiser, though the investigators were in the best position of anyone to address this very difficult issue; they had immediate access to witnesses and documents, and they had the broad expertise and manpower to assess them. The report does not even mention Toups's claim that he told Loutzenhiser to leave the Octagon House and that Loutzenhiser agreed to go; it does, though, offer the reasonable judgment that whatever Toups told Loutzenhiser was "not clear or understood." The investigation team may have been reluctant to confront directly the unhappy questions raised by Toups, perhaps out of deference to the fallen firefighters and certainly out of misgivings about Toups's credibility. The Forest Service chief investigator, Solverson, for one was adamant that Toups's account was far too elaborate to be believed. "He kept elaborating, from his log to his written account to his interviews," Solverson said. "We're supposed to believe this is the conversation? It became the briefing of a lifetime!" But the investigators had an obligation to make a greater effort to make their judgments clear in print, to be sure that the lessons learned are the right ones.

After the report came out, Toups wrote an angry critique to his superiors, complaining that his side of things had not been told in the report and citing more than twenty "gross inaccuracies"— alleged errors of fact and judgment about sequences, instructions to firefighters, the red-dot/green-dot map, and other matters. "Who made the decision to discount my testimony?" Toups wrote. "Why did the Department [Cal Fire] allow this document to be released as a 'Factual Report'?"

Toups gave no public interviews after the fire until he talked to me, though he fully cooperated with a string of official investigations. In fact, he was the only Cal Fire employee who agreed to be interviewed by the Office of Inspector General of the Department of Agriculture for its follow-on report, the one required by Congress's PL 107-203 legislation for fatal fires involving Forest Service personnel. The OIG report includes a brief summary of Toups's account, without comment, but immediately following that is a statement by Gearhart contradicting Toups. The placement cannot be purely coincidental. In fact, several firefighters said OIG investigators told them they did not consider Toups's account to be fully credible. The OIG report, though, did not come out until more than three years after the fire. Marginalized in public and blamed in private, Toups had cause to feel aggrieved and frustrated. One of his supervisors, for example, refrained from giving Toups a hero's award for saving civilian lives on the Esperanza Fire because Toups had become such a divisive figure. Finally, a firefighter of rank and long experience who is a friend of both of us prevailed on Toups to tell me his side of the story.

Toups and I talked by phone several times, and he willingly provided backup documents. These included his log sheet from the time of the fire, the verbatim transcript of his interview by fire investigators directly after the fire, and his critical letter about the first accident report. There was far too much material to cover by telephone; he and I agreed to meet and spend a day visiting the fire site and talking over the issues.

We got together for breakfast at a biscuits-and-gravy restaurant in Banning and ate heartily, knowing we had a long day ahead of us. Toups was 52 years old at this time and had retired from Cal Fire. He was still working, helping to develop computer programs to aid intelligence gathering and coordination during big fires, one of the more promising developments in firefighting technology. He looked younger than his age, even boyish, and was fit. He is shorter than most firefighters; his critics accuse him of having a Napoleon complex. His manner can be abrupt and insistent, a fact he acknowledged in a surprising way. As we talked at breakfast, he volunteered an account of how a superior had called him in for a job counseling session in the late 1990s. The superior was supportive and friendly but told Toups he was being too aggressive fighting fires and especially was guilty of acting without consulting others. Toups said he took the criticism to heart and mended his ways. On the Esperanza Fire, he said, he made a special effort to defer to the Forest Service captains and not order them around.

"These gentlemen I'm dealing with, you can see they're fire captains," Toups said. "These aren't young kids. They're all in their late thirties, forties. I respect those company officers. To micromanage them or tell them how to do their job is not my place. It is my place to see if there's a safety violation going on, to make sure that gets resolved."

Nonetheless, he made it clear that he thinks Loutzenhiser made a fatal error. "The only person who is at fault is no longer with us," Toups told me. "The company officer made a bad decision and killed himself and his crew. There's nothing more to pursue here."

One of the ironies of the Esperanza Fire is that Toups may not have been aggressive enough in making his points to Loutzenhiser. His final talk with Loutzenhiser came at a decisive moment, probably the last chance for Engine 57 to reorganize and pull back from the Octagon House. What happened during that conversation is central to two lingering questions about the Esperanza Fire: Why did Loutzenhiser set up at the Octagon House in the first place? And why did he stay?

Toups was never publicly blamed for the fatalities, and to this day the Forest Service captains do not hold him responsible. "I've never blamed Toups for what happened that morning; none of us have," Fogle said. "Lotzy and I went down there. We had plenty of time. We were in that area for two hours prior to the fire getting there. As engine captains, it is incumbent on us to make the call whether we stay and engage or leave. None of that lies on Toups's shoulders." The engine captains with the most intimate knowledge of the fire may not have blamed Toups, but he was indicted at the "whispering level." Many in the fire community privately blamed him for the fatal outcome, based in part on the false notion that Toups had directed Engine 57 to the Octagon House. Whatever else happened, it was Loutzenhiser's decision and his alone to set up and remain at the Octagon House, just as it was Fogle's to set up at the Tile House. The situation at the double-wide is different; there, Toups chose the ground.

All that aside, Fogle does not believe Toups's account of his talk with Loutzenhiser. Fogle, who kept in touch with Loutzenhiser by radio until the final moments, makes the point that Toups's account of his talk with the captain does not match what Loutzenhiser subsequently said—and did not say—on the radio. Loutzenhiser never mentioned the meeting or any proposed change in plans, which he surely would have done if he had agreed to a major redeployment such as leaving the Octagon House for the double-wide. "If *lying* is too strong a word, he is greatly exaggerating what he said in order to cover his butt," Fogle said of Toups.

After the fire, Fogle took it upon himself to make the best case for Loutzenhiser, his best friend. He studied the ground at the Octagon House like a detective and went on to participate in, criticize, and correct official and unofficial investigative efforts, including this one. Not least, he also provided sympathy, comfort, and counsel for the Loutzenhiser family. A devout Christian, he did these things in the name of his faith as well as in the name of his friend. Such a broad effort cannot wholly succeed; the forces arrayed against it are simply too great, the battlefronts too many. The attempt, however, is what is left for faith and friendship, and it can change things.

◆ ◆ ◆

ON OTHER ISSUES, the joint fire report is also silent about the general breakdown of radio discipline that caused so much frustration for the Forest Service captains during the fire, both before and after the burnover. The harping in the report on the use of "unauthorized" radio channels by the captains, when the authorized channels were clogged with often-routine chatter, is more an indictment of the fire communication system than the captains' behavior. Virtually every report on how to improve safety on big fires cites the problem of too many messages on too few channels; anyone listening to the chatter recorded by video cameras during the Esperanza Fire will come to the same conclusion. At the time, Cal Fire was helping develop a computer program to allow firefighters to communicate regardless of the amount of radio traffic, through an e-mail-like system. The joint report might have pointed to and encouraged such a hopeful effort rather than wag fingers at the Forest Service captains.

The finding that the Octagon House was "identified as non-defensible" by the 2002 red-dot/green-dot map fails to note two important points. First, the map was drawn up four years before the fire and does not address the status of the house in 2006, when it counted. Second, the map was primarily intended as a warning for politicians about the risks to life and property in that area and not as a guide for firefighters, according to Toups, who was responsible for making the map. The joint report also fails to mention the 2002 fire inspection report on the Octagon House that concluded "No violations—Thank you." The subsequent fourteen-page critique of the joint report by the four captains—Gearhart, Fogle, Dinkel, and Espinoza—along with Toups's separate critique, contains many additional technical points of dispute about fire behavior, communications, sequence of events, and other matters.

The arson case created special difficulties for fire investigators. The site of the fire was declared a crime scene and access to it was restricted for the fire investigation team. Once Oyler was arrested, there was an understandable reluctance to share any information that might adversely affect his trial. Cal Fire and Forest Service law enforcement officials took this a step further and began hoarding information, according to Solverson, and this led to many of the glaringly simple mistakes in the joint report. One example, he said, was the map that transposed Cerda's and Loutzenhiser's bodies, which was never subjected to full review. Despite Solverson's status as the chief Forest Service investigator, he was not allowed to conduct interviews and had to struggle even to obtain copies of interviews done by law enforcement personnel. "The investigation was the biggest challenge of my investigative career," said Solverson, who had thirty-five years of experience as a safety officer. "Cal Fire and Forest Service law enforcement wouldn't let go. They would not release the site. It was two weeks before I saw the transcript of an interview and I had to fight for it. They did all the interviews to the very end."

The joint report cited two "causal factors" as being the most responsible for the deaths: a loss of situational awareness, and the decision by Engine 57 to set up "at the head of a rapidly developing fire." The report, though, does not identify exactly what situation Engine 57 failed to anticipate; none of the other Forest Service engine crews on the ridge face predicted or expected an area ignition, which was the key event that caused the fatalities, and all of them were in exposed positions near Engine 57. Taken at face value, the finding is a caution against sending resources into any situation that might result in an area ignition. When Cal Fire's chief investigator, Jeff Brand, testified to the contrary during Oyler's trial, he sounded a more realistic note. "We still are going to send resources out to defend homes," he said. And when Team 8 night operations chief Phill Veneris drove down the face of Twin Pines Ridge the first day of the fire, he saw homes with electric lights on, indicating people were inside. "There were chunks of homes, chunks of light," Veneris said. "And I tried to figure what I would have done. There were people down there, homes down there. Any firefighter working in southern California would have gone down there—that's the job."

More specific is the joint report's contention that Engine 57 set up "at the head of a rapidly developing fire," a very dangerous position indeed. Firefighters who were there, however, dispute this description. Fogle and the other captains say the head had passed below Engine 57 by the time of the area ignition, which then sprang from a flank and not the head of the fire. Walker and some others say the head had swept past the Tile House and up Twin Pines Ridge *before* the area ignition occurred and that the area ignition was in effect one among several heads of the fire. Engine 57 was the unit farthest down the ridge face, but by only a couple of hundred yards. If Engine 57 is to be faulted on the issue of its position, then the fire supervisors who sent engines anywhere down Twin Pines Ridge or even stationed them along Twin Pines Road should be faulted, too, as should the Cal Fire and Forest Service captains who stayed on the ridge. Cal Fire Engine 3176 with Captain Jeff Veik and two crewmen had set up directly above the Octagon House and experienced everything that happened to Engine 57, minus the intensity and fatal outcome. Every fire progression map in the joint report shows that once the Santa Ana wind arrived, the fire turned and swept up and over Twin Pines Ridge.

Fatal fires are easy to second-guess in hindsight from a comfortable position far from howling winds and blistering heat. And in fairness, the same can be said about second-guessing official reports. The Esperanza Fire was an event of exceptional stress, with multiple fatalities, two separate agencies doing the investigating—one that lost the men and the other in charge at the time that happened, a prescription for extreme tension—*and* an arson prosecution. With the advantage of retrospect, two events stand out as being the most responsible for the fatalities. The first occurred when Toups showed up at the Octagon House less than an hour before the fatal run of fire. Regardless of what was said between Toups and Loutzenhiser, Toups's appearance was the last real opportunity for Loutzenhiser to take stock and reconsider a dangerous predicament. Toups's very presence provided a break, a fresh opportunity to adjust plans based on changing conditions. The moment passed and nothing came of it.

The second key event was the area ignition. The joint report identifies the area ignition merely as a "contributing factor" to the fatalities, one step down from a "causal factor," lumping it in with seven other factors such as a social culture that expects firefighters to take greater risks when defending homes. An area ignition is not a rare event, but it is an unpredictable one. Loutzenhiser had multiple warnings that he faced an extreme run of fire, from radio conversation with Fogle, from his talk with Toups, and from the runs of fire he witnessed at the Tile House and other sites. Loutzenhiser's statements on the radio show that he was confident Engine 57 could handle another run of fire that behaved like the others had. He most likely was right. If the fire had acted at the Octagon House as it had at the Tile House, the crew of Engine 57 would have had a rough time but almost surely would have survived; surely he was counting on that. But then the unpredictable happened: a golden nugget of flame in the bottom of the unnamed creek drainage blew out; a roaring jet of heat and flame, as though from a gigantic blowtorch, swept Engine 57.

The joint report came out in May 2007 and was followed in July by a second report by the Department of Labor's Occupational Safety and Health Administration, or OSHA. The fire community has mocked OSHA's past reports on fatal wildland fires as lacking in both expertise and common sense, and this one was no exception. The OSHA report cited the Forest Service with a serious violation because the crews of engines 52 and 57 were observed "without turn out gear." On the contrary, Toups had cautioned the crews to get into proper wildland gear, not heavy turnouts, and they complied. OSHA offered an overly credulous two-sentence version of Toups's account of his talk with Loutzenhiser and said that Toups had "ordered" Loutzenhiser to fall back to the double-wide. "Engine 57 did not follow orders that was [sic] communicated by the Branch Director." That went too far even for Toups, who says he strongly suggested but did not order a withdrawal.

Other matters cited as violations by OSHA included fighting fire at night, in hot, dry conditions, or with the wind increasing or changing direction, conditions common to almost every wildland fire. "If we stop fighting fires and people die from the uncontained spread of forest fires and towns are burned due to the fact we can't engage because OSHA said firefighting was dangerous, what will your follow-up report say then?" was a typical firefighter comment, this one on a popular wildland firefighter website. After the report's release, OSHA and Forest Service representatives got together for a talk, and OSHA dropped two of its six charges.

The potentially most upsetting report was the one produced by the Office of Inspector General, charged with oversight of the Forest Service. The OIG report could have led to criminal charges against firefighters. Surprisingly, it produced some positive results. The OIG report, which came out three years after the fire, showed that the office had learned something from past blunders. The OIG had been much criticized within the fire community for its report on the Thirtymile Fire and for another on the Cramer Fire of 2003; two firefighters died in the Cramer Fire, and legal action was taken against the incident commander, who was forced to resign and accept a term of probation. The OIG acknowledged in its Esperanza Fire report that many potential witnesses had refused to talk to the agency's team. The OIG, which has no oversight authority for Cal Fire, asked fourteen Cal Fire firefighters for interviews. All but Toups said no. The Forest Service survivors, over whom OIG did have authority, demanded and received a grant of immunity before they submitted to interviews, which meant their statements could not be used for criminal prosecutions.

The OIG's Esperanza Fire report noted several steps the agency had taken to educate its investigators about real-life conditions on the fire line. The OIG created a Wildland Fire Investigation Team and sent five special agents to a Basic Fire Academy class in Boise, Idaho, and other training venues. The agents also visited active fires not under investigation "to observe firefighting operations and enhance their understanding of wildland fires." Time spent in reconnaissance is never wasted. The OIG report, which came out in November 2009, states that there was "no criminal wrongdoing" by Forest Service or Cal Fire personnel on the Esperanza Fire. The finding was welcome, but it was also an easy call. Less than two weeks after the fire, the joint Forest Service–Cal Fire investigation team contacted an assistant U.S. attorney, Joseph Johns, section chief for environmental crimes of the Criminal Division of the Central District of California. Johns later confirmed to me that he told the team there were no grounds to prosecute any of the firefighters. It no doubt helped that by that time, Oyler had been charged with murder and arson. (This is the same Joseph Johns who two years later successfully prosecuted the case against Steven Emory Butcher, who was sentenced to forty-five months in jail for negligently starting the 2006 Day Fire in southern California.)

The OIG report also straightened out factual lapses in previous reports and gave more space to Toups's account. It corrected the errors in the *Esperanza Fire Accident Investigation Factual Report* about unified command, the red-dot/green-dot map, and the placement of Loutzenhiser's and Cerda's bodies. It also supported the use of unauthorized radio channels by the Forest Service captains as the only way they had to communicate effectively. The report devoted several paragraphs to Toups's account of his meeting with Loutzenhiser and included his key assertion that Loutzenhiser had agreed to withdraw to the double-wide. The OIG report made a few mistakes of its own: it gave the time of Loutzenhiser's death as the evening of October 26 (it was shortly before noon) and the date of Cerda's death as October 30 (it was the next day, October

31). Those mistakes did not affect the report's findings, but family members found them upsetting. Firefighters must continue to be wary of criminal, civil, and administrative liability when something goes wrong on the fire line. "The whole investigation process is broke," said Dietrich. "Now a serious injury accident automatically starts out as a criminal investigation. The ramifications are huge."

The most clear-cut lesson of the Esperanza Fire concerns arson: if there had been no human fire starter, there would have been no deaths, no gutted homes, no mass evacuations, no traumatic aftermath. The successful prosecution of Raymond Oyler, the first-ever conviction for murder for setting a wildland fire, was a resounding statement of intolerance for arson in the critical zone where human habitation and wildlands meet. The conviction means that in the future, when an arsonist lights a wildland fire and deaths occur, the arsonist faces the very real possibility of murder charges and the ultimate penalty. The trial, however, did not answer the questions: What kind of man was Oyler? What kind of man would light fire after fire until he killed someone?

Following the death penalty hearing, Oyler was driven to San Quentin State Prison and placed on Death Row, which has been described as an "antiseptic hell." Oyler himself used similar terms to describe his life there in a correspondence with me that began more than two years after he was incarcerated. "This place is a very lonely and dark place, the food is the worst it could be," he wrote,

---

Since the Supreme Court opened the door in 1976 for states to reinstate the death penalty, California has carried out thirteen executions, the last one in 2006. A federal judge stopped executions in California in February 2006 over concerns about the state's method of execution, lethal injection. Six years later, in November 2012, California voters rejected a proposal to repeal the penalty altogether and replace it with sentences of life in prison without parole. Californians traditionally have had an ambivalent attitude toward the death penalty: they want the option but not its frequent exercise. California has by far the highest number of Death Row inmates of any state, accounting for nearly a quarter of the national Death Row population, but it ranks in the middle among states in number of executions. As of this writing, California has a Death Row population of 724, which is almost double

and he offered details of daily life on Death Row. He is allowed to socialize for three or four hours a day with other prisoners, though he complained about being "forced to live with killers." He can take a shower about three times a week and likes to watch NASCAR racing on television. Otherwise, he is given cold food in his cell and spends most of his time there. He must wait five years before he is eligible for a job, but he plans to work once he can.

Oyler has repeatedly protested his innocence, but he has never explained his actions, including in his correspondence with me. During his trial, Oyler and I had a few words together during breaks, and he agreed to an interview. The interview never happened, but after he was jailed in San Quentin, I wrote Oyler and reminded him of the agreement. A representative wrote back for him that Oyler did not want to "talk about himself or his case." Loneliness and boredom had an effect, however, and two years later I found a note from him posted on the Internet on the site of an anti–death penalty group. In the note, Oyler said he wanted to "to enlist some quality longterm penfriends" to help him grow emotionally and spiritually in what he called "this lonely concrete jungle—home." When I wrote him again after reading his plea, he wrote back right away and said he was eager to correspond. He also asked for help finding an appeals lawyer. "I'm fighting for my life [for] the act of another," he wrote.

---

that of the No. 2 state, Florida, which has an equivalent population of 402. There are 704 male inmates in San Quentin awaiting execution and twenty female inmates on Death Row at the Central California Women's Facility in Chowchilla. An average of two new inmates are added each month. California's thirteen executions place it at No. 17 in number of executions, or exactly in the middle, among states that exercise the death penalty, plus the federal government. California's tally is far below the No. 1 state, Texas, which has executed 482 inmates, and the No. 2 state, Virginia, which has executed 109. Death sentences in California are automatically appealed, but it takes an average of four to five years for a lawyer to be assigned to an appeal and ten to fifteen years or longer to resolve the appeal. If loved ones of victims want justice by execution, they can wait a full generation or longer for it.

I made an inquiry about finding him an appeals lawyer and was told there was no way to hurry the process. I reported this news to Oyler. But I also told him that I thought he had received justice. "I think I better make a couple of things clear up front," I wrote to him. "I will not lie to you. I think you received a fair trial: I attended the trial and I've interviewed several of the jurors. The jury struggled with the evidence and came to a unanimous decision. I accept their verdict. Their decision to recommend the maximum penalty also came after debate and discussion."

In a subsequent letter to Oyler, I listed several factual matters that contradict his denials that he has never addressed. "You've made the point several times that you are innocent of taking the lives of the five Engine 57 firefighters," I wrote. "One problem I have with that, Ray, is that you've never explained yourself, except to claim your innocence. There are a number of things that link you to arson fires in the Banning Pass in 2006, such as your DNA being found on two arson devices from fires in June of that year; eyewitness testimony placing you in the vicinity of a number of arson fires over the summer; and your claim to having been at the Morongo Casino when the Esperanza Fire was set, when the casino's many surveillance cameras that were operating at the time do not show you where you said you were."

I did not make this additional point to Oyler, but the convicted firefighter-arsonist John Orr well describes in his book, *Points of Origin*, how an arsonist can explain away the death of innocent victims in one of his fires. "He rationalized the deaths as he did everything," Orr says of the arsonist character in his book. "It wasn't his fault."

Oyler's replies were respectful, but he offered little hope that he would be more forthcoming about his past actions anytime soon. With his legal appeal in mind, he wrote, "John, all I can say is I'm not the person who started the Esperanza Fire. In time it will come out. They will investigate to the fullest every aspect of the case and it will prove me innocent. I can't speak about the other fires." His state of mind as disclosed in his letters is that of a man who is lonely, scared, and searching for forgiveness. In one letter, he confided that he was in the process of becoming a Roman Catholic. "I think as long as you believe in God your spirit goes to heaven," he wrote, indicating that his spiritual journey had just begun.

Oyler could appear devilish or meek, formidable or wimpy—and during his arrest and trial, he was all of that. Under pressure he caved in to hysteria, falling off his chair in a police station after his arrest and then hallucinating about little men dancing across the defense table during his trial. He was an admitted heavy pot smoker; his sister, Joanna, testified that he—and she—used crystal meth. After the trial was over, I asked Douglas Allen, the veteran California arson investigator, what traits of a serial arsonist he saw in Oyler. Allen said Oyler fit only a general profile for an arsonist: he had low self-esteem, a need for power, and an addiction to excitement that required ever-greater stimulation. "Arsonists are on a power trip. They can control the emergency services with that one match," he said. Arsonists often try to join police or fire departments, seeking a uniform and a badge as a way of acquiring power, he said. In fact, it came out in court testimony that Oyler had approached Andrew Bennett, the fire's first IC, on the street in Beaumont several months before the fire and asked him where he should go to apply to join a local volunteer fire department. A check of records disclosed that Oyler had applied to the Beaumont department in 2000, took half a dozen classes, but never completed training.

If there was a sexual element in Oyler's fire setting, it hadn't been made apparent; the butt pat of the woman recorded by a surveillance camera at a gas station after he left work the day of the Esperanza Fire, however, is suggestive. Allen said that in his experience, only about 5 percent of male fire starters are sexually motivated, but the excitement of lighting a fire can stimulate subsequent sexual activity. Like other serial arsonists, Oyler stopped setting fires only when a major change occurred in his life: the hiatus after his girlfriend Crystal Breazile threatened to leave him unless he stopped, and the full stop following his arrest.

Breazile, who gave crucial testimony, never asked for any of the $550,000 reward money. Two years after the trial, however, Oyler's cousin Jill Frame, who had told the court the bizarre story about him threatening to set a mountain on fire so he could release his pit bulls from an animal shelter, asked to be rewarded. She was miffed, it was said, because the defense had accused her during the trial of turning in Oyler for money, and the Oyler family had treated her like a turncoat. The prosecutors and sheriff's police conferred with Riverside County supervisors and determined that Frame's cooperation had helped but also that she hadn't come forward until after Oyler's arrest. The supervisors awarded her $50,000, or half the $100,000 they had pledged to the reward fund. In explaining the amount, prosecutor Hestrin said the recipient, who was not publicly named, "was able to establish an intent of Oyler to start the fire and was crucial in establishing what was going on in Oyler's mind." Later on, her identity was established for this account.

Other prosecutors lost no time in taking a cue from the Oyler case. Directly after Oyler was sentenced in June 2009, the district attorney in neighboring San Bernardino County began to consider a similar prosecution for Rickie Lee Fowler in connection with the 2003 Old Fire, in which five people had died of stress and heart attacks related to the fire. The Old Fire burned 91,281 acres, destroyed 1,003 homes, and wiped out entire neighborhoods in San Bernardino and surrounding mountain communities.

The circumstances of the Fowler case were complex. Fowler, while serving a lengthy prison term on unrelated burglary charges, had confessed to starting the Old Fire. He later recanted. In January

2010, six months after Oyler's sentencing, District Attorney Michael Ramos announced Fowler's indictment for murder and arson connected to the Old Fire and said he would seek the death penalty. Ramos said he was not motivated by the Oyler case, but the timing, charges, and physical proximity of the two fires spoke otherwise. Fowler's case was a special challenge because the five victims had died of heart attacks, several after the fire. Fowler next was convicted in early 2012 of three counts of jailhouse sodomy and sentenced to 75 years to life. Then after a trial on the Old Fire charges later in 2012, a jury found him guilty of five counts of murder and recommended the death penalty. His own lawyer, Don Jordan, described Fowler as "despicable." A frequent first reaction, though, is that Fowler and Oyler may not have intended to kill anyone and so the death penalty and murder convictions were excessive. California's penal code, however, states that when a homicide occurs during commission of certain felonies, including arson, prosecutors may assume intent and bring first-degree murder charges.

After Oyler's conviction for the Esperanza Fire, District Attorney Pacheco, impressed by Detective Michaels' swift capture of Oyler, hired him as an investigator for the district attorney's office, where he was assigned to complex fraud cases. Michaels said he doesn't miss the homicide beat and is happy where he is. In 2010 Pacheco lost a race for a second term as district attorney to former Superior Court judge Paul Zellerbach, who retained the Oyler prosecutors, Hestrin and Mayman. Pacheco joined the white-collar and investigations unit of SNR Denton, an international law firm with offices in Los Angeles and San Francisco.

The four surviving Forest Service captains from the San Jacinto District all advanced, one temporarily, to the rank of battalion chief; Dinkel decided after a trial period that she preferred a less administrative post and at her own request returned to her former post as captain of Engine 54 at Cranston. Koeller remained a favorite of the fire community. "He has been our supporter from the beginning," Walker said in announcing Koeller's presence at the fifth-anniversary memorial dinner held near Idyllwild. At the time of the fifth anniversary, Koeller's wife, Denise, said she thought Greg's near-obsession with clearing up the site and building the stone memorial was his way of dealing with deep and troubling emotions about the role his home had played in the fire.

◆ ◆ ◆

WITHIN MONTHS OF the fire, a new kind of crop sprang up where chaparral once had been: real estate signs advertising land for sale. Realtors are keenly aware that it's easier to sell land you can see than land covered by dense and highly inflammable brush. The housing bust of 2008 slowed development in the old burn area, as it did everywhere. But it did not stop it. Less than a year after the fire, a development company announced plans to build 150 upscale homes on 610 acres in the Poppet Flats area, doubling the population. The proposal by Kajima Development Corporation violated a key recommendation of a Fire Hazard Reduction Task Force set up by Riverside County supervisors immediately after the fire: to limit growth in wildfire-prone areas. The developer said many steps would be taken to reduce fire risk, among them building buffers between houses, increasing water pressure, and using fire-resistant materials. It is possible to build a community that can withstand wildland fire, but it takes a great deal of money, community cohesiveness, and work. At the five-year mark, the Kajima project remained in the planning stage. Other recommendations of the fire hazard task force also faced setbacks. The year of the Esperanza Fire, the federal government provided $28.1 million for dead tree removal and forest safety grants to deal with the incendiary conditions on the San Bernardino National

Forest. Five years later, in a time of governmental budget cutbacks, the figure had slipped to $2.2 million.

The Esperanza Fire adds another chapter to the chronicle of tragedy fires, the multiple fatality conflagrations that enter the collective conscience of the wildfire world. There are no easy answers to living with fire, not when forests and wildlands pose a bewildering checkerboard of challenges, when human encroachment into wildlands rolls on governed by widely divergent regulations or no regulation, when fires have grown bigger and hotter, when numerous laws can be used to derail and delay work in the forests, and when state, local, tribal, and federal firefighters come to the fire ground with unresolved differences about missions, levels of competency, and communications. Every fire season proves it: consider the 2012 season that set records for high temperatures and acreage burned. In one state, Colorado, once known for its "asbestos forest," because wildlands in the state were so resistant to fire, winds in March whipped a prescribed burn back to life days after it was supposed to be controlled. It went on to kill three people, destroy twenty-five structures, and blacken six square miles of forestland. State officials ordered a halt to all prescribed burns, relieved the state forest service of firefighting duties, and created a special commission to investigate. Two major fires followed, one near Fort Collins and the other near Colorado Springs, and set state records for size and destruction of property. The common cause was a nationwide drought on a scale not seen since the 1950s, with no promise of relief in sight. On average, more homes have been destroyed by wildfire each year since the 1960s, jumping from 250 homes a year to a present level of over 2,700. There are plenty more homes around to destroy: Of 17 million homes built from 1990 to 2008, 10 million were in the wildland–urban interface.

Tragedy fires cost lives but they also drive policy changes, most of them for the better. Motivated by the fourteen fatalities in the

1994 South Canyon Fire, the federal government the following year approved the Federal Wildland Fire Management Policy and Program Review in an effort to forge a national approach to wildland fire. The review was updated in 2001, the same year Congress passed the National Fire Plan. As a result of these initiatives, communities at risk were identified, guidelines on how to prepare for fire were established, forest health was measured, clearing work was undertaken, and much was done to make fire services more competent and compatible. But overall, the problem grew worse, not better. A federal report on the state of wildland fire in 2009 acknowledged that solutions have not caught up with the problem.

"The past two decades have seen a rapid escalation of severe fire behavior, home and property losses, higher costs, increased threats to communities and worsening conditions on the land," the report stated. That same year, 2009, Congress passed the FLAME (Federal Land Assistance, Management, and Enhancement) Act to continue efforts to restore the national landscape, encourage fire-adapted communities, and respond in a more coordinated fashion to wildland fires. It is not naive to think that federal efforts, coupled with similar initiatives at other levels of government and in the private sector, will in time bring benefits to the land, communities, and firefighting practices; they already have. But nature has the last word, and it can be shattering.

The Esperanza Fire is a cautionary tale for everyone within reach of wildfire, from the fire line to the nation's capital. Firefighters cannot answer every alarm expecting an area ignition, but they should be aware it could happen. Homeowners who work hard to prepare for fire, and receive good marks from fire inspectors, should not be haunted for life if things go wrong. And firefighters who do their best should not be blamed if nature unpredictably turns on them. But taking a second, skeptical look at a fire plan under conditions of extreme danger—especially when firefighters are above flames on a steep slope—pays honor to the memory of Engine 57. What will not change is the nature of wildfire itself. It will forever keep its cunning, its power to destroy and to defy expectations, and its ancient place as a creature of the wild.